A Geography of the
Third World

A Geography of the Third World

J. P. DICKENSON
C. G. CLARKE
W. T. S. GOULD
A. G. HODGKISS
R. M. PROTHERO
D. J. SIDDLE
C. T. SMITH
E. M. THOMAS-HOPE

All at the time of writing were members
of the Department of Geography,
University of Liverpool

METHUEN
LONDON AND NEW YORK

First published in 1983 by
Methuen & Co. Ltd
11 New Fetter Lane, London EC4P 4EE
Reprinted 1984

Published in the USA by
Methuen & Co.
in association with Methuen, Inc.
733 Third Avenue, New York, NY 10017

© 1983 J. P. Dickenson, C. G. Clarke, W. T. S. Gould, A. G. Hodgkis
R. M. Prothero, D. J. Siddle, C. T. Smith, E. M. Thomas-Hope,

Typeset by Scarborough Typesetting Services
and printed in Great Britain at the
University Press, Cambridge

British Library Cataloguing in Publication Data

A geography of the Third World.
Underdeveloped areas—Descriptions and travel
I. Dickenson, J. P.
910'.091724   HC59.7
ISBN 0–416–74170–3 Pbk

Library of Congress Cataloging in Publication Data

Main entry under title:

A geography of the Third World.

Bibliography: p.
Includes index.
1. Underdeveloped areas. I. Dickenson, John P.
II. Hodgkiss, A. G. III. Title.
HC59.7.G365 1983   330.9172'4   83–7927
ISBN 0–416–74170–3 (pbk.)

306609

For Robert W. Steel

CONTENTS

LIST OF PLATES

LIST OF FIGURES

LIST OF TABLES

ACKNOWLEDGEMENTS

Plates 2.1, 3.1, 3.2, 4.2, 4.3, 6.2, 7.1 were provided by W. T. S. Gould; 4.1, 5.1, 6.3, 7.5, 8.1, 10.1 by J. P. Dickenson; 6.1 by D. J. Siddle; and 7.2, 7.3, 7.4 by C. G. Clarke.

The authors and publishers would like to thank the following for the use of copyright material: the Independent Commission on International Development Issues for figure 1.1; Weidenfeld and Nicolson for figure 2.2; Lexington Books for table 3.3; *People* for figures 3.5, 3.7; D. Q. Innis for figure 4.4; C. G. Clarke for figure 5.2; *Journal of Asian Studies* for figure 4.5a; *Economic Geography* for figure 4.5b; G. Hollier for figure 4.5c; Croom Helm for tables 7.1, 7.2, 7.3, 7.4, 7.7; University of London Press for figure 7.2; *American Geographical Society* for figures 7.3, 7.12; Pluto Press for figure 7.4; *Journal of Modern African Studies* for table 7.5; Methuen for table 7.6; Longman for figure 7.5; Société Tunisienne de Topographie for figure 7.6; H. Franklin for figure 7.7; Sep-Setentas/Diana for figure 7.8; P. M. Ward for figures 7.9, 7.10; CNRS for table 8.1.

PREFACE

This book has been written in order to present and discuss current geographical approaches to the study of what is commonly known as the Third World. Changes in public attitudes and in geography itself, both in the affluent and in the poor countries of the world, have prompted changes in the ways that geographers consider the half of the world's land surface and the three-quarters of its population which constitute the so-called Third World. In the 1940s and early 1950s 'Colonial Geography' reflected the current world order, with geographers in the metropolitan countries describing the geography of the colonial territories. 'Tropical Geography', prominent in the 1950s and 1960s, considered poor countries primarily on the basis of the opportunities and constraints imposed by tropical environments. In the 1970s and 1980s the work of geographers on the Third World is set firmly in the wider context of the world economy and incorporates the changed approaches of the social sciences in general. These changes have been reflected in course and examination syllabuses in schools, colleges and universities, but not so readily in the texts used by students at these levels. We feel that there is a need to present a contemporary geography of the Third World, exploring systematic themes in the development process and examining spatial patterns of development and underdevelopment at various scales within the Third World. Clearly a fully comprehensive coverage in a form that is acceptable in size and accessible in price to advanced school courses, college and general undergraduate students is impracticable. However, we have taken the view that the key themes can be identified to provide a cohesive and informative structure, and that we constitute a group of geographers with diverse expertise in those themes and in most areas of the Third World, sufficient to produce a broadly based overview of its geography.

In the Department of Geography, University of Liverpool, we have been uniquely placed to contribute to the geography of the Third World in its contemporary global context. Merseyside has had substantial contacts with the Third World for a long period. A statue of Christopher Columbus in one of Liverpool's parks notes that he 'the discoverer of America, was the maker of Liverpool'. Since

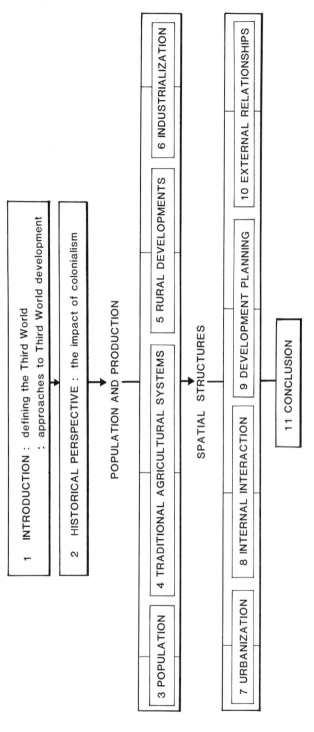

Figure P.1 The structure of this book.

the late sixteenth century trading contacts with the Americas, Africa and Asia have had a major role in the prosperity of the port and the city. Various Liverpool shipping lines were important in Britain's trade with the tropics, and tropical products of cotton, sugar, oilseed, leather and minerals have provided raw materials for industry. Well-established immigrant communities from Asia, Africa and the Caribbean form part of the social fabric of the city. The University of Liverpool has many close contacts with the tropics, particularly through its School of Tropical Medicine and Centre of Latin American Studies, and the Department of Geography has a long tradition of interest in the Third World. Three of the six heads of the department since the foundation of its Honours School in 1917 have fostered these interests, Roxby in China, Steel in Africa and Prothero in Africa and Middle America. Several of the present teaching staff have studied and taught in the Third World, and as a result a substantial number of graduates and postgraduates have worked on Third World themes and the Department has attracted numerous students from the Third World. The present authors have a wide range of experience of teaching and research in and about all the major areas of the Third World and have participated in programmes seeking to promote progress within it.

The structure of the book is summarized in figure P.1. It begins with a discussion of the characteristics of the Third World, and an examination of its evolution through time. The bulk of the text is concerned with major themes of spatial analysis and the development process and with the problems faced in securing social and economic advance, and it concludes with a global view of recent and possible developments affecting the progress of the Third World.

The writing of a co-operative venture has been a learning experience for all of us. Our method of working was first to identify the principal themes to be discussed as substantive chapters. The main topics to be included within each chapter were outlined by a principal author and then discussed by the group. Once the detailed contents had been agreed, chapters were drafted by individual or co-authors, then read and commented on by a discussant and circulated amongst the group for discussion, critical comment, suggested modification and the incorporation of case-studies and examples from our knowledge of the various parts of the Third World. Revised drafts were then produced and further discussed before being edited by two of us to massage the individual parts into a whole that has some uniformity of argument and consistency of style.

In preparing and completing the work we have incurred many debts of gratitude: to the people of the Third World with whom we have lived and worked; to our past and present colleagues and students in Liverpool and elsewhere upon whom our ideas have been honed; the several typists who have coped with various drafts in a variety of hands, some more legible than others; and the University of Liverpool for a small grant towards some of the costs of preparation of the book. Our spouses have tolerated our frequent disappearances to the Third World, to our studies and to editorial meetings. Finally, we wish to acknowledge our indebtedness to Robert Steel, pioneer in the geography of the Third World and colleague and mentor of our interests in the region.

Liverpool, January 1983

J.P.D.
C.G.C.
W.T.S.G.
A.G.H.
R.M.P.
D.J.S.
C.T.S.
E.M.T-H.

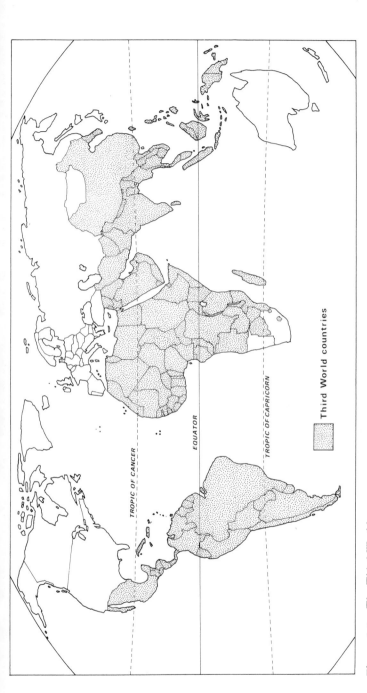

Figure 1.1 The Third World.

Defining the Third World is a controversial task. A variety of criteria may be used, and though these may clearly identify the core of the Third World, its boundaries will vary from one criterion to another. Some countries, such as those of Southern Europe, are marginal to the Third World. Their per-capita income levels, for example, are close to those of countries included here within the Third World. Even within the richest countries there are areas of their territories and segments of their populations experiencing profound poverty. Conversely some parts and social groups of the Third World flaunt great affluence.

Just as the more developed world is subdivided, primarily on the basis of ideology, between the First and Second Worlds, so it would also be possible to distinguish separately those less-developed countries, such as China or Cuba, that are pursuing overtly socialist paths towards development. Here, however, we have chosen not to make this subdivision. By many criteria South Africa should form part of the Third World but because of its peculiar political structure, and the dominance exercized by a rich white minority over the much poorer black population, we have excluded it from consideration here. Under majority rule it, and its dependency Namibia, would be taken as a Third World country.

1 INTRODUCTION

Defining the Third World

Over the past three decades or so there has been growing awareness of the contrasts in living standards experienced by people in different countries. It has been increasingly recognized that there are substantial contrasts in the wealth of some countries when compared to others. One might talk very broadly about 'rich' and 'poor' countries, but precise definitions are more difficult. Is 'wealth' to be assessed by the standards of a Texan multi-millionaire, or by those of the average 'man in the street' in Britain, France or Canada? Similarly, is poverty to be defined by the standards of a homeless beggar in Calcutta, or the average income of the people of El Salvador or Zimbabwe? Should 'wealth' be measured only in terms of money and the material possessions it will buy, or should spiritual and cultural values be assessed?

In spite of such difficulties attempts have been made to distinguish the poorer countries from those which are more affluent. The less-affluent countries have been variously called 'backward', 'underdeveloped', 'undeveloped', 'less developed' or 'developing'. All of these terms are relative. They make comparisons with 'advanced', 'developed' or 'more developed' countries. Two more recent terms to be used are the 'Third World' and the 'South'. The term the 'Third World' was first used in France in the 1950s and by the early 1960s formed part of a threefold division of the world on principally political and economic grounds: the First World of industrialized, market-economy countries, broadly the 'capitalist' or Western world; the Second World of centrally-planned economies (the 'communist bloc' or 'socialist camp'), and the Third World of poorer countries, many of them recently independent from colonial powers. The 'South' is a term which has come into use particularly since the publication in 1980 of *North South: A Programme for Survival. Report of the Independent Commission on International Development Issues*, more generally known as the Brandt Report. The Commission distinguished between the 'rich', 'developed', North and the 'poor', 'developing' South (figure 1.2).

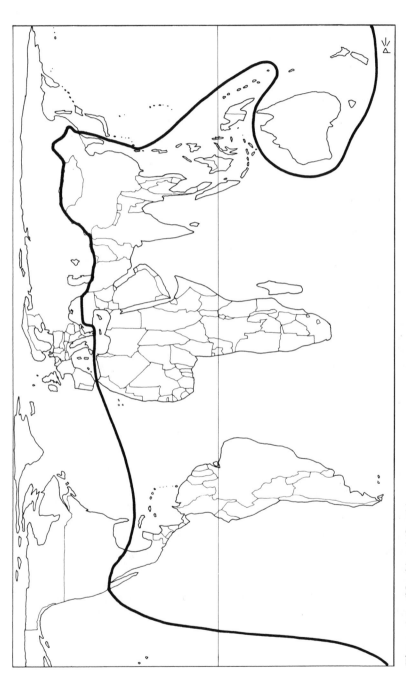

Figure 1.2 'North' and 'South'.
The Brandt Report distinguished between the countries of the rich North and the poor South, and this map has become the symbol of recent concern for the problems of the Third World and its interrelations with the more developed world. The map itself is based on the recently developed Peters Projection, rather than the more commonly used Mercator Projection. It provides a less Eurocentric representation of the world. Its surface distortions are distributed at the poles and the equator; the more densely peopled parts of the Earth are, it is claimed, in proper proportion to one another.

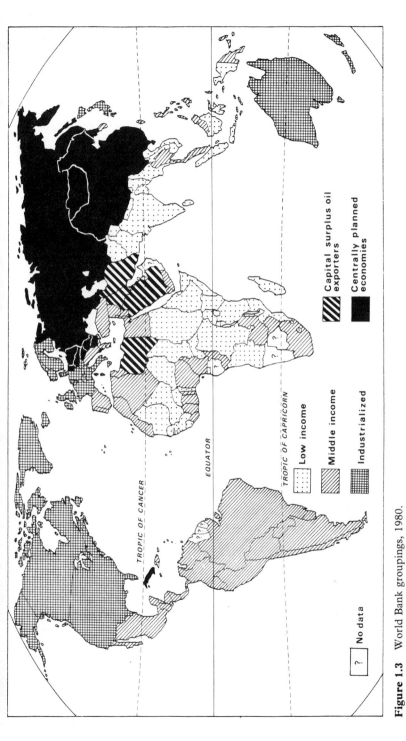

Figure 1.3 World Bank groupings, 1980.
The Bank uses economic and political criteria to distinguish five groups of countries with differing levels of development and development strategies.

Source of data: World Bank, 1980: 110–11.

3

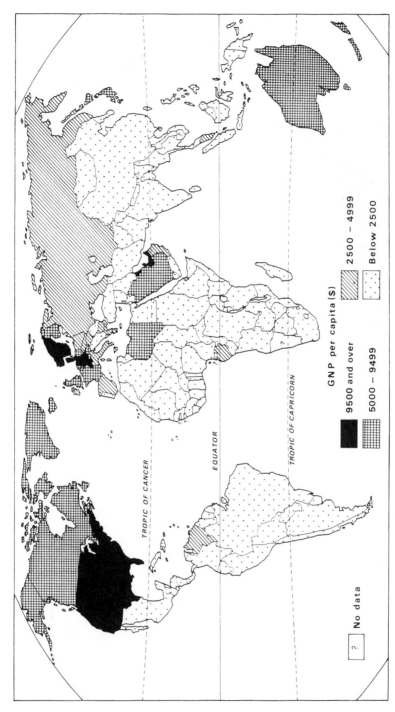

Figure 1.4 GNP per capita, 1978.

Source of data: World Bank, 1980: 110–11.

4

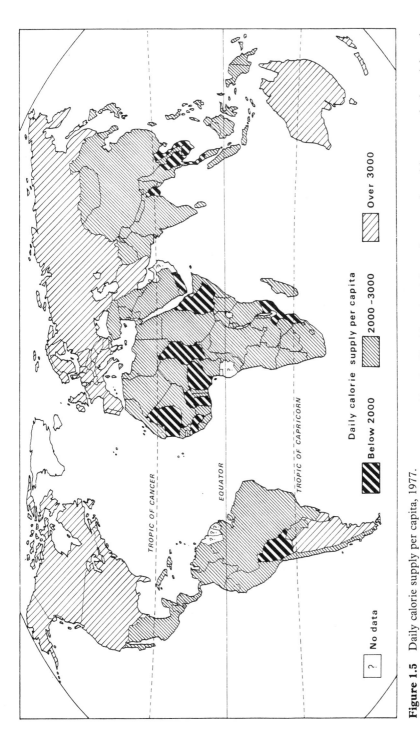

Figure 1.5 Daily calorie supply per capita, 1977.
The daily intake of calories necessary to sustain a person at normal levels of health and activity varies somewhat with age, sex, body weight and environmental temperature, but averages about 2200 calories per day. The map shows that several Third World countries have major calorie deficiencies, whilst in most of the developed world consumption is in excess of essential need.

Source of data: World Bank, 1980: 152–3.

Daily calorie supply per capita

Below 2000

2000–3000

Over 3000

? No data

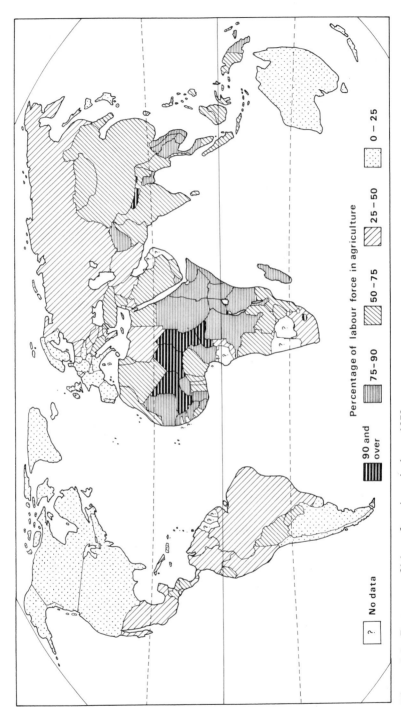

Figure 1.6 Percentage of labour force in agriculture, 1970.

Source of data: World Bank, 1978: 102–3.

Percentage of labour force in agriculture

90 and over

75–90

50–75

25–50

0 – 25

? No data

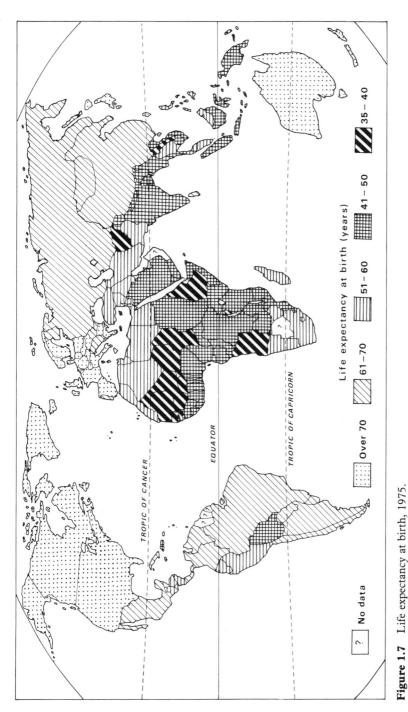

Figure 1.7 Life expectancy at birth, 1975.
This measure indicates the number of years a newborn child might be expected to live if subject to the mortality rates prevailing in the country of birth in the period 1970–5.

Source of data: World Bank, 1978: 108–9.

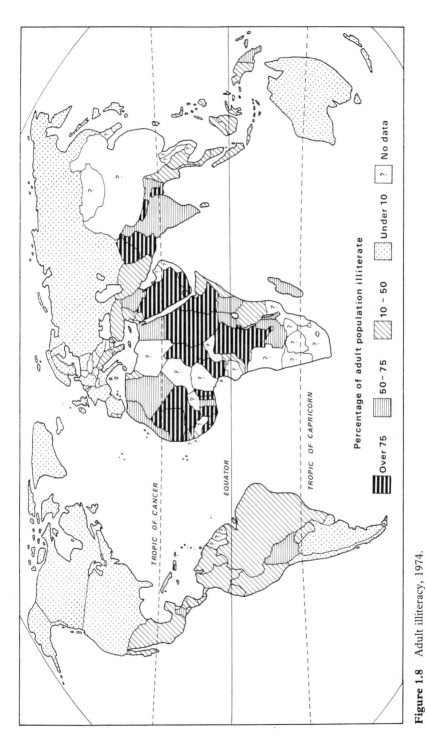

Figure 1.8 Adult illiteracy, 1974.
The map shows the percentage of the population aged over 15 years unable to read and write.

Source of data: World Bank, 1978: 110–11.

Percentage of adult population illiterate

Over 75   50 – 75   10 – 50   Under 10   ? No data

TROPIC OF CANCER

EQUATOR

TROPIC OF CAPRICORN

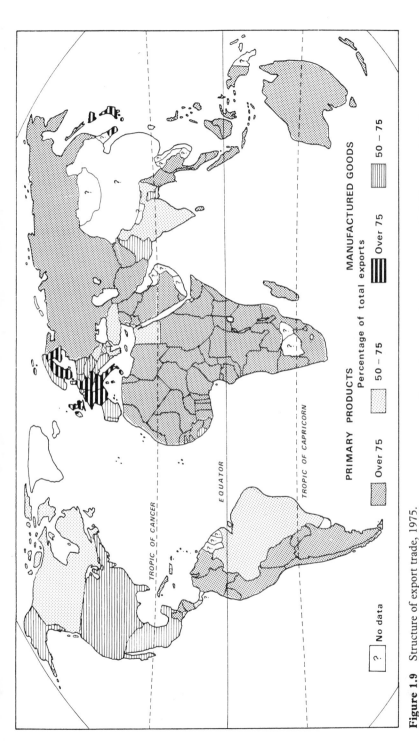

Figure 1.9 Structure of export trade, 1975.
The map shows the contribution made by primary produce and manufactured goods to the total export trade. It illustrates the limitations of using a single criterion to define the Third World. Most Third World countries have a heavy dependence on primary produce in their export trade; but so too do Australia, New Zealand and the USSR.

Source of data: World Bank, 1978: 88–9.

The World Bank, in its report for 1980, used monetary criteria, expressed in Gross National Product (GNP) per capita per annum, to categorize the countries of the world into five groups (figure 1.3). The less-affluent countries were divided into two groups – the 'low-income' countries whose GNP per capita in 1978 was below US $370, and 'middle-income' countries whose GNP per capita ranged from $370 to $3500. This middle-income group overlapped with the 'industrialized' countries, where GNP averaged $8070 per capita, but ranged from $3470 to over $12,000. The 'centrally-planned' economies include the USSR, the countries of Eastern Europe, Cuba, China and North Korea, and their GNP per capita ranged from $230 to $5700. A fifth small group of countries consists of those that have benefited from the escalation of world petroleum prices since 1973 and are identified as 'capital surplus oil exporters'. The World Bank excluded from its classification countries with less than one million inhabitants, and thus created a grouping which included countries as diverse as Guinea-Bissau and Comoros with GNP per capita below $300, Iceland and Luxembourg with GNP of over $8000 and oil-rich states such as Qatar and the United Arab Emirates where GNP per capita is above $12,000.

If the peculiar circumstances of the oil-rich states of the Middle East are excluded, the USA, Sweden and Switzerland might be generally accepted as rich, developed countries against which others might be measured. In 1978 these countries had GNP per capita figures of around $10,000. Figure 1.4 shows those countries that, in 1978, had GNP per capita figures of (a) at least half of this (b) those where the sum was between $2500 and $5000; and (c) those below $2500.

Using such figures we might argue that countries with a GNP per capita below $5000 a year are 'poor', those above 'rich'. A crude measure such as this, however, begins to reveal its own limitations. Britain, with a GNP of $5030 per capita, would *just* fall into the 'rich' category, while Ireland, Italy and New Zealand would be defined as 'poor'.

Of course income is only one measure used to indicate levels of development. Generally, the 'poor' countries have other characteristics of their societies and economies in common. Figures 1.5–1.9 indicate some of the spatial patterns shown by other criteria. When compared to the 'rich' countries, the people of the poor world have diets which are deficient in quality and quantity. There tend to be more people working in agriculture than in manufacturing. The average duration of life tends to be lower. A higher percentage of the population is illiterate. The export economies depend on primary products, from agriculture to mining, and often only one or two of these generate the majority of the export earnings.

A quick look at these maps suggests that there is a broad group of countries that share these characteristics. These and other measures can be used to try to define what has been called a 'commonwealth of poverty'. A closer look, however, reveals that these measures do not always include all of the same countries, so that the boundaries of the Third World are not very precise. Furthermore, the number of countries included or excluded can be altered by minor manipulations of the criteria used.

It should also be apparent that there are notable variations even within this

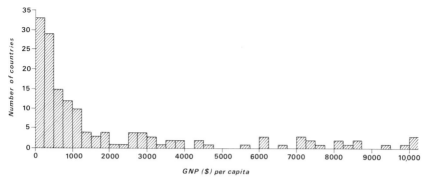

Figure 1.10   The global pattern of income distribution, 1979.
This graph shows the concentration of the large number of low-income countries (with annual GNP per capita below US $1000), and the spread of more affluent countries. Note that the largest single category is that of the lowest GNP group, below $250.

Source of data: World Bank, 1981: 134–5.

broad grouping. Even the monetary measure of GNP per capita uses a sub-division, and in 1978 the per-capita figure among the low and middle-income countries ranged from $90 in Bangladesh to $3500 in Israel. Of the thirty-eight countries with GNP figures below $370 per capita, which the World Bank identified as the 'poorest' countries, twenty-five are in Africa, twelve in Asia and only one, Haiti, is in Latin America. On such evidence one might claim that Latin America is less poor or less underdeveloped than Africa or Asia.

Such variations draw attention to the very important theme of scale in any discussion of the Third World. At the global scale we have identified contrasts in the level of development between the First and Second Worlds on the one hand and the Third World on the other. At a different scale, within that Third World, we can see other contrasts: some parts of it are poorer than others; some Third World countries are richer than others (figure 1.10).

Such contrasts also operate at other spatial scales. Using indices of economic and social development we can demonstrate that some parts of individual countries are richer and more developed than others (figure 1.11). It is also possible to demonstrate that, in general, the population of Third World cities and towns is richer and better provided for than are the people living in rural areas. The simple measure of per-capita income, at a global, national or regional scale, also presumes that measurable wealth is equally distributed amongst the whole population. It can easily be shown that this is not so (figure 1.12). Income distribution is 'skewed'; shares are unequal; some people are richer than others, whether in New York, Moscow, Asunción or Ouagadougou.

At these varying scales there is inequality. There is relative poverty in one country or region compared to another, between town and country, between one segment of society and another. In some places there is absolute poverty – the poverty of people whose existence is 'that of, at best, half men, living poorly and

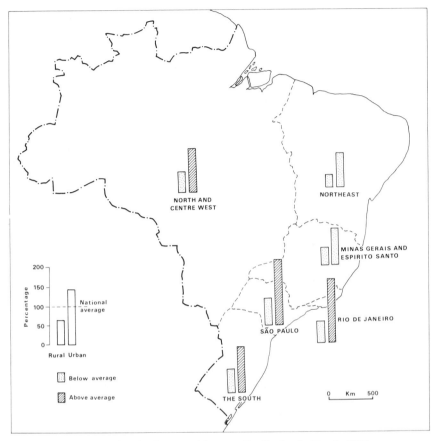

Figure 1.11   Regional and urban–rural income distribution in Brazil, 1970.
This map relates income levels for the rural and urban populations of the various regions of
Brazil to the national average figure. Rural incomes are everywhere below the national
average. Prosperity is greater in the urban areas of the South-East and South.

Source of data: Langoni, 1975: 107.

living briefly, living in the twilight world of the illiterate, living in the brutalizing
certainty that half their children would perish of hunger or preventable disease
before adolescence' (Buchanan, 1964: 108).

A crucial question is 'why should this be'? Why are some countries richer and
more developed than others? The fact that much of the Third World lies
between the tropics led to suggestions that the 'harsh' environment could
explain the lack of development. However, several of the countries identified as
'low-income' countries – Bangladesh, Afghanistan, Uruguay, or China for
example – lie partly or entirely outside the tropics. Moreover the tropical
environment is not uniform. It contains contrasts as extreme as those of the

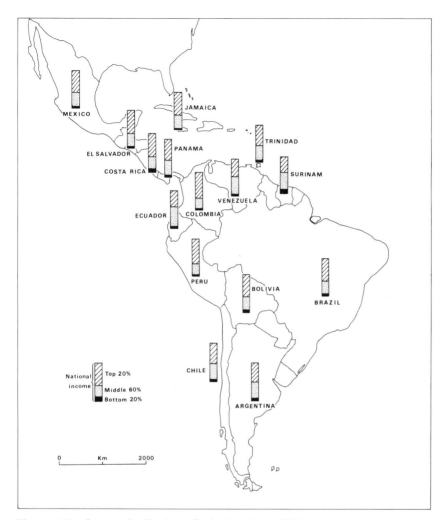

Figure 1.12 Income distribution in Latin America, *c.* 1970.
The graphs show the proportion of total national income received by three groups, the poorest 20 per cent, the middle 60 per cent and the top 20 per cent. In all cases the richest 20 per cent receive a share of total income greatly in excess of their proportion of the total population; conversely the poorest 20 per cent receive a disproportionately small share.

Source of data: Jarvis, 1973: 306.

Amazonian rain forest and the Sahara desert, or the Bolivian altiplano and the Irrawaddy delta.

It has been claimed that the Third World is deficient in the natural resources necessary to sustain development. Yet many Third World countries, dependent in their export trade upon a few primary products, are major sources of raw materials 'essential' to the economies of developed countries, such as iron ore, bauxite, coffee and sugar.

A recurrent image of the Third World is of the 'teeming millions' of people. Could over-population explain their backwardness? While it is true that countries such as China, India, Brazil and Nigeria rank among the world's more populous countries, many Third World countries have small populations. Fifty-four of the ninety low and middle-income countries identified by the World Bank in 1978 had populations between one million and ten million, while of the twenty-nine countries with below one million inhabitants, at least twenty-one could be regarded as Third World countries.

Because most of the richer countries have 'white' populations while many Third World countries are inhabited by 'coloured' people, racist arguments suggest that the 'natives' are 'inferior' or 'indolent'. Such an interpretation ignores the evolution of early human civilization and economic change in Egypt, Mesopotamia, India and China, now within the Third World, and the important technical advances made in China, India and Islamic countries during the European 'Dark Ages'.

Most Third World countries have been colonies of Europe at some time during the past 500 years; could the explanation be colonialist exploitation? If being a European colony is a prerequisite of poverty, how do we explain the present ranking of the USA, Canada or Australia? Third World countries experienced the rule of different colonial powers, Britain, France, Belgium, Spain and Portugal and others: the nature of colonial rule varied. So too did its duration: some countries have been independent of their colonial masters for over 150 years; many have achieved independence only since 1945; a dwindling few retain some form of colonial status.

It is unlikely that there is any one single factor which can be identified as the cause of Third World poverty. There are many countries; many contrasts; many causes. In recent decades there have been increasing efforts, by both the more-developed and the less-developed countries, to secure the development of the latter and to ease the poverty of the Third World and its peoples.

Approaches to Third World development

It is possible to argue that early Western theories and strategies for the development of the Third World emerged as a product of two traumatic events in world history: the great recession in trade in the 1930s and the end of the Second World War in 1945. The first allowed free rein to the ideas of John Maynard Keynes and his followers, the second created an atmosphere of freedom, idealism and optimism and provided the seedbed of the colonial independence movement. Keynes (1936) believed that the free play of the money markets would lead to booms and slumps of increasing severity, so that in the modern world no sophisticated social, political and economic system could survive without careful regulation of the economy. This did not imply any lack of enthusiasm for capitalism itself, but a belief that economic growth was more likely to be continuous and to benefit more people if it were stage-managed. The evidence of the 1930s brought this argument into sharp focus, and the post-war reconstruction of Europe was the first major attempt by European governments to use Keynesian economic strategies to regulate domestic economies and to plan 'aid' intervention on an international scale. The initial success of these measures through the Marshall Plan (the American Aid-to-Europe programme which allowed capital investment in new industries) encouraged development theorists to follow a similar reasoning process when they turned their attention to the poor nations of the southern hemisphere. The first theories of Third World development were, then, the product of three major influences: the Euro–American experience which had generated an enthusiastic belief in managed capitalist economic and social development; a new spirit of optimism about the future; and of growing determination in the colonies to make their own fresh starts.

In the 1950s political winds of change were sweeping the continents of Asia and Africa and many new and exciting ideas about social and economic progress were in the air. But at the same time most Western observers would have had no difficulty in identifying the Third World as a group of economically backward countries, generally in the tropics, which had been left behind by the socially, economically and politically 'more-sophisticated' nations of the northern hemisphere and southern temperate regions. This highly value-loaded view would have raised few eyebrows in the white Western areas of the world. What is more important, few who had dealings with Third World countries would have baulked at the inclusion of such words as 'ignorant', 'superstitious', 'corrupt' and 'primitive' in such a definition. There was a highly charged sense of cultural and (at base) ethnic superiority, moderated only by a genuine 'missionary' zeal to improve the lot of the under-privileged. Moreover, a firm belief in the virtues of cultural patronage characterized attitudes and values both on the part of the rulers and also on the part of the ruled. Even the radical intellectuals who served a political apprenticeship to independence in colonial gaols readily embraced the lineaments of this philosophy when it came to adopting development strategies for their new nations. Perhaps there was no other choice. As indicated above, there were strong historical currents feeding early development theory. It is therefore not surprising that the first theories of Third World development were characterized both by a strong belief in the power of interventionist economics and the superiority of the current Western model of economic (and by implication cultural) development, as a linear process directed towards the same kind of economic, social and political structures which characterized Western Europe and North America.

Walter Rostow (1960) gave an impetus to such thinking by likening the process of economic growth to that of an aeroplane setting off down a runway. After a long 'pre-industrial' taxiing process the economic engines are revved for a rapid surge towards 'industrial' take-off into the clear blue sky of sustained economic growth.

Although this was quickly recognized as a simplistic model, based on too limited a view of the European Industrial Revolution, the underlying assumptions of comparability were embodied in most early theories of Third World development. The argument is quite straightforward. Progress has been achieved in the West (and in the European East) by eliminating the rural character of economic and social relations. It is these 'primitive, backward, conservative, superstitious' elements which have all been removed in the progress towards an urbanized society. The Third World was characterized as having peasant social and economic attitudes and institutions of precisely the kind condemned by Western theorists.

Once having identified a clear continuum from rural poverty to urban affluence in the West, it was perhaps inevitable that the first development strategies should approach the problem of inducing change in the Third World by concentrating on the 'successful' end of this spectrum. If Western development had taken place through the generation of an urban industrial system increasingly geared to a sophisticated and capital-intensive technology, then this was the direction in which Third World economies should go. By this means the interaction of negative effects or 'the vicious circles of poverty', which perpetuated the adverse condition of poor countries and poor people, could be broken. If a man was poor, he could afford little food; if he was under-nourished, he was more prone to disease; if he was ill and under-fed his capacity to work was limited; if his work ability was limited, his income was low; and in consequence he could afford little food. There was then a process of circular causation of poverty. The Swedish economist Gunnar Myrdal (1963) and others argued that if this process could be broken and reversed by industrialization then economic progress might be achieved. There might then be a converse 'circular causation of cumulative development', a process which Myrdal linked to Rostow's 'take-off'. If some impetus could be given to a poor family, community or nation, there might be change for the better. For example, the location of a factory at a particular place might spur development there, providing jobs, higher incomes, and new services: transport, education and health. The population, place and country would benefit, and there would be a diffusion of the benefits of growth.

This process of diffusion, identified by Myrdal as 'spread effects' and by Hirschman as 'trickling-down' effects (1958), would provide the stimulus to economic progress and an improvement in the lot of the poor countries. Precisely what were the best initiators of this process were unclear, though there was a strong preference for the urban-based industrial developments which appeared to have been vital in the process of European economic revolution. The French economist François Perroux (1971) suggested the notion of *industries motrices* (propellent industries) which would provide the necessary stimulus; once these had been identified and established, they would form the nuclei of 'growth poles'. Perroux's idea was enthusiastically taken up, not least because it appeared to have spatial implications: growth would diffuse from the growth pole to other places. However, Perroux himself was concerned primarily with an economy in the abstract, suggesting only that growth might be induced, not *where* it might take place.

There had emerged, then, a development philosophy based primarily on the experience of capitalist Europe, in which industrial and urban growth were the keys to progress; and a belief that a major stimulus was needed to break the vicious circles of poverty. There were some uncertainties as to quite what the best stimulus was. There was also, from an early date, a recognition that economic progress could not be achieved everywhere at the same rate. Both Myrdal and Hirschman had recognized countervailing forces, 'backwash' or 'polarization' effects, that would inhibit equality of development throughout a country. Hirschman noted that, in a geographical sense, growth would necessarily be unbalanced. He believed that, over time, the trickling-down effects would outweigh those of polarization; Myrdal felt that this was unlikely unless there was intervention in the economy by the state.

Such ideas provided the basis for ideas of a 'centre–periphery' model, most clearly expounded by John Friedmann, one of the most influential writers in the development field in the 1950s and 1960s. He stated that

economic growth tends to occur in the matrix of urban regions. It is through this matrix that the evolving space economy is organized. The location decisions of most firms, including those in agriculture, are made with reference to cities or urban regions.   (Friedmann, 1966: 28–9)

The cities then were the core of economic advance; around them was the area of more efficient agriculture, and beyond were the backward subsistence activities.

So it was that the city and the city region were identified as the catalyst of a process designed to engage the whole national space. Primary growth-poles comprising related industries would be identified and encouraged by a network of communications. Aid would be channelled down a hierarchy of minor centres. The focal growth impulses of industrial development would produce a flow of investment to trickle down this hierarchy of economic and spatial feeders to the smaller urban centres. Eventually even the smallest villages would receive the benefits. Like Rostow's runway analogy of economic growth, the idea of development trickling down a spatial infrastructure blurred a number of issues that are taken up later in this book. But it was enthusiastically adopted as a working spatial model for development planning (figure 1.13) and is still an implicit feature of many national plans. Indeed the process was given specific structure by planning theorists. Major industries could be implanted in major centres. They would provide jobs for the urban poor, create wealth that, when invested in subsidiary industrial enterprises, would generate more jobs. These in turn would generate further wealth. From this wealth taxes could be raised to invest in schemes of public health and education. It all seemed quite straightforward. All that was needed was to put what economists call the 'multiplier' to work. Why is it then that things have gone so badly awry? Thirty years of investment aid, technical expertise and national plans have not been successful in generally raising living standards. The gap between rich and poor continues to grow.

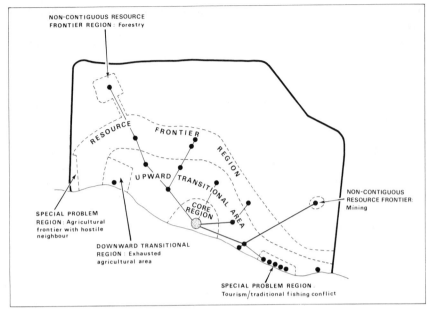

Figure 1.13 Development regions (the Friedmann model).
Friedmann identified five types of regions relevant to national planning policies. This diagram expresses them spatially. The core region is the focus of economic growth, with an urban nucleus. Around it upward-transitional areas are in the process of development. Their resource endowments and proximity to the core make them likely beneficiaries of further growth. Resource frontier areas represent the frontier of settlement or even leapfrog into virgin territory to exploit new resources of land or minerals, often with lines of penetration provided by new highways or mineral railways. Downward-transitional areas represent areas of settlement that are stagnant or declining because of decline in their resource base or industrial structure. They are areas which lose population and capital to more dynamic areas. Friedmann also identified regions with special problems, such as those at national boundaries, or where there are conflicting resource uses. At a less complex level, the core and upward-transitional regions could be identified as the 'core' and the remaining areas of the country as the 'periphery'.

Source: Based on Friedmann, 1966: 39–44.

The main cause of the failure has been an inability to appreciate the effects of such a policy 'on the ground'. Myrdal was one of the first to notice that 'back-wash' was a more significant effect of development intervention than trickle-down or spread effects, and that the tide of human migration towards major urban centres, overstimulated by aid-capital, is both a symptom and a cause of both rural poverty and urban imbalances, with many Third World cities developing a para-sitic role in relation to the surrounding countryside. It is scarcely surprising, therefore, that attitudes to the Third World have been changing during the last decade and that there is now a new crop of theories both to explain the past and to outline strategies for the future.

Moreover, important shifts of emphasis have also taken place in the world. The United Nations (UN) is now dominated, numerically, by the new nations of the Third World who have a voice on the international stage. Oil has been recognized as a scarce resource with important reserves in the Third World. The political exploitation of this perception in the Middle East is reflected in the way some of the rules by which richer Northern states abstract mineral wealth from poor ones have changed. The growth and consolidation of China as a world power has made an impact on the thinking of those who live in poor countries. Socialist revolutions have replaced some Western oriented post-colonial regimes by those seeking development by an alternative route. At the same time a new self-assertiveness is seen, not only in the UN but also in the growth of Islamic self-consciousness – a religious radicalism that has transformed the self-image of those who were previously culturally subservient. Matching these changes is the re-evaluation of the colonial (and post-colonial or neo-colonial) development period in theories, not of development, but of *under*-development. Many observers have noted that 'modernization' benefits only the élites of Third World countries. The new state apparatus tends to create an elaborate administrative hierarchy (a civil service). This in itself creates a wage and salary-earning class open to advertising and creating a market for Western style consumer goods. Imports of such goods rise, and in order to save foreign exchange Third World countries 'substitute' such imports by manufacturing locally. The local industrial economy is soon dominated by factories producing beer and spirits, soft drinks, cigarettes and tobacco, confectionary and milk products, transistors and refrigerators. Obviously only those with 'urban' incomes can buy such goods in any quantity. Most of the industrial plants are constructed with imported equipment and use foreign expertise. Spare parts are part of the deal and in this way suppliers ensure that development can only be serviced by external technologies. The manipulation of Third World economies by individual large-scale enterprises (multinational companies) with the connivance and encouragement of local élites is part of a wider malaise which some have identified as the domination of the 'periphery' of the global economy by those who live in the 'metropolitan-core areas' of Europe and America. At a national level, the core area of the primate city dominates the rural periphery. Frank (1969) argued that these connections between satellite and metropolis are channels through which the centre appropriates part of the economic surplus of the satellites, gravitating up towards the economic core of the capitalist world (figure 1.14). Dependency theorists also claim that some regions stifle local entrepreneurial initiative by an uncritical adoption of external assistance.

But a note of caution is appropriate. A righteous anger, even if it is tempered by collective humility, may be just as dangerous a basis for theorizing about Third World development as the old cultural arrogance. At their best such ideas may release productive energies in the direction of solving Third World problems.

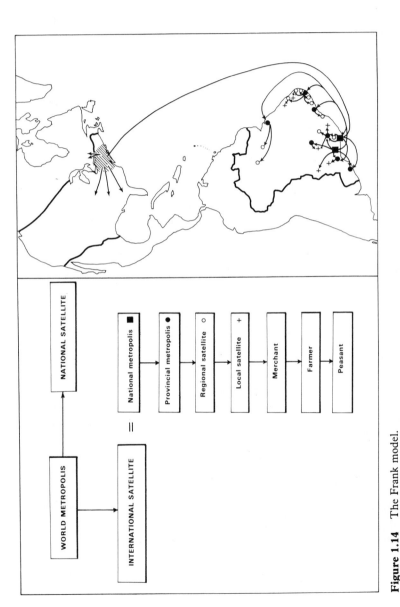

Figure 1.14 The Frank model.

Frank identified (1969) a process of exploitation in capitalist development, in which a metropolis exploits its satellite areas. He envisaged this operating at a variety of scales: at a world scale with the metropolis of the eastern USA exploiting other parts of the world; and at a national scale, with a national metropolis exploiting its satellites. This pattern is shown here both as a diagram of a metropolis–satellite hierarchy, and as a national and international map of the metropolis–satellite relationships of the USA and Brazil, in which the world metropolis exploits its own national satellites within the USA, and an international satellite in Brazil. The latter, São Paulo, becomes the national metropolis exploiting a hierarchy of lower satellites.

At their worst they encourage the substitution of one set of mistakes by another. In the last resort the debate between those who favour 'radical socialist transformation', those who favour a mixed economy with some state control, and those who believe in (more-or-less) unfettered capitalism is not just a Third World affair, and it will be no surprise to find differences of attitude reflected (as they should be) in the pages of this book. Indeed development experience provides us all with much more ammunition for discussion and debate between those who occupy different ideological, theoretical and political positions.

The arguments concerning the merits and demerits of collective control of the means of production, or unfettered free enterprise, are no longer presented in terms of empty theories. Socialist attempts to reduce poverty have now been tried and tested in the same furnace of experience. These sometimes bitter experiments have taught radical regimes that political dogma cannot replace economic reality, that circumstances alter cases. Not all countries are 'ripe for socialism'. Not all regions within a country are going to respond in the same way to uniform policies. Sometimes the political machinations of superior forces (or super-powers) subvert honest attempts to achieve a local initiative. Progressive strategies with any hope of long-term success must always be based on a recognition of the art of the possible. The arguments between those who favour free enterprise and those who prefer collective controls are often presented in the abstract or at a national or international scale of reference. But it is not only a question of either dictatorship or peoples' democracy, totalitarian police state or free and open elections. Against this large-scale ideological backcloth, real decisions are made at a local scale where compromises are more important than ideological confrontation. The resultant systems will surely develop some of the advantages of being able to choose the best from alternative forms of social and economic policies but equally, because we are human, some of the disadvantages of each ideology.

There are at least some hopeful signs that the poor of the Third World are to take an increasingly important part in the decisions about their own future. It took many years of development initiative before, in some countries at least, 'bare-foot' doctors began to replace large prestigious hospitals and rural schools began to teach rural science; before the shanty-town was recognized as a potentially viable social entity rather than an administrative inconvenience. It has taken many years of socialist planning for some communist countries to begin to recognize that personal initiative and private incentive are a vital part of life. There is at least some hope that we have all begun to learn by our mistakes and that the next decade of development will be enriched by this experience. One thing is certain: each day and each hour too many people will still continue to die of starvation for us to become complacent.

2 HISTORICAL PERSPECTIVE

It is not so much in their poverty as in their relationship with the rest of the world that Third World countries find some common identity. Most of these countries had been colonies of European powers at some time between 1400 and 1945. Only parts of Arabia, Iran, Afghanistan, Liberia, China and Thailand had never been under formal European government. Nevertheless, European power affected all of them. When European empires ceased to exist the Third World still bore the legacies of the preceding four centuries. It inherited political, economic and social structures that, even after the dissolution of formal empires, were still influenced by the twentieth-century forces of modern imperialism.

There was nothing new about the formation and expansion of empires, nor were European nations the only dominant world powers between the sixteenth and twentieth centuries. The Turkish empire stretched from the Mediterranean to the Indian Ocean and survived until the First World War. Hindus from India colonized South-East Asia in earlier times and, with the Chinese, controlled much of its trade. Muslim influence had extended from southern Spain and North Africa to India by the thirteenth century.

It was not until the nineteenth century that European empires affected the entire globe but, unlike their predecessors, 400 years of European expansion created an international world order from which virtually no country could exclude itself. A new global system evolved with Europe as the centre of military power, technological invention and wealth, and, with few exceptions, the rest of the world constituted a relatively weaker group of countries on the periphery of international developments. The exceptions included the former European colonies in North America and Australasia; European settlements in these areas produced a totally different variant of colonization. They became self-governing European societies overseas and were effectively extensions of Europe. Subsequently they evolved with their own identities, though still part of the global centre. A further group of colonized territories that do not form part of the Third World are those that were Russian possessions in Asia, which were incorporated into the USSR. Japan, which was also never colonized, has not only become an expansionist power since the late nineteenth century, it has also achieved a technological pre-eminence which currently rivals the industrialized countries in the West.

The historical processes associated with the changes that led to the emergence of the gap that now differentiates the Third World from the industrialized West are the subject of diverse interpretations. The question that many have raised is: did European expansion and influence cause Third World economies and societies to retain traditional and outdated methods of production and social institutions? If this were the case, then it would be pertinent to ask whether this was due to European exploitation of overseas territories, or whether traditional methods of Third World production were so deeply entrenched that they were unable to respond promptly and fully to the modernizing influence of Western development. An alternative view questions whether expansion of the world capitalist economy drew the countries which lay outside the central core of global developments into an international system of capitalism, within which they were not only exploited, but with which their internal systems were unable to cope.

The impact of European expansion was not uniform throughout the world. The pattern of expansion varied, so did the motivation for it, and the countries affected were themselves varied in character, historical background and exploitable resources. However, one thing is clear: the gap in wealth and technology which currently exists between Europe and the European settler colonies on the one hand, and the countries of the Third World on the other, is relatively new.

The Third World on the eve of European expansion

At the time of the European 'Age of Discovery', some indigenous peoples in the Americas, Africa, Asia and Australasia had highly developed sophisticated cultures and technologies. In each continent there existed a range of cultural levels, from simple hunter–gatherer tribes to more advanced, urbanized civilizations.

In Latin America the Aztecs had developed a complex, highly stratified society, with a nobility which held military, secular and priestly authority. Skilled craftsmen worked gold and other precious metals. Intensive agriculture supported a dense rural population and a large, sophisticated urban system, culminating in the capital city Tenochtitlán, which so impressed the Spanish conquerors on their arrival in 1519. In western South America the Incas had also developed an extensive empire. Agricultural techniques included irrigation, terracing and use of the foot plough. Contact between the widely scattered rural communities and the imperial centre at Cuzco was maintained by a well-developed system of roads. Impressive monuments and fortresses further demonstrated the cultural level achieved by the Incas.

In Asia even more advanced civilizations were to be found. China by the time of the Ming dynasty in the fifteenth and sixteenth centuries had inherited a long tradition in philosophy, art and literature. Few technological achievements elsewhere could compare with China's abacus, fine silks, lacquers, porcelains and explosives. Throughout much of South-East Asia Hindu trading empires were contemporaneous with the European Dark Ages. At a time when Western Europe was a collection of small feudal principalities, much of South-East Asia was integrated into a loosely structured, but culturally and commercially sophisticated unity.

Early development in Africa, as in America and Asia, varied greatly. There were, for example, marked contrasts between the societies of the Egyptian, Ethiopian and Sudanese empires on the one hand, and the pygmies of the Congo and the hunter–gatherers of the Kalahari Desert on the other. Some states had well-established trading and agricultural systems, as in the kingdoms of West Africa and Zimbabwe.

Muslim culture, centred on the Middle East, made important contributions to learning in the fields of mathematics and astronomy. In medicine, considerable progress was also made and hospitals were a feature of the principal Muslim cities as early as the eleventh century. Knowledge of chemistry and other natural sciences was advanced and Muslim cartography greatly influenced medieval European map-making in the Mediterranean.

Thus, by the time European expansion began, the continents which now comprise the Third World had nurtured highly complex civilizations with high levels of cultural, technical and social development. Some of these areas were not 'undeveloped' or 'under-developed'. Rather they were what Buchanan (1967: 21) has called 'pre-developed', with societies which had achieved a high degree of cultural, economic and political development before the arrival of Europeans, and in some cases in advance of progress in Europe itself. Their relative backwardness today is due, at least in part, to the impact of European colonialism on their development, which created a particular pattern of relationships between colonizer and colonized, and profoundly modified the internal structures and patterns of the colonized territory. European expansion affected most of the world, and created a pattern of unequal relationships between a European core and a periphery of dependent lands.

Early European expansion

The era of European overseas expansion lasted from the late fifteenth century to the mid-twentieth. This period falls into two distinct phases: the first between 1450 and 1800, and the second the nineteenth century and the period before 1945. The first phase of colonialism was largely in the Americas and associated with considerable settlement by European migrants. During this phase several other parts of the world were as powerful as Europe. However, this phase laid the foundation for later expansion and by the end of the eighteenth century the relative power of Europe in military, scientific and financial spheres was such that the establishment of a core–periphery pattern at a global scale could begin. The second phase of European expansion was more rapid than the first: within 120 years Europe had claimed most of the rest of the world. This phase focused upon

Africa, Asia and the Pacific. Europeans were active in the new colonies in various administrative and commercial capacities, but with some important exceptions such as Algeria, Angola, Mozambique, Rhodesia and Russian Central Asia and Siberia, these were not colonies of settlement.

EUROPE IN THE AMERICAS

Conquest of Latin America was carried out by the Spanish, Portuguese, French, Dutch and British. Spain secured the largest, richest and most diverse territory; and did so with great rapidity. Within seventy years of Columbus's arrival in the Caribbean, Spain had overthrown the Aztec and Inca empires, and occupied most of middle and western South America. Portuguese occupation of Brazil was less rapid, and initially remained close to the seaboard. It is significant for this process of European conquest that the lands of the New World, discovered or undiscovered, were divided between Spain and Portugal by the Pope in 1494. The other European powers came later to the region, securing smaller territories in the Caribbean and Guianas.

These invasions were motivated by economic considerations. The Spaniards in particular sought precious metals, exploiting gold in the Caribbean before 1510; major sources of silver in northern Mexico and upper Peru from the mid-sixteenth century; and lesser mineral deposits from Mexico to Chile. Mining was the key to the early Spanish colonial economy, providing wealth for export to Spain, the impetus to urban growth, and fostering extensive development of ancillary activities to serve the mines – producing food, pack animals, timber, and salt and mercury for use in silver processing. This economy was exploitative not only of land but also of labour. The mines required substantial manpower, which was obtained by imposing forced labour on the indigenous population. Initially the Indians were also required to provide services and tribute to Spanish settlers, later they were induced or required to provide labour on the substantial landholdings the Spaniards created. Spain exercized close control over its colonies, regulating administration, the urban pattern, controlling trade and restricting the development of manufacturing. The colonial territories were exploited in the interests of the metropolis.

Portuguese occupation of eastern South America was less rapid. After initial small-scale extraction of forest products, the Portuguese developed a plantation economy producing sugar in the north-eastern coastlands. The large landholdings were worked initially by Indians, but after these had fled or died, slaves were imported from Africa and provided a major element in the Brazilian economy until after 1850. The Portuguese envied the mineral wealth of Spanish America, and exploration of the interior resulted in the discovery of gold and diamonds in the late seventeenth and early eighteenth centuries. This prompted the first significant settlement of interior Brazil, and also contributed to the westward push of Portuguese territory beyond the 1494 demarcation.

Sugar was also a major element in the colonies of the other European powers, in the Caribbean islands and the Guianas, again based on plantations and the use of African slave labour. The wealth generated by sugar made these possessions the most valuable parts of the emerging empires of eighteenth-century Britain and France. The sugar monoculture of the plantation had a stultifying effect on other sectors of the rural economy, limiting the production of basic food crops and fostering the need to import essential foodstuffs. Plantation society was dominated in the first instance by Europeans, and later by people of mixed European and African or Asian ancestry. Slaves formed the lowest echelon of this society, and, even after emancipation, their descendants found themselves at the base of a highly stratified and status-conscious society. The plantation system left pervasive influences on both the economy and society in the Caribbean. It had cultural implications as well, engendering a belief in the intrinsic worth of everything European and the negation of anything African or local.

Throughout Latin America three centuries of European rule brought profound change. Vast areas of land had been brought into cultivation, major mineral resources were exploited; cities, routes and ports had been built; and trade, albeit closely controlled and narrowly based, had been developed. Yet most of the benefits accrued to Europe, or to European settlers in the region; consequences for the indigenous population were limited and often adverse. European lifestyles, language and religion were, with varying degrees of success, imposed on the aboriginal populations. In many areas of Latin America the demographic implications of conquest were considerable. As a result of warfare, enslavement and disease the Indian populations of the Caribbean, Middle America, the Andes and Brazil were substantially reduced. Substitution of the indigenous labour force by black slaves also profoundly modified the demographic pattern. Slavery was most important in Brazil, the West Indies and the Guianas which received an estimated seven to eight million African slaves during the period from 1550 to 1850. In consequence, in much of the Caribbean and in the canelands, goldfields and early coffee plantations of Brazil, blacks became numerically dominant in the population. In addition miscegenation between whites and blacks, and the surviving Indian elements elsewhere, gave rise to the substantial proportion of people of mixed race that exists in much of the continent.

INDEPENDENCE OF THE LATIN AMERICAN COLONIES

European colonization in the Americas reached its peak by the late eighteenth century. Shortly afterwards Brazil and the mainland colonies of Spain became independent. In the Caribbean, by contrast, although French St Domingue secured its independence (as Haiti) in 1804, colonization persisted much later into the 1980s.

The movement to independence was shaped by both internal and external influences. In Spanish America locally born Spaniards came to resent the inferior role forced upon them in administration, and the close control of trade exercized by and in the interest of peninsular Spain. There was resentment at all levels of society, by negro slaves and Indian serfs, mestizos and creoles, and recent immigrants. This internal dissatisfaction was compounded by external influences. The colonies had been exposed to the liberal ideas of eighteenth-century Europe, which were made explicit in the French Revolution. The achievement of independence by the USA demonstrated that freedom from colonial power could be secured. Napoleon's invasion of Spain considerably weakened the link between the colonies and the Spanish Crown. Revolutionary movements began in Mexico and elsewhere in 1808, and more extensive wars of independence soon afterwards. These uprisings were spontaneous and local, but were responses to similar circumstances. Mexico, Venezuela, Colombia, Argentina and Chile were the principal nuclei of the independence movement, culminating in the fall of Lima in 1821. In the space of fifteen years the Spanish empire was reduced to Cuba and Puerto Rico.

Yet independence brought no profound change to Spanish America. There had been no real social revolution, for the urban creoles merely replaced the Spanish administrators, and in the countryside the *caudillos* ('strong' men) fought against the new authorities. For the bulk of population little had changed. Nor did the end of Spanish trading restrictions bring greater prosperity from the substantial mineral resources, diverse agricultural products and abundant uncultivated land.

Brazilian independence was achieved less violently, for Portuguese rule had been less harsh than that of Spain. Again Napoleon was the stimulus to independence, forcing the Portuguese court to flee to Rio de Janeiro, which became the capital of the Portuguese empire. When the court returned to Lisbon Brazil was unwilling to accept a return to colonial status and declared its independence in 1822.

Independence in Latin America did not bring immediate and rapid progress. In the former Spanish territories there was strife, disorder and dictatorship. It was not until the 1850s that economic transformation began to take place and the continent's resource assets began to be realized. Countries of Western Europe, particularly Britain, began to provide the capital, coal, manufactured goods and technical skills the continent lacked in return for raw materials. There was economic advance with the building of railways and telegraph lines, the introduction of steamships, and improvement of the ports and urban services. Such developments, however, were in the interests of Europe as much as Latin America and some of the economic and spatial patterns that evolved were essentially to serve the emerging European core, rather than the newly independent states.

When the European empires in America began to crumble, in Asia only the foundations of empires had been laid. The Spanish and Portuguese had several trading and naval bases throughout the region and Spain controlled the Philippines. The main objective of the Dutch, English and French in the East was to acquire wealth through trade without necessarily controlling territory. However, the private trading companies received official patronage and were exceedingly powerful in the areas where they operated. The Dutch East India Company was especially prosperous in Indonesia, and the English East India Company in India.

The state-owned French company held sway in Indochina and challenged the English in India, though with limited success. Meanwhile, European penetration of Africa was still in its early stages and confined to coastal trading posts, but, as in Asia, the foundations for later intervention had been established.

The pattern of European economic penetration into independent Latin America in the second half of the nineteenth century was paralleled by a more comprehensive role elsewhere, in Africa and Asia, involving the creation of new empires. The period of the nineteenth century and up to 1914 was an age of imperialism. The countries of Western Europe, motivated by political rivalry, militarism, a desire for markets and for sources of cheap raw materials, sought control of territory in the tropics. These incursions brought some advantages in the establishment of law and order, the introduction of medical skills, and the creation of large-scale economic activities: mines, plantations and transport systems. Yet if imperialism was a stimulus to economic and social change, it also created a distorted pattern of development. The new colonies were not seen as areas to undergo balanced development; instead they were major sources of raw materials for European cities and industries, and potential markets for the products of those cities and industries. The direction of development was, therefore, in the interests of the imperial power, not of the colonial territory and population.

European expansion in the nineteenth century

European empires went on to expand faster during the nineteenth century than at any previous time. In 1800 Europe and its possessions (including ex-colonies) covered about 55 per cent of the land surface of the world (figure 2.1); in 1878, 67 per cent; in 1914, 84 per cent and yet more by the outbreak of the Second World War in 1939.

The industrialization of Europe made tropical colonies desirable as markets for manufactures, advantageous places for the investment of surplus capital, and as assured sources of raw materials. Overseas expansion was also an expression of European nationalism and a growing sense of superiority over the rest of the world. Christian missions were established everywhere and explorers penetrated what they regarded as 'dark continents' and 'unknown lands'.

By the end of the nineteenth century the 'scramble for Africa' had resulted in virtually all of the continent being divided between Britain, France, Germany, Portugal, Belgium, Spain and Italy. Territories in the Pacific had been claimed by Britain, France and Germany, the USA and Spain. Russia occupied Central Asia as far as the Afghanistan border and the British increased their control over the Indian subcontinent as far as the North-West frontier. The latter two powers agreed to preserve the neutrality of Afghanistan and Persia (now Iran) as non-colonized buffer states. Similarly, Siam (now Thailand) lost its empire and was subjected to unequal economic treaties, but remained independent as a buffer between British and French possessions. With this one exception, South-East Asia was completely

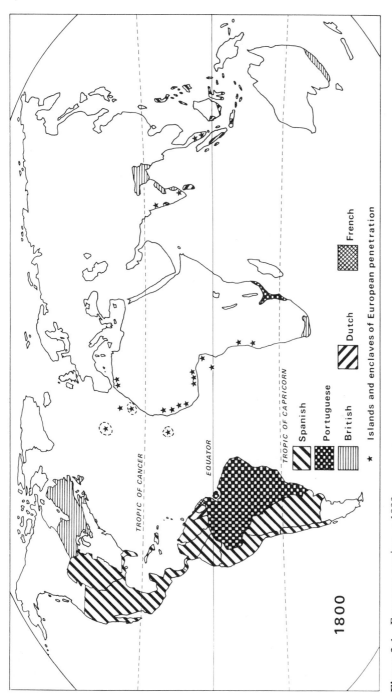

Figure 2.1 European empires, *c.* 1800.

divided between the Netherlands, Britain, France and the USA by 1914. The Chinese empire survived the encroachment of the European powers and the expansionist designs of Russia, Japan and the USA, but while diplomatic deadlock preserved China's political independence, economic imperialism prevailed through informal control over its government. The colonial powers also secured extraterritorial rights in the Treaty Ports.

AFRICA

In Africa the precise type and impact of colonial expansion varied. After 1870 European countries sought to expand their economic and political influence. In some cases, such as Kenya and Algeria, settler colonies were established. In others, such as the Ivory Coast and German Cameroons, plantation economies controlled by metropolitan import–export companies were created. In yet others, such as Zambia and the Congo, mineral resources provided the basis for exploitation. In some cases essentially negative influences prevailed – in Uganda and Chad political control was taken to prevent the expansion of other colonial powers. However, the establishment of a dual economy, of a modern, European export-orientated sector alongside and undermining the traditional economy, was common to all. Internal conditions and local peoples were no longer the determinants of subsequent events. The African territories became part of an international economic and political system controlled from Europe.

In the Islamic states of North-West Africa the French and later the Italians and Spanish, acquired land primarily by conquest. French settlers engaged in the production of three major export crops: olives, wheat and vines. This export sector tended to occupy the best land and use machinery, though the pattern of exploitation varied. In the earliest colony, Algeria, the French encouraged large-scale immigration of small landowners; in Tunisia and Morocco the creation of very large commercial enterprises was more common. Throughout these territories though, the modern, export-orientated agriculture stood in contrast to the traditional agriculture and extensive pastoralism of the native peoples.

In contrast, European activities in Egypt were primarily commercial. Financial indebtedness brought Anglo–French control over governmental and financial affairs, and then British occupation in 1882. Exports of cotton drew Egypt into the world economy, with Europe providing the industrial and financial skills and Egypt the raw materials. The British encouraged the development of irrigation and an extension of the cultivated area. Cotton output increased substantially, but it continued to be an export crop, rather than the basis for a local textile industry, despite the fact that cotton textiles constituted one-third of imports.

In West Africa the European impact was markedly different. It occurred initially through missionaries and explorers whose activities aroused considerable public interest in their home countries. Until the 1860s European activity was associated with suppressing the slave trade, and there was little expansion inland. A flourishing commerce began to develop in vegetable oils and groundnuts. These products were grown and collected by Africans, with little intervention by Europeans. However, the trade required extensive commercial contacts and led to rivalries between British, French and German trading companies, and prompted increased European control over the region. Gradually treaties made with local rulers became more binding until they led to the virtual loss of indigenous control. In both British and French West Africa economic policy subordinated African interests to those of the metropolis. Though there was less alienation of land than in some other parts of Africa, and peasant farmers produced most of the groundnuts and palm oil, the colonial system forced them to concentrate on export crops, rather than on producing subsistence foods.

East Africa was drawn inevitably into the network of world trade after the opening of the Suez Canal in 1869. Rivalry between the European powers ensued, with Britain eventually emerging as the dominant influence. Initial interest was in the suppression of the slave trade, but by the early twentieth century efforts were being made to make the colonies profitable additions to the empire, mainly by agricultural development. New systems of land use and land tenure were introduced, particularly in Kenya. Large-scale immigration was encouraged and substantial areas of land were alienated. The pattern was not uniform, however, for in Uganda export cotton was primarily a peasant crop. In those areas where land was sold, leased or given to Europeans by the authorities, traditional African economic activities were disrupted. The pastoral and nomadic tribes were severely affected and some put up considerable resistance, which the British quelled, frequently by force. Labour shortages were overcome by a system of taxation which forced the Africans to work for monetary wages while at the same time preventing the accumulation of capital within the African reserves.

In Southern Africa the local economy and social systems were irreversibly altered with the penetration of Dutch settlers from the seventeenth century onwards. Traditional seasonal grazing lands were appropriated and disease, particularly smallpox epidemics, decimated large numbers of the population. The Africans had no option but to work for the Europeans or to retreat into less-hospitable desert areas, for their cattle were seized or killed and a system of taxation was forcibly imposed. The Rural Reserve policy, generally applied in the second half of the nineteenth century (except in Rhodesia − now Zimbabwe − where it came much later), introduced a new element into the territorial relations between Europeans and Africans in the southern part of the continent. The best land went to the Europeans, with the reserves generally on the more marginal areas, and suffering from overcrowding.

Discoveries of gold and diamonds in the second half of the nineteenth century brought about further and even more fundamental changes in the political economy of Southern Africa. A system of migratory labour evolved and men left the reserves for varying periods of time to work in the mines. This gave the mining magnates full control over the workers. It also greatly influenced the character of the urban areas which developed and the social and economic relations between European and African.

THE INDIAN SUBCONTINENT

There were major contrasts between the colonial regimes that developed in Africa and in the Indian subcontinent, and also within the latter. These differences reflected the varying conditions within which the colonial systems operated as well as the diverse purposes the colonies were intended to serve.

In India the British consolidated earlier trading interests and extended their influence until, in 1849, they controlled the whole country. The Indian empire became an important source of agricultural exports, particularly of cotton, jute, hides, oilseed and tea, but competition from British producers destroyed the existing artisan cotton textile industry.

English became the medium of official communication and of education, and India eventually adopted British political institutions. Acceptance of alien rule was fostered principally by making very few changes in the basic structure of Indian life. Moreover, members of the established social groups, the aristocracy, the merchants, bankers and educated professionals, were absorbed into the expanding civil service which gave them the illusion of power. The advantages of British rule to India probably lay most in its imposition of law and order over a vast, hitherto divided subcontinent; the provision of a system of centralized government; and the construction of a comprehensive system of roads, railways and canals which could facilitate subsequent large-scale industrial and agricultural growth.

The colonial experience of Ceylon (now Sri Lanka) was dominated by the development of a plantation economy. While rubber plantations were able to attract peasant labour as the work was intermittent, local people refused to work on the coffee and tea estates. Tea production was largely carried out by Tamil immigrants imported from southern India. The increase in plantation production led to the eventual neglect of the irrigation systems, and decline in rice production. The system of compulsory labour for maintenance of the irrigation system was effectively destroyed by the British administration and with it much of the power of village councils. Self-sufficiency in food production was lost and rice, the staple food, had to be imported, especially in the dry zone.

The expatriate plantation sector grew rapidly and created great wealth. Little of this wealth ever reached the Ceylonese, though there were some exceptions. An upper class of indigenous landowners had existed long before the arrival of the British, making their profits by renting out rather than cultivating land. The rise of the coffee industry gave them an impetus for engaging in production; and later many began to produce tea, coconuts and rubber. Because the owners of such estates were local, the profits remained in Ceylon.

SOUTH-EAST ASIA

The countries of South-East Asia were once basically self-sufficient but were changed into suppliers of primary commodities for Western markets by the impact of colonialism. They were thus brought into almost total dependence on the fluctuations of a world market over which they had no control. Where a labour supply was not forthcoming immigrants were brought in or came spontaneously to occupy positions as middlemen in colonial commercial activities. Meanwhile, the majority of the region's indigenous inhabitants became increasingly marginalized within their own society, and dependent upon the new monetary economy into which they were forced.

Dutch control of Indonesia and, in particular, Java, was intensified in the nineteenth century under the 'culture system' which created a planned economy on a vast scale, and converted Java into a massive producer of sugar, coffee, tea and other foodstuffs for the Dutch market. This system led to the diversification of crops, the introduction of scientific methods of production including modern irrigation works and a great improvement and extension of the communication network. With all the prosperity that ensued from the culture system went gross exploitation of the Javanese cultivators, and forced labour when voluntary workers could not be recruited. The problem of acute poverty was far more widespread in the prosperous island of Java than in the less-developed islands of Indonesia. Less-intensive colonial contact in the outer islands of the archipelago meant that people were less involved in the production of export crops and relatively unaffected by the rising demands and expectations involved in the coming of a monetary economy.

The experience of the British colonies in South-East Asia differed only in detail from that of Dutch Indonesia. The wealth of Burma which had undoubtedly been developed through the production of rice, tea, lead, rubber, copper and other export goods, was largely in alien hands. *Laissez-faire* colonial policies permitted free trade, British control of resources, and the immigration of Indians who acted as commercial middlemen and moneylenders. Poverty revolved around the agrarian problem and the plight of the peasantry whose new financial commitments kept them in a state of continual indebtedness. From a self-contained subsistence economy focused upon the social life of the village, at least 50 per cent of the Burmese peasants had become landless agricultural tenants and labourers by 1940. At the same time progress in the Western sense had occurred in Burma as it had throughout the rest of the colonial world. British rule had liberated the Burmese from many of the restrictions and abuses of traditional society and there had been some improvements in health. Balanced against these benefits was the fact that the Burmese had a disproportionately small share in the great prosperity of their country and for the majority, life had become marginalized as they strove to survive within the framework, though on the fringe, of the new international system.

Malaya's transformation into a leading producer of tin and rubber was associated with large-scale Chinese and Indian immigration so that in its peninsular states a multiracial society emerged where the immigrants outnumbered the indigenes. The port of Singapore became the centre of British financial and commercial interests in the region, and virtually a city of Chinese traders.

While development on the peninsula was rapid in the regions of Chinese-dominated tin mining, the rest of the country was little changed and the social imbalance between the immigrants and indigenous Malays became very clear. The development of the west-coast states was further increased by the British construction of roads and railways linking the mining areas, plantations and ports.

In contrast to the situation in most of South-East Asia, in Malaya there existed the preconditions of a balanced agrarian policy. There was an abundance of land relative to population size and a highly prosperous tin industry that financed public works and other developments without resort to a rigid taxation system. Furthermore, the high level of Chinese and Indian immigration obviated the need for coercing Malays into working on the plantations. Smallholders were not seen to be in competition with the estates, so that in contrast to other colonial situations the British authorities in Malaya also encouraged the development of small-scale farming.

In Sarawak, Brunei and Borneo European enterprise was minimal. The countries were poor in resources and, in the case of Sarawak, the paternalistic administration deliberately discouraged modern commercial exploitation. The result was a far slower rate of economic growth or development of an infrastructure than was the case elsewhere in the region. In 1940 Sarawak was little changed from what it had been a century before, with much of the land still covered in virgin forest and the greater part of the population engaged in subsistence farming. Of its known resources only oil was of any real significance for the outside world. The advantage was that large numbers of people had not become marginal within their own society and economy. Yet by the mid-twentieth century even Sarawak could not escape being part of an international world, existing within the framework of a global monetary economy.

Contrasts in colonial activity also existed among the French South-East Asian territories of Vietnam, Cambodia (now Kampuchea) and Laos. However, the differences were more of degree than of kind. The pre-existing differences in the development of the northern and southern parts of Vietnam were further exaggerated by the colonial regime. The densely populated north was largely left to its traditional self-sufficient subsistence economy based on rice production. The south bore all the imprints of the classic colonial situation: large-scale commercial enterprises and the creation of a distinct dual economy. Development, which was concentrated in the more sparsely populated southern region, was associated with the appalling poverty of the peasants, their continual indebtedness to moneylenders and other middlemen and an ever growing population. Immigrants to Vietnam were mainly Chinese who had been going there long before the beginning of colonial commercial activities, but who went in increased numbers during the colonial period. They played the role of middlemen operating between the Europeans and the Vietnamese peasants.

Cambodia and Laos, like the neglected eastern territories of Malaya, were perceived to be countries of low economic opportunity and were, therefore, omitted from the mainstream of colonial activities. They remained areas where a simple subsistence pattern of life prevailed. In the case of Cambodia the economy contributed small amounts of rice, rubber, maize and pepper to the international market, and Laos produced some teak, tin and coffee. As elsewhere in the colonial world, even the small amount of commercial activity that developed was monopolized by outsiders – in this case, French, Vietnamese and Chinese. The simple, though highly refined, cultural life of the Khmer people of Cambodia and likewise the traditional world of the Laotians were, as a consequence, only minimally affected by the direct influence of colonialism. However, they were not to escape the many indirect implications of being poor unsophisticated societies in an increasingly prosperous and technological world.

The Philippines shared many of the features of colonialism in the region. Typically, there was a dual economy: foreign-owned plantations produced a few primary goods for the world market while the subsistence sector was characterized by poverty and indebtedness to a group of middlemen comprised mainly of Chinese immigrants. On the other hand, Philippine society differed from any other in South-East Asia in that at the end of the nineteenth century its history of colonization by Europeans – the Spanish – had already lasted for three centuries. By the time the island societies came under US colonial rule they were in many respects Westernized in terms of culture and attitudes. This factor was of major importance to the pattern of US penetration in the twentieth century. The traditional Asian self-contained subsistence economy had already been influenced by one oriented towards the world markets. A basic infrastructure existed and the range of commercial agencies and credit facilities characteristic of a monetary economy were an accepted part of Philippine life. The major economic change under US rule was the spectacular rise of the sugar industry which altered the economy into a virtual monoculture.

THE PACIFIC ISLANDS

Traders, whalers and missionaries accounted for most of the Europeans in the Pacific in the nineteenth century. These were mainly British and some French nationals. By the end of the century the US also had significant commercial interests in the region. The implications of colonization for the Pacific islands were broadly similar to those of other Asian countries affected by the spread of the plantation economy. The earlier small-scale trade in sandalwood and sea-slugs for the Chinese market was replaced by a much larger export trade in coconut oil and guano. Both of these products were controlled by small settlements of Europeans in the islands. Demand for plantation labour led to many social and political disturbances, and as a consequence by the 1860s the political systems in Fiji, Samoa and other island groups were beginning to disintegrate.

The impact of colonialism

The process of colonization within any one country or group of countries was conditioned by the pre-existing historical circumstances and the attractiveness of its resources to the colonizers. In turn, these affected the degree of exploitation and the nature of the developments that took place and consequently the level of marginalization that occurred within the economy and society. The communities least attractive to European settlement, such as Laos and Cambodia in South-East Asia, remoter islands of the Pacific and the more isolated areas of central Africa, were among the least exploited. Yet, their greater retention of indigenous social traditions and economic practices did not enhance their possibilities for future development. On the contrary, they have remained among the poorest of Third World countries. In so far as they gained from their isolation, it has only been because the lower levels of Western material expectations have been aroused. On the other hand, Malaysia, well-endowed with resources for which there is international demand, or the Philippines with its cultural sophistication, are examples of countries which though exploited by the colonial system have, nevertheless, emerged with the facility to compete favourably by comparison with other Third World countries.

The net balance in the advantages versus the disadvantages of colonial penetration was not, in the last analysis, a measure of the total influence that European expansion had upon the countries of the periphery. It was being on the periphery of global events and the internal marginalization of large sectors of the population with which this was associated, that made the vital difference to future developments.

It is not surprising that the preservation of political sovereignty in China, Afghanistan, Thailand and Iran was in no way sufficient to isolate these countries from the effects of an evolving global power balance, which they were in no position to counter. They were all the victims of unequal trade treaties with European countries and undoubtedly part of the colonial sphere of influence in the Middle and Far East. The Open Door Policy imposed upon China by Britain, France, the US and Japan virtually made China an economic satellite of the imperial powers until the communist revolution of 1949.

Other countries which maintained political autonomy also bore significant hallmarks of colonialism. Thailand's economy, for example, depended on the export of four primary products – rice, teak, rubber and tin – of which only rice was controlled by Thais. In return, manufactured goods were all imported. A typical colonial economy developed, with a foreign-owned export sector and a traditional agricultural sector and even rice was transformed from being a subsistence crop to a commercial one. As in the formal colonies, peasants were forced into a marginal way of life in relation to the country's mainstream of production. While Thailand gained none of the apparent advantages of a formal colony, such as European medical and educational services or a communication system, its slower pace of change might well be viewed as a net advantage. Thailand escaped many of the socially disruptive effects of colonialism that were experienced by neighbouring Vietnam and Burma.

Colonial status was primarily a political phenomenon but the economic aspects of European dominance in the world, which colonialism heightened, did not necessarily depend on formal relationships. Economically, therefore, all the world outside of the settler colonies of North America and Australasia came under the domination of Europe and, later, under the influence of these former settler colonies as well (figure 2.2).

Decolonization

In 1939 the colonial empires in Africa, Asia and the Pacific were at their peak; by 1965 they had virtually ceased to exist. There is no simple explanation for this rapid decolonization. It was undoubtedly due to a combination of factors, and varied with different territories. The demand for independence came both from the colonies themselves and also from external forces which eventually militated against the continuation of empires.

The nationalism which crystallized the response in the colonies against alien rule was a European phenomenon until the Second World War, but through exposure of the colonial élite to Europeans and European education, nationalist ideas were ultimately transmitted to the colonies themselves. In addition, the period of European occupation of the colonies had brought about such fundamental change in the indigenous societies that the conditions which had made alien rule possible in the first place had been destroyed by those societal changes themselves. Large-scale mining and agricultural operations produced both an urban and rural landless proletariat. Growing populations led to a shortage of land, improved communications broke down the isolation of village communities. Religious teaching and secular education created an awareness of the differences between Europeans and colonial subjects, and the rising expectations developed through the increased awareness of Western forms of modernization and technology all combined to produce the conditions that made nationalism an easily generated force among colonial populations at large. Further, it is likely that within certain societies, in particular those of Islam, the preconditions for nationalism and opposition to Western, Christian domination were already latent at the time of colonization and it was simply the opportunity for self-assertion that came later. However, it was not essential that these preconditions should exist within each society, for once the trend had been set by some countries the process spread to others. Just as it had been impossible for countries on the periphery to avoid the influence of European power during the expansion of overseas empires so, later, it was only a small number of territories that were not carried along by the waves of decolonization which swept the empires away.

External influences also contributed to the dissolution of empires. The Russian Revolution gave impetus to the notion of mass movements and class struggle. It generated anti-imperialist sentiments which had their impact on West European thinking, encouraging the view that colonial domination was intrinsically immoral. The USA also began to exert pressure on the European powers as it pursued its own expansionist goals in the mid-twentieth century. However, the Second World War had the most direct impact upon the relationship between

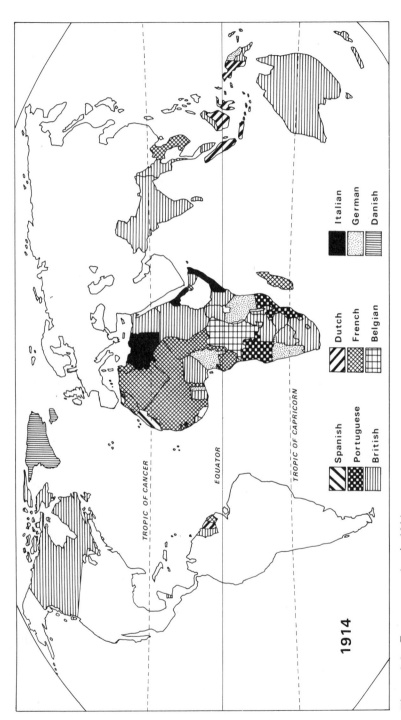

Figure 2.2 European empires in 1914.

Source: Fieldhouse, 1966: 241.

colonies and their metropolises. During the war France, Belgium and the Nether-lands were cut off from their dependencies and it was largely impossible to return to full colonial rule after the war. Other colonies were less affected, and in the long-established Caribbean colonies, for example, the notion of Britain as the 'mother country' was greatly encouraged by the sense of allegiance that the war fostered. Yet the war brought fundamental changes to the colonial world, and during the 25 years after 1945 substantial decolonization took place in two main waves. Most of the states that achieved independence in the first phase of decolon-ization, from 1945–50, were in the Islamic Middle East and Asia. In the second phase, the majority were in Africa (figure 2.3).

All that remained of European empires by 1965 were either territories that had been fully incorporated into the colonizing state, or those that were so small or poor that they did not think independence feasible. France incorporated its Caribbean colonies as Overseas Departments, and its small Pacific dependencies as Overseas Territories. Portugal still held most of its empire and was only forced to relinquish Mozambique and Angola after the fall of the Salazar regime in 1974. The British and Dutch retained some of their island colonies, many of which became independent in the 1970s. Spain incorporated the Canary Islands, relinquishing its West African colonies in the 1970s. Russia incorporated all her colonial territories as part of the USSR, and the USA incorporated Hawaii and retained its other possessions in the Caribbean and the Pacific as self-governing dependencies. The only countries outside these categories were Zimbabwe, South West Africa and the Republic of South Africa in which large European settle-ments had become established, but which differed from the settler colonies of North America and Australasia in that the European population never became a numerical majority. Similar situations existed in Algeria, Zambia and Kenya and independence was resisted for some time. However, all three finally became sovereign states before 1965. In the remaining anomalies, white minority rule prevailed until 1979 in Zimbabwe and continues in South Africa and Namibia.

The consequences of colonialism for the periphery

The colonial experience had drawn the countries of the Third World into close linkages with the colonial powers of Europe, but the relationship that emerged was not a reciprocal one; the benefits that accrued to the core were greater than those received by the periphery. Even after independence the balance, with the possible exception of the impact of the OPEC (Organization of Petroleum Exporting Countries) oil crisis, tended to favour the former colonial powers. Indeed, the unequal nature of the exchange tended to favour the continued economic advance of the rich North to the detriment of the poor South.

The colonial experience should not, of course, be seen entirely as a negative process. We can only speculate what the experience of the colonized territories (and the colonizers) might have been without this major episode in world history. The colonial period did witness a diffusion of economic ideas and technology.

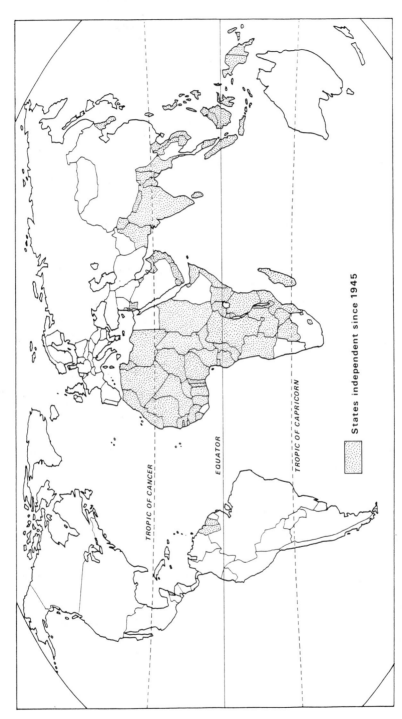

Figure 2.3 Countries obtaining political independence since 1945.

States independent since 1945

Colonial governments provided a basic infrastructure of railways, ports and highways, or provided the stability which encouraged private investment in these fields. Such projects were primarily in the interests of the colonial power, but they did provide a basis, even if an imperfect one, for later independent development.

In some cases colonial governments established law and order, provided a basic administrative structure, and, together with the churches, introduced improved medical and educational systems. Colonialism also generated contact with ideas and scientific advancements in the West, providing models of economic development. These models have largely been retained by the former colonies after independence. Thus, many Third World countries still maintain close linkages with the First World, structuring their policies for development according to patterns in the West, while others have been more deeply influenced by the ideologies and development processes of the Second World.

The nature of the colonial experience has posed many problems for Third World countries. In the typical colonial administration non-Europeans had virtually no share in government at the higher levels of control and authority. After independence, national governments had to take over from administrations that had no deep sense of identification with local interests. Their predecessors had in all cases followed a conservative path, having lacked the wider public support and thus the confidence to institute major change. Other political consequences lay in the Balkanization of regions through the creation of national boundaries bearing little relationship to pre-existing tribal or cultural zones. Unrelated, even hostile ethnic and tribal groups were brought together and a homogeneous colonial authority imposed on them. With independence, the emergent states have in some cases been divided and disrupted to the point of open and persistent warfare as tribal conflict is exacerbated by political competitiveness and the domination of one group over the rest.

Patterns of land ownership and land use were profoundly disrupted in many areas by the impact of colonialism. In the old empires of Central and South America, as in the later empires in Asia and Africa, ownership of land by the colonizers was directly related to production but most of what was produced was for consumption in the metropolis.

The plantation colonies, whether for sugar or coffee in Brazil and the Caribbean, tea, rice and rubber in South and South-East Asia, cotton, cocoa and coffee in Africa or coconuts in the Pacific, formed part of an expanding export sector. The predominance of this sector forced the producing countries of the periphery into a precariously vulnerable position in relation to international financial systems and market demand. The wealth it created went, for the most part, to the European and North American metropolises. Meanwhile, interest in resources available for local production declined; wage labour superseded exchange and communal obligations; and the financial rewards of the economic system were rarely invested in the producing country.

Among other effects of the dual production system were its lasting social and demographic consequences. In most cases plantation agriculture involved the inflow of large labour supplies. Millions of Africans were imported as slaves to the sugar plantations of Brazil, to Spanish America and to the Caribbean. Later, after the abolition of slavery, Indian labour was contracted for plantations in the islands of the Caribbean, Pacific and Indian Oceans and in East Africa. Tamil workers from south India filled the labour deficits for coffee and, later, tea plantations in Sri Lanka. Likewise, Indians and Chinese went to the plantations and mines of East and South-East Asia in large numbers. In some of these areas, such as Sri Lanka, Malaysia, Indonesia and the Caribbean, ethnic and racial tension has developed and in some cases it has taken on major social and political significance producing highly disruptive forces.

The advantages of medical services established in the colonies – especially in the fields of combating prevalent debilitating diseases which reduced working capacity – were balanced by the implications they had for the demographic structure. The prolongation of lifespan, coupled with the continuing economic and social prestige of having large families, resulted in rapid increases in population size. In many areas increases in food production were less rapid, with obvious serious effects. The orientation of economic systems towards monetary reward and the attractions of Western consumer society have encouraged people to seek paid jobs. Lack of such jobs in both the countryside and the city has contributed to the persisting population problem.

In addition, empires were not built solely on economic relationships. They involved cultural and psychological factors that affected different social groups in various ways. The prestige of the colonizer was important in the accomplishment of effective colonization. Indeed, it was a fundamental feature of dominion that the masters believed implicitly in their own judgements and constantly sought to reinforce them. Ethnocentricism, combined with the motivations of expansion, provided a powerful component of colonialism. By the turn of the nineteenth century, people in the industrialized countries of Europe and America perceived the world as essentially comprised of themselves and a vast majority of 'natives'. Their unquestioned belief in their own superiority over 'the natives' represented the outcome of the intellectual structures and philosophies that both accompanied colonization and, at the same time, helped to make it possible.

Racism and a sense of superiority became factors used to justify colonization while, at the same time, they were also a consequence of it. The romanticized version of the American Indian and the African as noble savages in European literature which persisted as late as the nineteenth century gave way in popular interpretation to that of the uncivilized and indolent native. Similarly, the exotic image of the Orient and respect for the Eastern sage were obliterated after the eighteenth century by the view that Asians were inferior. In the late nineteenth century when colonialism, conquest and imperialism were at their height, Europeans no longer had any doubt about their superiority over the rest of the world, its peoples and their cultures. Eventually, what was 'good' for the colonized was seen from the viewpoint of the colonial masters. Of equal, if not greater, significance was the fact that even the colonized peoples themselves came to believe it.

Plate 2.1 External elements in the Third World landscape.
a) Norfolk Hotel, Nairobi, Kenya. The European settler population in Kenya, as else-where, created a landscape and infrastructure in the image of the metropolitan country.
b) Even in Third World countries which were not colonies, developed world influences may be noted: a bar in Thailand.

Education, like technology and social patterns which evolved under changing conditions in the West, became superimposed and partially adopted elsewhere. This has encouraged imitation of Western ideas rather than innovation within local environments on the periphery. In turn, this trend has multiplied the implications of Western contact. Language provides one example of the superimposition of new structures upon colonial cultures. The local élites, and in some cases entire populations, came to accept the language of their colonial masters, rather than the foreigners learning theirs. Thus, throughout the world, numerous languages and tribal and regional dialects became subordinate to the few pre-eminent European languages.

Whether aware of the consequences or not, those in the periphery who have been educated in the European tradition form a group who are fundamentally removed, if not altogether alienated, from their own environment. This has had the effect of reducing and in some cases even preventing creativity and inventiveness within an indigenous setting. Furthermore, large numbers of people have continued to be educated for roles that they could not, or would not, play locally but could more readily assume in the metropolises of the centre. The migration of the highly skilled from Third World countries to such metropolises has produced a self-perpetuating depletion of trained people and created a drain on investment in human resources.

Perceptions and goals conditioned by the West through the mass media and other aspects of disseminated Western technology, bear no relation to the reality in much of the periphery. To the large numbers of people in the Third World who have become marginal in an economic sense may be added many more who have become alienated by the emergence of unrealistic expectations.

Conclusion

The era of European expansion overseas irreversibly affected and altered the non-European world in two fundamental ways. At the international level it created a dependency relationship of the periphery upon the centre, while at the national scale this same relationship brought about the marginality of local internal structures. The effect of the economic relations that evolved, or were otherwise established, was a reflection of the balance of power between Europe and the rest of the world, in particular the increasing strength and sophistication of European industrialization, financial acumen and military strength. The peripheral countries came to depend on Western capital for their own developments. The net effect was the increase in the wealth and power of Europe, and their commensurate decline in the rest. The control the West exerted over the resources of its colonies was through agricultural and mineral production as well as the direction and terms of trade. The sheer discrepancy in global power that was reflected in the evolution of the centre–periphery relationship, permitted the continued and renewed penetration of the Third World by imperialist powers in the second half of the twentieth century. The centre–periphery relationship has therefore been perpetuated to the present time and on this hinges most factors that determine the characteristics of the present Third World.

By 1965, the era of formal empire was virtually over, yet the industrialized Western countries were still able to dictate terms of trade and other economic arrangements. Clearly, a force far greater than mere economic or political controls had been generated during the age of empire. Apart from economic profit, empires had provided Europe with a world it could dominate not only militarily, but also in the technological and intellectual spheres. Western-oriented cultural systems, with their accompanying tastes, fashions and consumer habits, became an intrinsic part of internationally accepted goals. The 'machine-age', which had evolved in the West, had unquestioningly come to represent 'modernization' and 'advancement' everywhere – regardless of its consequences. 'Development' policy and planning have, therefore, frequently exacerbated the processes of underdevelopment by treating the symptoms rather than the causes of poverty. Yet progress has continued to be measured against Western models.

However 'rich' a country may become, unless its institutional characteristics and social structures, cultural values and world view, industrial competitiveness and military power, approximate to European standards, it will still be included within the concept of the Third World. It was only in the aftermath of the Second World War that the myth of European superiority was exploded. It was then that the colonized began to regain confidence in themselves and sought once more to control their own destinies. The shape of their respective futures, their options and the methods by which they may be achieved reflect in all respects the ways in which their economies, societies and international role have been moulded by the global historical processes of the recent past.

3 POPULATION

There are now more than 3000 million people in the Third World out of a global population of over 4000 million. This high proportion has come about through persistently high rates of population increase, largely resulting from the decline in death rates accompanied by continuing high birth rates. The population of the Third World as a whole and of most of its parts has grown exponentially. Rates of natural increase range, for the most part, between 2.0 and 3.5 per cent per annum, at which a population can more than double within the lifetime of a generation (approximately twenty-five years) (see table 3.1 and figure 3.1). By contrast, in the more-developed parts of the world, where population increase is now mostly below 1 per cent per annum, it would take more than 100 years for a population to double.

Table 3.1 Global and regional population indices.

	Population (millions) 1977	Average annual rate of growth (per cent) 1970–7	Birth rate (per '000) 1975–7	Death rate (per '000) 1975–7	Area ('000 km²) 1977	Density (per km²) 1977
World	4,124	1.9	31	13	135,830	30
Asia	2,355	2.2	34	13	27,580	85
Latin America	342	2.8	37	9	20,566	17
Africa	424	2.7	46	20	30,319	14
Oceania	22	2.0	23	10	851	3
Europe	478	0.6	16	10	4,937	97
North America	242	0.9	17	9	21,515	11
USSR	226	1.0	18	8	22,402	11

Source: UN Demographic Yearbook, 1977.

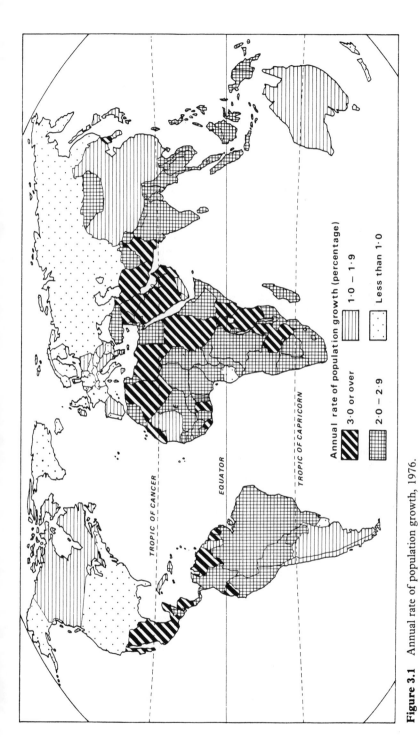

Figure 3.1   Annual rate of population growth, 1976.

Source of data: US Bureau of Census, 1977.

For much of the Third World it is difficult to know accurately the numbers and characteristics of the population. Census data that provide the main source of information are deficient. There are still countries where censuses are incomplete though there are now very few where they have yet to be taken for the first time. Censuses are relatively costly and difficult to conduct in poor countries with low levels of literacy; people often do not understand the reasons for certain questions and may resent them as an intrusion on their privacy – for example, the counting of people is often associated with attempts to collect tax. Some census data are more difficult to collect than others. Women, for example, are reluctant to divulge the number of their children, both alive and dead, and it is very difficult to collect accurate data on ages. Even where censuses are taken they may be the subject of controversy because of political interference and official dissatisfaction with the results. In Nigeria three successive censuses (1962, 1963 and 1973) have been the subject of such controversy that their results have been abandoned. Thus, while there is no doubt that Nigeria has the largest population in Africa, precisely how large is not certain, and the characteristics of the population are known only from fragmentary and incomplete evidence. Though this is an extreme case, there are many Third World countries that are forced to undertake much of their socio-economic planning without adequate knowledge about the people for whom it is intended.

Population growth and characteristics

Notwithstanding the above difficulties, it is possible to make some general statements about population in the Third World. In the past population growth was limited through a combination of natural and man-made factors causing high levels of mortality and limited life expectancy. Environmental and human hazards produced limitations in food supply resulting in periodic serious shortages and famines. In subsistence economies such impacts have been very severe. Disease has combined with food deficiencies, wars and political disruption to limit population growth, and in some instances the population has been reduced. With high levels of mortality, particularly amongst infants, high levels of fertility were required to compensate so that populations might at least maintain themselves, and grow at low rates of increase in some instances.

Changes in the last fifty years have produced some amelioration of these conditions. Though major food deficiencies continue, more efficient transportation at all scales has made better distribution possible than was the case in the past. Although there is a much reduced dependence on subsistence production, shortages and famines continue to occur, though generally without devastating effects as in times past.

While the living standards for many people in the Third World have not been strikingly improved, some progress has been made in the control of disease, particularly the prevention and reduction of epidemics. This, together with improvements in public health through better water supply and waste disposal,

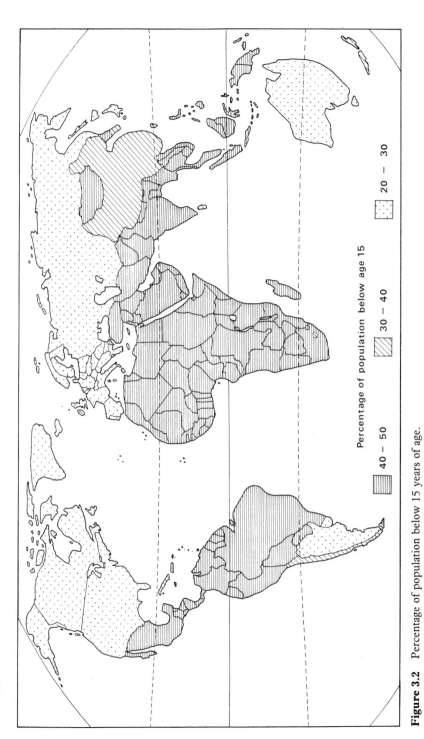

Figure 3.2 Percentage of population below 15 years of age.

Source of data: World Bank, 1978: 102–3.

Percentage of population below age 15

20 – 30

30 – 40

40 – 50

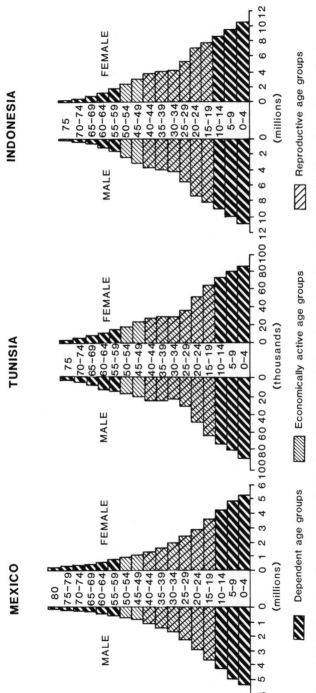

Figure 3.3 Typical age/sex pyramids for Mexico, Tunisia and Indonesia showing dependent, economically active and reproductive age groups.

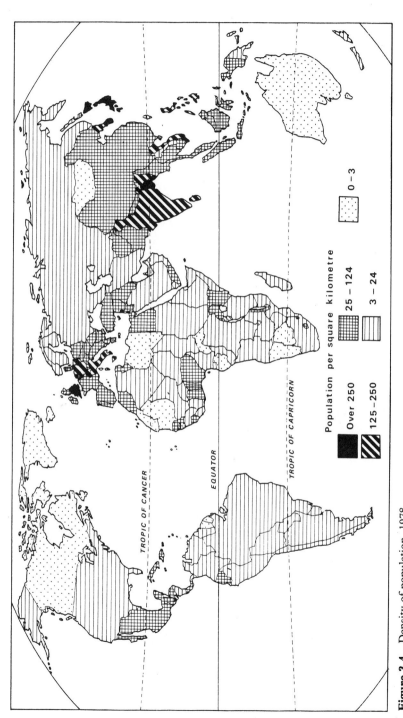

Figure 3.4 Density of population, 1978.

Source of data: UN Demographic Yearbook, 1978.

has reduced the mortality rate in all age groups. However, the most important factor contributing to population growth is the high proportion of people in the younger age groups. More than 40 per cent of people in the Third World are less than 15 years of age, with a further large proportion in the reproductive age groups of 15–40 years (figures 3.2; 3.3). The latter with their high levels of fertility produce high birth rates (30–50 per 1000) and this, related to falling death rates (10–15 per 1000), has resulted in high rates of natural increase.

While overall there are large and still increasing populations throughout the Third World, between one part and another there are important variations in numbers, structure and composition. Generalizations are difficult to make, for with analysis at progressively more detailed scales it very quickly becomes clear that modifications and qualifications are necessary. At a continental scale there are more people in Asia than there are in Latin America or in Africa. The same order is to be found in population density, which is highest in Asia and least in Africa (see table 3.1 and figure 3.4). Within the continents there are larger areas of high population density in Asia than there are in either Latin America or in Africa. Particularly in China, in the India subcontinent and in parts of South-East Asia, rural population densities above 1000 per km^2 are common. In Latin America and Africa high densities occur in limited areas only and there are large areas of low density, for instance in the largely uninhabited Amazon Basin and the great desert areas of Africa (figure 3.4).

There is a vast range of contrast in population numbers and densities between countries in the Third World. China (933 million), India (638 million) and Indonesia (145 million) are countries with some of the largest populations in the world and they also have some of the highest country-wide population densities (table 3.2, figure 3.4). There is nothing to compare with them in Latin America or Africa, and in population size only Brazil (115 million) and Nigeria (72 million) in any way approach them. In Africa countries with large areas, such as Zaire and Sudan, have only relatively small populations, low overall densities and very limited areas with high densities (table 3.2). For the most part, countries in Latin America and in Africa with small areas have small populations, though population densities in some of these may be high. Rwanda (4.5 million), one of the smaller African countries in area and population, has the highest country-based density on the continent (171 per km^2). High densities are also common in small island countries in the Caribbean and the Pacific. Size and density of population are important for several reasons. A large population provides a large man-power resource, though in Third World countries the majority of the people have only traditional skills and there are a limited number with modern education and associated skills. In the majority of Third World countries educational facilities are limited. Though improvements have been and are being made it is impossible to keep up with demand: for example, in Africa while the numbers enrolled in schools increase the numbers who remain without schooling increase also.

Large populations may be a disadvantage in terms of the resources required to meet their basic needs, especially when numbers are growing rapidly without an

Table 3.2   Representative country population indices.

	Population* ('000s) 1978	Average annual rate of growth* (per cent) 1975-8	Birth rate** (per 1000) 1976	Death rate** (per 1000) 1976	Area* (km²) 1978	Density* (per km²) 1978
China	933,032	1.4	30	11	9,596,981	97
India	638,388	2.1	36	15	3,287,590	194
Indonesia	145,100	2.4	38	16	2,027,087	72
Taiwan	16,793	2.1	26	5		
Singapore	2,334	1.2	19	5	581	4,018
Hong Kong	4,606	1.6	18	5	1,045	4,408
Brazil	115,397	2.8	39	10	8,511,965	14
Mexico	66,944	3.6	40	7	1,972,547	34
Jamaica	2,133	1.5	29	7	10,991	195
Libya	2,748	4.2	48	14	1,759,540	2
Egypt	39,636	2.1	39	13	1,007,449	40
Sudan	17,376	3.4	49	17	2,505,813	7
Nigeria	72,217	3.2	50	24	923,768	78
Zaire	27,745	3.7	47	17	2,345,409	12
Rwanda	4,508	2.4	48	21	26,338	171

Source: * UN Demographic Yearbook, 1978.
   ** US Bureau of Census, 1977.

expansion of resources at a corresponding rate. In many cases increases in population have not been matched by increases in food production. Countries such as India, Bangladesh and Pakistan, with large agricultural populations and limited land and financial resources, battle with this problem on a major scale. Brazil and Nigeria are more fortunate in having large land reserves in relation to their populations and they also possess other resources for development (oil in Nigeria and a wide range of minerals in Brazil). Conversely, small populations in large land areas may be disadvantaged in there being too few people to promote economic development.

In some areas land may be unused not only because of a lack of man-power but also because of factors such as disease, which in the past made large areas of savanna Africa of limited value for settlement because of infestation with tsetse-fly, which transmits sleeping sickness among humans and trypanosomiasis in cattle. The spread of disease has also been responsible for the desertion of lands previously inhabited: as has been the case in areas of the Indian subcontinent with high levels of malaria infection, and with river valleys in West Africa infected with river blindness. Projects for disease control and eradication are difficult and costly to organize and are not always successful. The hoped-for global eradication of malaria, which seemed a possibility in the 1950s, has proved impossible, and in the Indian subcontinent there has been a massive resurgence of this disease since the mid-1960s. Smallpox, however, has now been officially eradicated.

While population densities are a rough indication of relationships between people and land they must be interpreted very carefully. Some of the highest rural densities in the world are found in the Nile Valley in Egypt (c. 1500 per km²). They are evidence of a remarkable accommodation of people and land that has been developed over many millennia, though present-day densities are supported only at very low living standards. This is also true of somewhat lower, though still relatively high, rural densities in Africa, Asia and Latin America, and people may not be well provided for even in areas of low population density if agricultural systems and practices result in low productivity.

Over-population may occur where the needs of population exceed the available resources, both those used and those that are not yet fully developed. It is difficult to define these circumstances with any precision and relative over-population (where there are still resources to be developed) is more common than absolute over-population (where the limits of resource exploitation have been reached). Over-population is most commonly associated with rural areas and is manifested in such features as high rates of population growth coupled with low productivity, the uneven distribution of land, landlessness, unemployment and underemployment. These features are to be found in parts at least of all Third World countries. Over-population is an increasing feature in the urban areas where resources are inadequate to meet needs for food, shelter and employment.

Migration

Dissatisfaction with poor living standards in rural areas and the prospect, or expectation, of better standards elsewhere has been a major factor in the outflow of rural population to towns in many Third World countries (figure 3.5). So far urbanization has been relatively limited in Africa, but it is well-developed in Asia where there is a strong indigenous urban tradition and in Latin America where several centuries of European colonial influence produced major administrative and commercial centres. The populations of many urban places have mushroomed in recent decades, with growth rates several times the national average, particularly in major cities. For example, Lagos in Nigeria is growing at 14 per cent per annum and will have a population of four million by 1985. Urban populations grow rapidly not only due to in-migration but also because of high rates of natural increase since the reproductive age groups are well represented.

Much attention has been focused on rural–urban movements in all parts of the Third World, and they are important everywhere. They are most significant in Latin America and least important in Africa. However, they have tended to receive disproportionate attention and not enough has been given to the movements of people within rural areas. Only limited note has been taken of circulatory movements that are common both in rural areas and between rural areas and towns. These movements do not involve the permanent transfer of

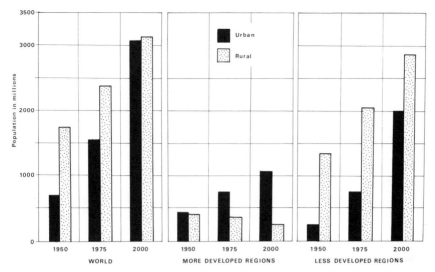

Figure 3.5 Past and projected comparative growth rates of urban and rural population – 1950, 1975 and 2000.

Source: People, 2, 1975.

population between one place and another: people move away from their places of residence for varying periods, sometimes seasonally and possibly for years, as farmers, traders and labourers, and for other economic and social reasons, and then return. In this way there is both temporary and permanent redistribution of population. Where there have been massive permanent transfers of people between rural and urban areas, continued high rates of natural increase in the former have prevented large-scale depopulation. However, depopulation may occur in limited areas through population pressure. It is much more common in small circumscribed territories such as Caribbean islands which have lost population to one another, and more recently further afield to North America and Europe.

Migration from the Caribbean
Emigration from the Caribbean has long been a part of the way of life. Movements of people from the islands began in the nineteenth century soon after the emancipation of the slaves. Leaving the sugar plantations and the islands to which they had been forcibly bound for so long, had major social and psychological implications. Migration was seen as an escape from many of the obstacles hindering personal, economic and social improvement, and eventually became an established pattern in the life of the society.

The desire of Caribbean people to emigrate has been encouraged by the opportunities for work which have occurred from time to time on the American mainland and in Europe. Discrepancies in the cost of labour between the Caribbean territories and the major cities of the North Atlantic, have meant that Caribbean people have provided a cheap supply of labour since the middle of the nineteenth century. In Central and South America, railway construction, fruit plantations, oil drilling and refining and the cutting of the Panama Canal, all associated with US and European companies, depended on large supplies of imported labour from the Caribbean islands. During and after the Second World War, the spatial shift in demand for labour brought about a commensurate shift in the direction of Caribbean migration, to the USA and to Western Europe.

The flows of people from different Caribbean islands to the North Atlantic metropoles reflected colonial and neo-colonial linkages, with immigration policies giving preference to colonial subjects. Thus the movement of people from British colonies dominated the West Indian migrations to Britain in the 1950s, until the imposition of the Commonwealth Immigrants Act of 1962 which prevented further entry. Most migrants from the Netherlands Antilles and Surinam (formerly Dutch Guiana) went, and continue to go, to the Netherlands. Unhindered access to France has been allowed to the citizens of the French Caribbean possessions. Likewise, Puerto Ricans and Virgin Islanders, as nationals of US dependencies, migrate without hindrance to the USA. In addition, large numbers of people from the Dominican Republic, Haiti and intermittently from Cuba have sought entry to the USA. Others from the English-speaking Caribbean territories have migrated there since the Second World War and to Canada since the lifting of restrictions on black immigration in 1962. Crude estimates of net migration figures (that is the numbers who entered specified countries minus those who left) are given for 1950–72 in table 3.3 (flows of less than 1000 migrants are not given). The total net migration between 1950 and 1972 accounted for approximately 10 per cent of the Caribbean population. The significance of even the smallest flows is better understood when the relatively small population of the Caribbean countries is taken into consideration. For example, in 1979 there were 180,000 Surinamese and 30,000 Netherlands Antilleans living in the Netherlands, while their home populations were only 350,000 and 240,000 respectively.

A major factor in the pattern of Caribbean international migration has been the emphasis in North American immigration policies on attracting highly skilled migrants and limiting the entry of the unskilled and semi-skilled. Although these policies have been in existence since the mid-1950s, they have been variously implemented and have had an increasing effect on Caribbean migration since the late 1960s. Of the total number of migrants from Guyana between 1969 and 1976 going overseas to work (that is excluding dependents and students) some 55 per cent were in the professional, technical, administrative and clerical categories, though these groups comprise less than 20 per cent of the total workforce in Guyana itself. Of the total number of emigrant workers from Jamaica between 1967 and 1978, approximately 76 per cent were the white-collar groups and if the emigration of students were included the figure would be further augmented. Such high levels of emigration from the highly educated and trained sectors of the

Table 3.3 Estimated net migration from the Caribbean to North America (1950–72).

Countries of migrant origin	Countries of migrant destination				
	Canada	France	Netherlands	UK	USA
Barbados	10,000			28,400	30,000
Bahamas					8,000
Belize					6,500
Guyana	18,000			28,100	12,000
Jamaica	35,000			168,600	200,000
Leeward & Windward Islands	10,000			59,000	45,000
Trinidad & Tobago	40,000			23,800	65,000
Guadeloupe		45,000			
Martinique		55,000			
French Guiana		5,000			
Netherlands Antilles			10,000		
Surinam			30,000		
Cuba					620,000
Dominican Republic					250,000
Haiti		4,000			200,000
Puerto Rico					860,000

These figures include estimates for illegal migration.

Source: The table is adapted from figures given in Segal (1975).

population mean losses in educational investment as well as the depletion of skills to the labour force.

Similar pressures in some parts of the Third World, coupled with demands for labour in more economically developed countries, have resulted in emigration from North African countries and from India and Pakistan to Europe, and from Mexico to the USA. These outflows have been mainly of unskilled or semi-skilled labour though they also include the 'brain-drain' of professional people (especially doctors) from Third World countries to the more-developed countries of the northern hemisphere.

While movements occur for economic reasons above all else, and may be made under direct economic pressure or with the prospect of economic gain, there are movements in many parts of the Third World which are otherwise determined. Environmental hazards (droughts, earthquakes, hurricanes, tidal waves) force people to move, and nowadays because of the increasing population more are affected by these catastrophes. Political actions are important factors producing much refugee movement, and since about the middle of this century there have been major forced movements of populations in the Third World. In the 1940s millions of Muslims and Hindus were displaced with the partition of the Indian subcontinent, and many Palestinians became refugees after the establishment of the state of Israel. In the last decade refugee movements have been common in Africa and in South-East Asia, in the latter particularly during and after the Vietnam war. The numbers involved as refugees are counted in millions; for example at the present time among the Somali in the Horn of Africa.

During the era of European colonialism there were permanent and temporary movements of population from the metropolitan countries in Europe to their colonial territories. In some instances these produced considerable racial intermixture especially in Latin America and the Caribbean where slaves imported from Africa added to the racial complexity. Though colonialism is now almost entirely ended, European minorities remain in Africa and in Asia, most particularly in South Africa where they dominate the politics and economy.

Factors in population change

The movements referred to above have distinctive flow patterns that influence and sometimes alter the distribution of population. They also influence the structure of population, causing the higher proportions of younger reproductive age groups in Third World cities, and the loss of young, active people from rural areas. However, population size in countries, continents and in the Third World in general is determined mainly by the balance between births and deaths.

Mortality rates have fallen dramatically during recent decades in all age groups, though, for example, they remain high for children (150–200 per 1000) in sub-Saharan Africa, where life expectancy is less than 50 years. All people welcome measures that result in some control over death and that contribute to the lengthening of life. Furthermore, communities at local, regional and national level can now undertake steps to reduce mortality – for example, by reducing disease and improving public health – and these actions can be carried out without specific reference to individuals. Thus mortality rates in Third World countries are now fluctuating at relatively low levels, with periodic, short-term, upward trends in limited areas as a result largely of natural or man-made catastrophies.

Though there has been some recent evidence of a slight reduction, fertility rates among Third World populations generally remain high. Decline has occurred mainly in China and in Latin America but there has been no significant decline, and possibly some increase, in Africa and much of South Asia. Though, in general, high levels of fertility are no longer necessary to maintain numbers, it is difficult to change people's attitudes and practices so as to effect substantial reductions. Men's virility and women's fertility are demonstrated by the births of large numbers of children. Where people are dependent on low levels of technology, particularly in agriculture, numerous children may be regarded as economically advantageous, notwithstanding the extra mouths which have to be fed. Sons augment the family labour supply and provide some security for parents in old age, while daughters may bring dowries into the families into which they marry. Children are regarded as socially prestigious and are valued as economic assets.

In contrast to mortality it is thus far more difficult to influence fertility behaviour by either direct or indirect action. Communal measures are more difficult to operate than is the case with mortality, for the decision whether or not to have children has to be taken by individuals. Governments may introduce policies to exhort or even to coerce changes in behaviour but such policies are difficult to put into practice. To effect changes in fertility patterns there must be incentives for people to plan and control the size of their families as well as the means to make this possible.

Among governments as well as among individuals there are variations in attitudes towards fertility. Countries with small populations often wish them to be larger for reasons of prestige and to promote economic development. Such is the case with Libya, which wishes to develop with its large oil revenues for investment. There are countries with large populations that for similar reasons wish to see them even larger. Conversely there are both small and large countries where the pressures of population on available resources of all kinds are so great, resulting in low economic and social standards for the majority of people, that they make efforts to check further growth. Egypt which is immediately adjacent to Libya, has in contrast a large rural population and very limited financial resources for investment and seeks to limit its population.

Governments can institute both direct and indirect policies to promote or to limit the growth of population (figure 3.6). Those wishing to increase numbers hold out the promise of greater economic development and political power if there are more people to exploit existing resources. Taxation can be adjusted to favour large families and family allowances may be paid. Conversely, when limitation on growth is necessary governments may encourage people to limit their families by presenting the prospect of a more favourable economic future if there are smaller numbers to be supported, and may penalize those with large families by taxation or withholding of allowances. In these ways China on a large scale and Singapore on a small scale have been working towards limiting their populations. China, with the largest population in the world, has developed on socialist principles since the 1940s and now has major programmes for planning and controlling the number of its people. In the majority of its central provinces, with large total populations, annual growth rates are now below 1 per cent (figure 3.7). Singapore has reduced its birth rate from 45 to 16 per 1000 and its annual growth rate from 4.0 per cent to 1.6 per cent in the last twenty years.

Factors in population control

Family planning and control have figured importantly in discussions on population in the Third World in recent decades – with various and often vigorous reactions. Planning and control have often been considered only in terms of limiting or reducing population, whereas they should be seen more objectively as the means whereby the best potential is fulfilled for people both nationally and individually. However, the planning and control of population are very emotive

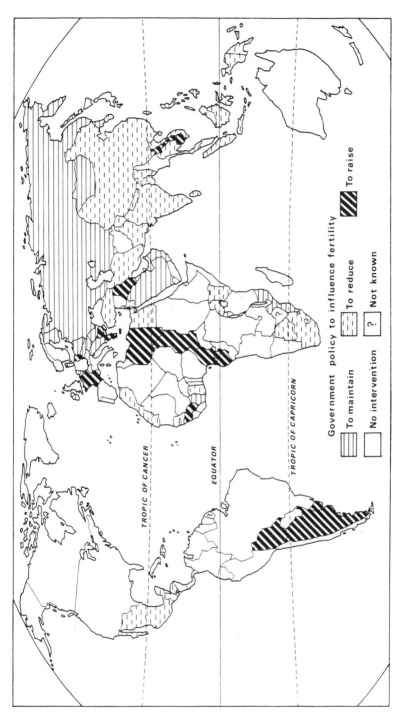

Figure 3.6 Government policies on family planning.

Source of data: After *People*, 8, 1981: 32.

issues about which it is difficult to be objective. Reactions are influenced by political, religious, social, cultural and economic factors.

Suggestions for planning and control of population have been interpreted by some in the Third World as an attempt by the more-developed parts of the world to limit numbers and reduce the threat which they might otherwise pose. It is also felt that the pressures of population in many parts of the Third World could be reduced if existing political, social and economic structures were changed. Some religions and cultures have blessed and encouraged large numbers of children, viewing with outright disapproval some of the means available for family planning. The Roman Catholic Church, for example, condemns artificial means of birth control though it is not against all means of planning and control. Together with a lack of commitment for other reasons from people themselves to reduce fertility, this attitude has contributed significantly to burgeoning numbers in many predominantly Roman Catholic countries: in southern Europe in the past and in Latin America at present.

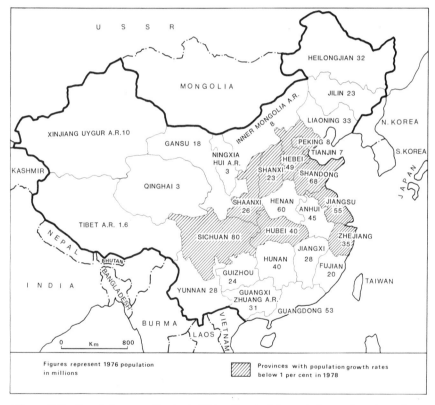

Figure 3.7 Population growth rates in China. Provincial population totals and provinces with annual growth rates below 1 per cent.

Source: People, 6, 1979: 18.

A major concern with population on a global scale in general and in the Third World in particular has developed especially since the middle of the present century. Notwithstanding continuing deficiencies of data, sufficient information has become available to make the magnitude of growth fully evident. National and international organizations have increasingly developed the means for acquiring information; they include national census organizations and institutions for the study of population, with international involvement within the UN (for example the Population Division of the Economic and Social Council) and its special agencies (World Health Organization, Food and Agricultural Organization, International Labour Organization and the World Bank). Within the last decade the UN Fund for Population Activities (UNFPA) has been set up as a special focus for work on population: to provide support for better investigation and to contribute ways and means of alleviating and possibly solving the wide-ranging problems which population presents. The political, cultural and religious attitudes which have been indicated do not make this work easy: for example, they prevented the direct involvement of the World Health Organization in aspects of population control for more than two decades after this body was set up.

In retrospect many of the approaches applied to population planning and control in the 1950s and 1960s can be seen as crude and lacking in insight. They were paternalistic on the part of the more-developed world towards the Third World, and were, to a large extent, responsible for the belief that the former wished to control the numbers of people in the latter. Methods for control were introduced which while they were acceptable in some parts of the world were found to be unacceptable in others. These approaches were made possible because of important advances in contraceptive methods, particularly the contraceptive pill and intra-uterine devices which were more efficient than aids previously available. It was thought that these new methods could be applied on a very large scale among people with limited or no knowledge of what they involved or implied.

Official and unofficial bodies in the USA in particular were responsible for the development of many of these approaches and for making the new means of contraception available. Through official and unofficial organizations in Third World countries, investigations were undertaken of people's knowledge of, attitude to and practices in family planning, and programmes were set up to make family-planning measures more widespread and effective. These programmes have had varying effects and degrees of success. Some of the more significant successes have been achieved among relatively small populations: here it has been possible to develop motivation for the acceptance of family planning and to provide the means for effecting it. Notable examples have been in Asia, in Hong Kong, Taiwan and Singapore. The most significant impact for countries with very large populations has been that claimed for China. There the contemporary official authority has combined with traditional acceptance of authority to achieve remarkable reductions in fertility rates in a very short time through contraception and abortion, without any assistance from outside the country (see figure 3.7).

India has had variable success in its measures to control population growth. Attempts to spread the adoption of family-planning measures have ranged from encouragement to coercion. Those of the latter kind were contemplated in India in the last decade, involving legislation which would have made sterilization compulsory after the birth of three children to a couple, or four if the first three were all of the same sex. These moves were strongly resisted and reaction against them was an important factor in the downfall of Mrs Gandhi's government in March 1977. The evidence from the 1981 census is that population growth at 2.5 per cent per annum in the last decade has been only minimally less than that in the 1960s. In Mexico, a country with what may be described as a medium-sized population which has been growing rapidly, an important reduction in fertility has been achieved in a matter of a few years. Since 1977 the annual rate of increase of population has been reduced from 3.4 per cent to less than 3.0 per cent as a result of a comprehensive family-planning programme. Even with such reduction the Mexican population will still be capable of doubling its numbers within 25 years.

The means to plan and control population is not enough, to be effective these means must be applied on a large scale. They must be used by large numbers of individuals to have any impact at regional, national and subglobal levels. These individuals must therefore be able to appreciate the advantages gained from reducing the numbers of children born to counteract the previously perceived advantages of having many children. The processes through which such changes in attitude can be realized are complex and by no means clearly understood.

To maintain a population at replacement level, with a balance between those who die and those born, requires 'zero growth'. As yet no country in the Third World approaches this, in contrast to the developed world where all countries have low growth rates (many below 1.0 per cent per annum) and some have negative growth, with the result that their populations are being reduced. The succession of stages through which changes can occur in the relationship between fertility rates and mortality rates has been established as the 'demographic transition'. However, the factors which influence changes to produce these stages in the transition are difficult to identify and evaluate, and there are considerable differences of opinion about them. The demographic transition that has occurred in the more-developed parts of the world can be studied only retrospectively, and as it is studied in more detail it becomes clear that it was not uniform in character. Likewise the changes occurring in the Third World at the present time are not common to all its many and varied parts.

Economic development is undoubtedly an important factor in reducing fertility rates. For example, improved economic status with higher living standards encourages people to have fewer children. Those Third World countries that have substantially reduced their rates of population growth have also experienced important advances in their economies, which have affected a very considerable proportion of their populations. This extension of economic benefits is most important. Where wealth is enjoyed by only a small minority (as, for example, in many of the major oil-producing states at the present time) its effect will be minimal in changing the attitudes and practices of the mass of the population towards the production of children.

Economic development provides the means for bringing about improvements in public health through financing curative and preventive medicine on a large scale. As a result mortality rates decline overall, but most important are reductions in infant mortality through the better care of mothers and infants. As a consequence parents are more likely to come to accept that large numbers of children are not necessary to ensure that sufficient survive to provide for family needs.

Plate 3.1 Schoolchildren in Western Kenya receiving milk.
Kenya has one of the highest birthrates in the world, and over half the population is under 15 years old. Most Kenyan children now go to primary school, and almost one-third of government expenditure needs to be allocated to education expenditures. The school-milk programme has been recently introduced as a means of improving the nutrition of the children.

Economic development also allows for levels of education to be raised. Improvements in literacy and progressive advancement to higher standards of education attainment are important influences in reducing the size of families. Education provides people with new perceptions of economic opportunities and the appreciation that one factor in achieving these is to have fewer dependent children. Better educated people are better able to understand the methods and techniques of birth control and can appreciate that it is not sufficient to follow the exhortation to

Practise family planning this weekend

which appeared some years ago on a wall in India.

The education of women, not surprisingly, is of great importance and recent studies in Africa have shown that it is probably the most significant factor in influencing women to have fewer children. However, in many Third World societies women have traditionally occupied positions in which they are socially and economically inferior to men. As a result, advances in education have come more slowly to women and they seriously lag behind in literacy and in other respects. This is a situation that needs to be changed radically and rapidly, not only for greater acceptance of family planning but also for women's rights to equality.

Clearly, a great many factors operate in complex relationships with one another to determine the need for controlling population numbers. Understanding why control is necessary is essential for the widespread acceptance and practice of methods of family planning. People cannot simply be forced to accept and to practise it. Greater attention must be given to these problems in the Third World as they are determined and interpreted from within the Third World itself. More needs to be known of the attitudes and feelings of countries, ethnic groups, families and individuals towards the problems they face. Any suggestion of direction or dictation from the more-developed parts of the world on such delicate and personal matters, however well-meant, is likely to be rejected.

Viewpoints on population

Thinking on issues concerned with population has been profoundly influenced by a number of different viewpoints. Nearly 200 years ago Thomas Malthus advanced the theory that population increased geometrically while resources to meet the needs of people increased only arithmetically. As a result the former would outstrip the latter and any balance between them would be maintained only when population growth was limited by natural and human calamities, or by other means of control. These ideas were challenged in the nineteenth century by Karl Marx and more recently by those who derive their views from him. Marxist scholars see the present imbalance between population and resources in the Third World as a result of the unsatisfactory control of the distribution of resources and the means by which they are used. They maintain that the capitalist system inevitably leads to a minority of people enjoying a good life at the expense of the majority who work to provide it. They argue that socialist control of production and distribution would provide the means for the more effective use of resources, which could be made available to people in general. These views do not exclude forms of population control through family planning, but these need to be effectively integrated with control over the production and distribution of resources.

The gloomy predictions of Malthus were not fulfilled in the nineteenth century in the now-developed parts of the world, even though their populations increased rapidly. New sources of primary products from colonial possessions and improved methods of production provided sufficient resources to meet increased needs within the capitalist system. However, by the middle of the twentieth century, with well-established and still accelerating rates of population increase in the less-developed countries, the Malthusian spectre, as it has been described, has appeared again. Large proportions of Third World populations exist at very low standards of living at all times. Periodically, through natural and man-made disasters, some of them are reduced to famine and starvation. They are trapped in these circumstances. The means by which they may be extricated involve promoting more efficient production and better means of distribution. This requires a reduction in the demands of the more-developed world, as well as the reduction of numbers of people in the Third World. Until the last decade the major thrust has been towards the reduction of numbers to lessen the Malthusian threat. Hence the emphasis on the introduction of family planning and the need for it to spread on a very large scale.

The results have not been as satisfactory as anticipated for reasons already given. According to the International Planned Parenthood Federation, approximately 100 million couples in Third World countries now use modern means of contraception, but 500 million couples of child-bearing age still remain without access to such methods of family planning. Fertility control is important but alone it is not sufficient.

Within the last decade Third World countries themselves have made their views on population and its related problems much more widely known. This reflects their increasing impact and influence on a range of global concerns. Focus on these concerns has come in a series of international conferences organized by the UN and concerned with the environment, with habitat, with women in particular and with people in general. The last of these themes was discussed at the World Population Conference held at Bucharest in Romania in 1974, at which the participants were the political representatives of their respective countries. The conference discussed a draft World Plan of Action on Population prepared by the UN and based on wide-ranging consultations. In this discussion participants from Third World countries, with support in particular from China, seriously criticized the proposals. They argued that the main problem was not that of numbers of people as such, but their poverty and the need and means for alleviating this. Population was identified as a symptom rather than as a cause of problems in the Third World. By alleviating poverty and with consequential higher living standards for a greater number of people the prospects would be greatly enhanced for reducing numbers through lower fertility rates. However, to achieve higher standards there would need to be a major redistribution of resources on a global scale.

The final agreed World Plan of Action on Population provided for a variety of new directions in thinking about, and actions concerned with, population. Probably the single most important recommendation in the plan was

that countries wishing to affect fertility levels give priority to implementing development programmes and educational and health strategies which, while contributing to economic growth and higher standards of living, have a decisive impact upon demographic trends, including fertility. International co-operation is called for to give priority to assisting such national efforts in order that these programmes and strategies be carried into effect.

Developments were listed which could effect improvements; among these were reduction in infant and child mortality through improved nutrition and care, greater involvement of women in socio-economic development, protection for children and the aged, and wider educational opportunities.

In placing emphasis on the needs rather than on the numbers of people it has been said that the conference at Bucharest and the agreed World Plan of Action 'drove a stake into the heart of old Malthus', casting aside family planning as the only means of solving population problems. The new theme to be followed was 'development is the best contraceptive'. While changes in attitudes and approaches are of great significance they will not in themselves lead to rapid solutions to population problems in countries of the Third World. In any case it must be remembered that patterns of population growth and structure in these countries are already largely set for the remaining decades of this century and can only radically alter by catastrophic events.

At Bucharest the complexities of the issues relating to population came to the fore, underlining that there is not one problem but many. Third World countries with population policies felt that the importance of these had been emphasized and that they might be widened to involve other aspects besides control over numbers. Control through family planning remains of prime importance, though with greater concern for human rights and family welfare in the strategies devised. Greater emphasis on integrating various approaches to population and to development is necessary. The Conference charged the more-developed parts of the world with the need to continue their aid to activities concerned with population, setting these in the wider context of aid for development rather than in the previously narrow context of aid to limit population.

The need to tackle poverty and to institute more broadly based development in the Third World has been taken up and elaborated in the Report of the Brandt Commission. The Commission emphasized that priority attention be given to the poorest countries to remove poverty and to abolish hunger. It proposed an emergency programme for the first half of the 1980s to involve the large-scale transfer of resources from the rich countries to the poorest countries. In this way a contribution would be made to breaking 'the vicious circle between poverty and high birth rates'. The Commission recommended that development policies should include national population programmes aimed at achieving a balance between people's needs and the resources available to meet these, given that means for family planning would be freely available. It also stated that migrant workers should be better protected through co-operation between governments and their immigration and emigration policies, and that the rights of refugees to asylum and legal protection should be strengthened. All of these matters should be considered in the broader context of conserving and improving the global environment on which the future existence, let alone the well-being, of all people depends.

There is some encouragement to be gained from the fact that within the last decade people, resources and environment have received more attention and wider discussion than has ever been the case in the past. Wider appreciation leads to greater concern, which in turn may lead to greater pressure upon national and international authorities for action to be taken. The problem of population has become a major global issue. It must remain so until solutions can be found. While we may write of achieving a balance between population and resources we must not lose sight of the fact that people are the most important of all resources. Numbers of people in Third World countries, their characteristics and qualities, their distribution and their movements are of crucial concern. Without people all other resources have no meaning.

4 TRADITIONAL AGRICULTURAL SYSTEMS

Agriculture is crucial to the prospects of development in the Third World and in recent years has been given higher priority in development plans. It is evident that agriculture is the source of food supplies both for the rural population and also for the expanding urban sectors of Third World countries. In many cases, it must also provide the bulk of exports to support the external balance of payments, and is the source of raw materials for processing and manufacturing sectors (for example, cotton textiles). Less obviously, perhaps, it is a source of capital for investment in non-agricultural sectors, especially in countries where mining and industry are relatively unimportant. Yet it is also evident that the raising of agricultural productivity has, in many countries, proved to be a very difficult task. The first part of this chapter examines briefly the characteristics and recent trends in agricultural production in the Third World, drawing attention to basic differences between its component major regions. For most farmers in the Third World, agriculture is part of a way of life rather than simply an occupation, and an integral part of complex, traditional cultures involving religion, kinship and the whole fabric of rural society. Partly because of this wider involvement, consideration of rural sectors of Third World countries is a much broader issue than consideration of agriculture alone, quite apart from the inclusion of rural settlement, population and rural–urban relationships.

Traditional peasant societies have evolved agricultural systems with a limited technology which seeks to balance on the one hand their needs for subsistence and for exchange, and on the other hand their need to conserve the environment in such a way as to preserve the possibilities for future production. Traditional ecological and cultural systems in the rural sector are almost everywhere challenged and modified by the impact of modern pressures to produce more for the market and to supply rapidly growing populations, and the extent to which they have successfully adjusted varies widely in different parts of the Third World. The second part of this chapter will be concerned with these issues.

Peasant farmers make up the vast majority of agricultural producers in the Third World, but in many areas large-scale estates play an important, and sometimes dominant role. This aspect of Third World agriculture is highly varied: the origins of large plantations in tropical Africa and South-East Asia, for example, are to be sought only in the last century or so; but in much of Latin America the large estates are deeply rooted in colonial history from the sixteenth century. It is a characteristic of the modern world that governments have come to intervene deeply in rural life and in the direction of agricultural change, but land reform, colonization of new land, planning for rural development and the encouragement of agricultural production have not always met with unqualified success, and new forms of development may be needed in order to lay the spectre of Third World hunger about which so much has been written. These are issues to be taken up in the next chapter.

Agricultural production and recent trends

It has already been pointed out that most countries of the Third World are predominantly rural, which in itself suggests the dominant role of agriculture. In the Third World as a whole, 60 per cent of the working population is employed in agriculture, but there are very considerable variations from one area to another (figure 1.6) which broadly correspond to differences in GDP per head. It is generally the case that the poorer the country, the greater its dependence on

Plate 4.1 Cultivation techniques, Tunisia.
Much of traditional agriculture in the Third World is associated with simple techniques, in this case the use of a draught animal and a small metal plough.

agricultural employment: on average it accounts for less than 50 per cent of total employment in South America, where income levels are relatively high for the Third World, but over 80 per cent in much of tropical Africa. But the differences within the Third World are less striking than the contrast with the developed world, where the average dependence on agricultural employment is only 13.1 per cent, and falls to as low as 2.1 per cent in the UK, 2.3 per cent in the USA, 4.3 per cent in West Germany and 5.3 per cent in Canada.

The predominance of the rural sector and the dependence on agricultural employment are two important characteristics of Third World economies. A third major feature, especially in relation to the advanced industrial world, is that Third World exports consist very largely of the products of primary industry, either of minerals, or foodstuffs and raw materials of agricultural origin. It is this fact that has been seen by some as a basic reason for the lack of progress in development and for the dependency of the Third World. The role of agricultural products in the trade of the Third World is fundamental, though in recent years it has been overshadowed in the politics of world trade by mineral exports,

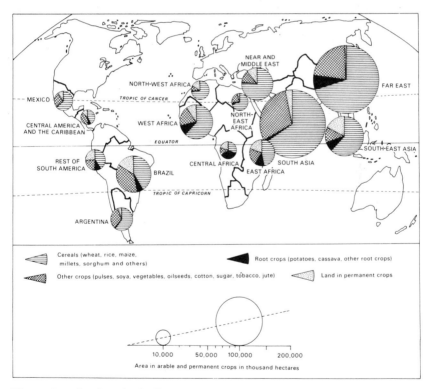

Figure 4.1   Land use in the Third World, 1979.
Source of data: FAO, 1980.

particularly of oil. In 1978, about 35 per cent of exports (by value) from the developing world (excluding China) were of agricultural origin (58 per cent from Latin America; 42 per cent from the developing countries of Africa; 19 per cent from the developing countries of Asia, including the Middle East).

Oil production has reduced the dependence of some countries on agricultural exports (for example, Mexico, Ecuador, Nigeria, Indonesia). But countries not endowed with workable mineral deposits such as oil, iron ore, copper, bauxite or tin, remain heavily dependent on the export of agricultural products. In Latin America, over 70 per cent of exports from Argentina, Uruguay, Paraguay, Colombia and most of the Central American republics are of agricultural origin. Dependence on agricultural exports reaches over 90 per cent in many African countries: Burundi, Chad, Ethiopia, Malawi, Somalia, Uganda, Upper Volta; and over 70 per cent in Ghana, Ivory Coast, Kenya, Mali, Sudan, Uganda and Tanzania (see figure 1.9).

The composition of agricultural production in the Third World in relation to land use and the production of selected crops is shown in figures 4.1 and 4.2, based on the official statistical series of the World Food and Agricultural Organization (FAO). It should be stressed that these are derived from national returns,

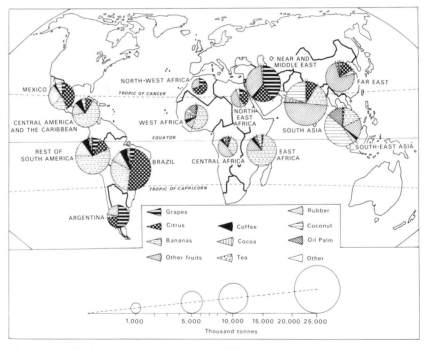

Figure 4.2 Production of permanent crops, 1979.

Source of data: FAO, 1980.

which are not always as accurate as one would wish. Areas cultivated, yields, production and trends are often based on estimates rather than careful data collection, and it is obvious that poor countries can rarely afford to maintain expensive statistical services. There are also variations in how different categories of land use and production are defined. But they are the best figures available on which to base quantitative estimates.

Figures 4.1 and 4.2 are based on the use of arable land in crops and land in permanent tree or shrub crops such as coffee, tea, oil palm and fruits. The first point that emerges from consideration of figure 4.1 is that a very large proportion of land in all regions is devoted to the production of basic staple foodstuffs providing energy in the form of carbohydrates. Cereals and root crops together occupy about a half or more of cultivated land, and in much of Asia and in North and West Africa over 70 per cent. Pulses (beans of various kinds and peas) also play a significant and widespread role, and are often the major source of protein in the diet, though soya beans, while of great importance as an indigenous crop in the Far East, are associated elsewhere chiefly with the more commercialized of the Third World economies.

In more detail, patterns of specific cereals and root crops show an adjustment to environmental conditions which can only be briefly summarized. Wheat is the major staple in subtropical or temperate regions: Argentina and Chile (where production is highly commercialized), North-West Africa (with barley as the other major staple), the Near and Middle East, northern India and Pakistan and north China. Rice is of overwhelming importance in the more humid, tropical regions of South and South-East Asia and the Far East, and it is also a significant staple in parts of Latin America, but much less so in Africa. Maize is of particular importance to Latin America, and also in East Africa. Millets and sorghum are of more regional importance as staple crops in areas of highly seasonal, often highly variable rainfall in South Asia and the Far East, and in the savanna lands of West Africa and the Sudan, but sorghum has also become a commercially important crop in some other regions – in Argentina and Mexico, for example. There is a similar variation in patterns of root-crop production: cassava, which is adapted to hot and humid climates, is the major staple (in terms of the land it occupies) in Central Africa, parts of West Africa and the Amazon basin, but in West Africa yams share primacy of place among root crops with cassava, and sweet potatoes are locally of importance in Latin America.

Patterns of specialization in specific cereals and root crops as staple foodstuffs, on the world scale and at more local levels, reflect many other factors besides environmental conditions. At the broadest level, the choice of staple foodstuffs is bound up with cultural preferences and traditions. Patterns of food preferences change slowly, and agricultural practices associated with specific crops may involve long-standing skills, customs and even religious practices. Rice has symbolic value in much of the Far East, just as maize has in parts of Latin America. The pressure of population on land resources may put a premium on crops of high nutritional value which yield well in terms of calories per hectare: rice is often preferred to cassava on such grounds, for example. Also strategies of crop production may need to trade off risks due to climatic variability against maximizing the production of food. Thus a balance may need to be struck between high-yielding crops such as rice, which may be liable to fail if rainfall is insufficient in an exceptional year, and crops such as millets, which are lower-yielding, but can withstand greater climatic variation. Finally, of course, among more commercialized economies pressures expressed through price structures, access to national or international markets, government policies, and the introduction of new varieties of crops affect patterns of production in ways that will be explored later.

Most of the cereals, root crops, pulses and vegetables are for domestic consumption within the Third World countries themselves, and often within the villages in which they are produced. Oilseeds, cotton and sugar enter far more into national and international trade. Sunflowers and linseed (for vegetable oils) occupy some 15 per cent of Argentina's arable land in crops; the Sudan has a high proportion of land devoted to the production of sesame, and both countries export vegetable oils. Although India, China, Brazil and Pakistan are leading Third World producers of cotton, it is widely grown in Africa and Latin America both to supply local cotton-textile industries and the international market. Sugar production dominates the land use of the Caribbean region, where it occupies 27.6 per cent of land in crops, and the region is of great importance in the international sugar trade.

A substantial proportion of cultivated land is devoted to tree and shrub crops, particularly in humid tropical regions (figure 4.2). Attention tends to be focused on highly commercialized plantation production of tree crops such as rubber, tea, cocoa, coffee and bananas, but on the whole they tend to occupy a *relatively* small proportion of total cultivated land. Coffee occupies less than 4 per cent of cultivated land in Brazil; cocoa less than 6 per cent in West Africa, and tea only about 14 per cent in Sri Lanka. Production of highly commercialized plantation products for export tends to be mainly localized, with easy access to ports, railways and good roads, and in small countries may dominate land use as sugar does in Cuba. While the output of such crops has a significance extending far beyond the proportion of land they take up, it is also important to recognize that, as with the production of cereals, a large proportion of the output from tree and shrub crops goes for domestic consumption within the Third World. Bananas, commercially important as export crops in Central-American republics, parts of the Caribbean and in Ecuador, are also important in the internal consumption patterns of tropical Africa and other parts of Latin America. Other fruits, such as mangoes, avocadoes, papayas, and many others, constitute important elements of diet, and are often an integral part of village agriculture.

Agricultural production for external markets plays a key role in some Third World countries, and increasingly must supply raw materials such as cotton for national industries, but these facts should not detract from the overriding importance of maintaining food production for internal consumption. In many Third World countries, food supplies are barely adequate, and although there has been some slight improvement since 1961–5 (see figure 1.5 and table 4.1) in all of the

Table 4.1 Indices of agricultural production, yields and area cultivated, 1979 (1969–71 = 100).

	Third World	Africa	Latin America	Near and Middle East	S and SE Asia	Far East	Developed market economies
Population	122	129	127	128	124	114	107
Total volume agricultural production	129	115	133	129	124	136	120
Production per head of population	105	89	104	101	100	118	112
Cereals							
Wheat: production	160	94	124	141	162	193	133
yields	130	110	104	135	129	137	110
area cultivated	122	86	120	105	126	141	121
Rice: production	123	130	131	104	119	126	110
yields	113	106	111	114	112	114	109
area cultivated	108	123	119	91	106	110	101
Maize: production	122	101	110	128	117	145	156
yields	111	89	111	110	107	116	132
area cultivated	109	113	100	115	110	125	118
Root crops: production	116	119	94	157	150	111	87
yields	103	99	91	122	121	106	112
area cultivated	112	121	104	129	124	105	78
Pulses: production	117	110	109	110	109	133	73
yields	106	103	100	100	100	111	116
area cultivated	111	107	109	111	109	120	85
Meat: production	133	114	120	120	125	150	118
number of stock	117	107	119	118	108	107	117

Source of data: FAO Production Yearbook, 1979, vol. 33.

Note: (a) Africa excludes the Republic of South Africa, and also Egypt, Libya and the Sudan, which are included in the Near and Middle East.
(b) Far East comprises China, the Korean Republic and Vietnam.
(c) Latin America includes the Caribbean islands.
(d) Near and Middle East includes Egypt, Libya and Sudan; the eastern margin includes Afghanistan.

major regions of the Third World, the averages for South Asia and even Africa imply that many of the poor must suffer from malnutrition, and many more are so near the margin of subsistence that drought, excessive or unseasonable rain, frost or hail may bring disaster. In some cases, the inadequacy of internal production requires that foodstuffs, sometimes essential ones, must be imported. Scarce reserves of foreign currencies have to be used to finance imports of this kind. In the late 1970s, for example, foodstuffs constituted about 20 per cent of all imports into Peru, and 12 per cent of all imports into Venezuela. Peru was then importing 86 per cent of its wheat, 32 per cent of its barley and 12 per cent of its rice. To raise the productivity of agriculture for domestic consumption is at least as important, in many countries, as raising productivity for export. In Peru, for example, the rising bill for food imports inspired legislation in 1972 requiring that at least 20 per cent of arable land in coastal areas be devoted to food crops for internal consumption.

Low productivity is one of the most obvious characteristics of Third World agriculture. It is, however, essential to distinguish between productivity of land and of labour. Productivity of land may imply productivity in terms of market value, volume of output or even nutritional value. Use of different criteria would produce different measures of productivity, though market value is the conventional method. But in another sense, productivity of land implies both the choice of crop or product and the yields of specific products per hectare. One of the reasons for low productivity of land in the Third World is that farmers remote from urban markets, and reliant on their own production, must concentrate their efforts on crops necessary for their own subsistence, which may be highly productive in terms of *nutritional* value, but command low prices both in national and international markets. For example, it has been observed that in Venezuela, productivity on farms created by agrarian reform was only three-quarters of the value per hectare of the national average, but this low productivity was at least as strongly related to the concentration of the agrarian reform sector on crops of low market value (maize, beans and rice) as it was to low yields of any one crop.

Yields of specific crops are, nevertheless, low in the Third World as a whole (see table 4.1), and the contrast with the market economies of the developed world is particularly clear. The average yield of wheat is only 62 per cent of that of developed market economies; of maize only 23 per cent, of rice, 35 per cent, and of sugar, 65 per cent. But overall figures conceal very considerable and significant variations. Low yields may be associated with environmental factors, the lack of capital, the use of poor seed, lack of fertilizers and low technology, and they are sometimes the consequence of long continued cultivation of poor, exhausted and eroded soils. Yet wheat yields per hectare in Mexico (3618 kg/ha) and Egypt (3176 kg/ha) are twice those of Canada (1690 kg/ha), where the productivity of capital and of labour are more important than the productivity of land.

Yields per hectare are of the greatest importance where there is pressure of population on resources to the extent that it is essential to maximize production from restricted areas of cultivable land, and peasant farmers in the Third World sometimes display considerable expertise in coaxing high yields from small plots of land by highly intensive methods; but in general terms it is the productivity of labour in agriculture that determines levels of income and in this respect the contrast between the Third World and advanced industrial economies is even more striking. Table 4.2 indicates, for selected countries, the value of agricultural production per head of economically active population in agriculture. It is clear that the range of variation is much greater than that of yields, and it is also clear that the values reported for some of the poorer countries point to abysmal levels of poverty.

Indeed, it is clear that productivity of labour in agriculture varies with average values of GDP per head. (The figures given in table 4.2 show a Spearman's rank correlation coefficient of +0.95 when compared with GDP per head.) Argentina heads the list among the Third World countries included in the table, and most of the Latin American countries show values of over US $1000; the lowest values are those for Ethiopia, Bangladesh and India.

Table 4.2 Productivity per head of economically active population in agriculture (for 1977 unless otherwise stated: 1977 US$).

		Latin America		*Asia*		*Africa*	
USA	23,360	Argentina	4229	Turkey	1063	Egypt	802
Canada	13,851	Venezuela	2627	Philippines	738	Morocco	694**
Australia	11,736	Ecuador	1145	Sri Lanka	512	Nigeria	440**
UK	11,071	Brazil	1123	Indonesia	478	Zimbabwe	396
		Mexico	1026*	Pakistan	403*	Kenya	338
		Bolivia	530**	Thailand	334	Tanzania	268
				Afghanistan	265*	Ethiopia	118**
				India	189*		
				Bangladesh	176		

* 1976.
** 1975.

Source of data: UN Statistical Yearbook, 1978.

Many reasons may account for the low productivity of agricultural labour and some are identical to those responsible for low yields per hectare, but perhaps the major factors may be grouped under two headings: lack of capital and the lack of adequate land for peasant farming. Lack of adequate land may be a result of the pressure of population, leading to the fragmentation of family farms, or it may be, less directly, the result of encroachment by large estates on to the land reserves of small-scale peasant farmers. In either case the problem is that of too many people working on too little land to the point at which additional labour applied to the land brings very little return in the form of additional yield. Chronic under-employment is one of the features of peasant farming systems in the Third World. But low productivity is also a result of the lack of capital for the purchase of seed, fertilizers, farm animals and implements or for investment in systems of water control, storage facilities, pest control and mechanization. Low productivity implies a low standard of living and the impossibility for the peasant farmer of accumulating capital; too often it implies malnutrition, which itself limits productivity. This has long been identified as the vicious circle of poverty from which it is so difficult to escape.

Is there any evidence, on an international scale, that conditions are improving? World organizations such as the FAO, the UN Conference on Trade and Development (UNCTAD) and other international conferences have repeatedly drawn attention to a world crisis of food production. From time to time, human disasters on a massive scale are given publicity by the media: for example, the perennial crisis of drought in the African Sahel, and the repeated droughts and famines in north-east Brazil. They may be seen as natural disasters, most liable to occur in areas characterized by a high variability of rainfall: they may indicate a deteriorating environment brought about by over-grazing, the unwise clearing of forest or cultivation of land. They may, in short, be seen from an ecological point of view, but it would be grossly inadequate to ignore the fact that disaster strikes most quickly and most seriously those who are already at the margin of subsistence. Yet there is general evidence of at least some slight improvement.

The volume of agricultural output in the Third World has shown an upward trend in the 1970s, increasing at a slightly faster rate than that of the industrial world (see table 4.1). But growth of agricultural output has been uneven between different parts of the Third World, and should be seen against the rate of growth of population (see figure 4.3). In general terms, the fastest rates of growth have been registered in China and Latin America, followed by South and South-East Asia and the North East. It is in the developing countries of Africa, however, that the increase in agricultural production has fallen far short of world averages. In South and Central America most countries have registered an increase which is well above the rate of population growth, though there are important exceptions: Chile, Peru, Guyana, Uruguay, Mexico and Venezuela. In much of the Far East and South-East Asia, too, the rate of increase of agricultural production has been higher than that of population, though again there are exceptions, notably Kampuchea and Laos, torn by political troubles during the 1970s. But it is in Africa that trends have been most depressing. Food and agricultural production has increased more rapidly than population in only nine African countries, but has failed to do so in thirty-two of them (see figure 4.3). It is, in general, the poorest countries, together with some that have experienced internal political turmoil or exceptional drought conditions, such as Ethiopia, that have suffered a crisis of agricultural production – all the more serious since most of them depend almost exclusively on agricultural production not only for domestic consumption but also for the bulk of their exports.

How far have increases in output in the last decade or so resulted from increases in the area under cultivation or from the increases of yields on existing cultivated land? In some parts of the world, reserves of potentially cultivable land are running out, and it can be argued, for example, that in much of South Asia and in parts of Latin America, increases in output are more likely to come from intensification of production on existing agricultural land than from colonization of new land. The question of colonization is to be raised in more detail in chapter 5, but the statistics suggest that both processes have been at work in the recent past. In the Third World as a whole, land in arable and permanent crops has increased by 12 per cent from 1961–5 (average) to 1978, and this has been achieved largely at the expense of forested land. In Latin America cultivated land in arable and permanent crops shows the biggest increase in the Third World (22 per cent) and permanent pastures have also increased by 8 per cent, mainly as a result of deforestation, chiefly in the Amazon basin. In Africa cultivated land has expanded by 14 per cent, with the largest increase in tree and shrub crops, but at the expense of both permanent pastures and of forest. It is in South and South-East Asia that the increase in cultivated land has been lowest, no more than 8 per cent. All of these percentages are far below the rate of increase of population, and it is clear that the expansion of cultivated land is by no means keeping pace with population growth.

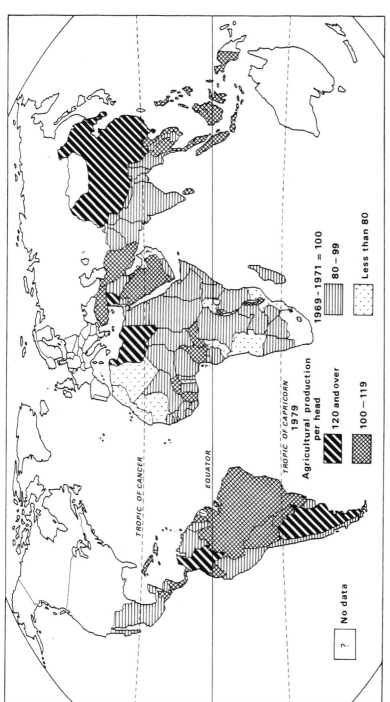

Figure 4.3 Trends in agricultural production per head 1969/71 to 1979 (1969/71 = 100).

Source of data: FAO, 1980.

But they are also less than the increase in the volume of output of agricultural production in the 1970s, which suggests that yields of agricultural products have, in fact, increased over the period. A more accurate comparison may be made by examining the extent to which changes in output of some arable crops stem from changes in the area cultivated or in yields per hectare, and this may be done from FAO statistical returns (see table 4.1).

In the Third World as a whole, it is encouraging that yields of the major cereals, with the exception of maize, have increased rather faster than the area under cultivation, and have indeed increased at a faster rate than among developed market economies, though they started from a very much lower base level in 1969–71. But this is not the universal experience. In Africa, for example, maize yields have fallen and production has been maintained only by an increase in the area under cultivation. Wheat, not an important crop in Africa, has declined both in area under cultivation and output, and expansion in Latin America of wheat and rice has been sustained mainly by increases in the area under cultivation. In South and South-East Asia it seems possible to attribute increases in yield of major crops such as wheat and rice to the effects of the Green Revolution (see chapter 5), which created its own social problems, but it is in the Far East that expansion of output, from increases both in yields and area under cultivation, appears to have been most remarkable, though the statistics from China may be suspect. There has been notably less advance in the production of pulses and root crops (cassava, potatoes, yams, sweet potatoes, etc.) which have received less attention from plant geneticists in the developed world, and advances have been achieved mainly by increases in the area cultivated. Finally, it is disturbing that meat production and the increase in livestock numbers in most major areas has fallen short of the rate of growth of population, particularly in Africa. The most notable exception is again in the Far East, representing some recovery, perhaps, from the political turmoils of the early 1970s.

So far attention has been focused on the characteristics and recent trends of agricultural production as a whole in the Third World and its major regions. Agriculture plays a key role both in the employment structure and in the contribution it must make to the maintenance of food supplies for growing populations and to the supply of materials for export. Yet agricultural production has expanded relatively slowly in many parts of the Third World, and in some areas has failed to keep pace with the growth of population. Growth has in part been due to increases in areas cultivated, and in part to a modest increase in yields, but productivity is low compared with the advanced industrial world, both in terms of yields per hectare and in terms of labour employed. It is clear that there are substantial variations within the Third World, however, both among the major regions and within them at the level of individual countries, and it is necessary to look more closely at agricultural production in the context of the rural frameworks and the physical environments of the Third World.

Peasant farming and rural societies

Very different interpretations have been put upon the dominant processes at work which underlie both the current crisis of food production and the social unrest, dislocation and poverty of the rural sectors in many Third World countries. They include the growth of population, the 'revolution of rising expectations', the difficulties and strains involved in the transition from subsistence to commercial farming, the increase in social and economic inequalities, or at a more generalized level, the impact of capitalism and the emergence of a wage-paid proletariat. Some economists have suggested a distinction between 'modern' and 'traditional' sectors in relation to the development problems of the Third World, but the clarity and validity of this distinction have been called into question, and it may be more useful to focus, first of all, on peasant farming which is by no means as static and unchanging as the term 'traditional' may imply. And it can be argued that the distinction between peasant farming and large-scale agriculture, represented by the plantation in the Caribbean, the *hacienda* in Spanish Latin America, agribusiness in Africa or South-East Asia, or collective farms in China, is clearer and more useful than that between 'traditional' and 'modern'.

Who, then, are the peasantry? They have been defined in various ways, but the essential features of definition would seem to be: (a) that a peasant has access to land as a means of production – he may own it, or he may be a tenant working the land and paying rent, but he cannot be simply a wage-paid labourer; (b) that he works the land to which he has access primarily by his own or his family's labour; (c) that the land is his primary source of income and/or subsistence; and (d) that he participates in a cash economy, usually in a subordinate status, and therefore is part of a wider society. Peasant farming is thus not *necessarily* associated with subsistence farming only, but with both subsistence and commercial production. It may be, and often is, strongly oriented to production for the market. Nor is it *necessarily* associated with low technology, though this is often the case in the Third World, but rather with small-scale technology – the hand cultivator rather than the tractor. Finally, while peasant farmers must by definition have access to land, it unfortunately does not follow that they have access to enough land to support themselves at a satisfactory level of living in the light of local expectations. It is often this fact, and the lack of economic opportunities, that is responsible for low productivity, and not an intrinsic lack of capability among peasant farmers.

At a rough estimate, perhaps 80 per cent of the farm families of the Third World would fall into the category of peasant farmers as defined above. Small-holdings are the most characteristic feature of Third World agriculture, as may be seen from table 4.3 which lists the median sizes of holdings in a broad selection of Third World countries. There are some provisos to be made: some African countries give figures only for 'traditional' holdings and fail to give data on large holdings or plantations; some only give data relating to land actually in crops, excluding fallow land, etc., and in other cases, holdings may be supplemented by common grazing rights over large areas.

Table 4.3   Median size of agricultural units in Third World countries

Less than 1.0 ha		1–1.9 ha		2.0–3.9 ha		4.0 ha and over	
Asia		*Asia*		*Asia*		*Asia*	
Bangladesh		Philippines	1.5	Pakistan	3.5	Thailand	4.0
(1977)	0.5			Burma	3.6	Iran	5.8
Indonesia	0.5					Iraq	7.5
India	0.6						
Singapore	0.6						
Sri Lanka	0.6						
Taiwan	0.7						
Africa		*Africa*		*Africa*		*Africa*	
Egypt	0.7	Zambia	1.0	Senegal	2.1*	Niger	4.4
Gabon	0.7*†	Cameroon	1.2*†	Uganda	2.2	Botswana	4.6*†
Togo	0.8*†	Malawi	1.2*	Chad	2.3*†	Algeria	4.9
Liberia	0.9	Zaire	1.2*†	Mali	2.9*	Tunisia	5.0
		Mozambique	1.3	Sudan	3.0		
		Ghana	1.4*	Morocco	3.1		
		Congo	1.4*†	Ivory Coast	3.9*†		
		S. Leone	1.5*†				
		C. Afr. Rep.	1.5*†				
		Kenya	1.9				
Latin America		*Latin America*		*Latin America*		*Latin America*	
Haiti	0.9	El Salvador	1.1	Surinam	2.2	Honduras	4.0
		Jamaica	1.1	Trinidad	2.3	Belize	4.5
				Guatemala	2.3	Costa Rica	5.0
				Ecuador	2.7	Paraguay	5.6
				Mexico	3.1	Venezuela	7.0
				Colombia	3.3	Nicaragua	7.0
				Peru	3.7	Brazil	9.0
				Dominican		Uruguay	27.0
				Rep.	3.9	Argentina	40.0

Notes: * Area in crops only.
   † 'Traditional' sector only, excluding large estates or a modern farming sector. Dates of surveys are the most recent available.
Source: Land Tenure Centre, Wisconsin (1979) *Land Concentration in the Third World.*

The outstanding fact to emerge is that in almost all parts of the Third World, except some countries in Latin America and parts of the Middle East, median farm sizes are less than 5 hectares, and in most of the countries listed that are predominantly in the humid tropics, median farm size or the area in crops is less than 2 hectares. To some extent, the figures relate to environmental factors. In Africa, countries with a high proportion of savanna lands such as Botswana, Chad, Mali, Niger, Senegal and Sudan, tend to show higher figures for the median farms than those of the humid tropics. Farm sizes are, however, affected by many factors other than the area needed to supply the needs of an average farming family under different environmental conditions. Holdings in areas of intensive rice production are quite small: Bangladesh, Indonesia and India have the lowest figures in the table. Pressures of population are clearly reflected in the small size of the median farm in India and Bangladesh, but in central Africa the small size of the cultivated area of the median farm reflects the difficulties of cultivating anything more than a few hectares by traditional methods of clearing and hoe cultivation. Median farm sizes tend to be larger in Latin America as a whole, though over-populated El Salvador and Haiti are exceptions.

Table 4.3 gives no more than a general guide confirming the predominance of small-scale peasant farming in the Third World. It is necessary to look more closely at the relationship of peasant farming to environmental conditions, levels of technology, and rural marketing. Traditional farming systems have evolved in different environments that are often quite finely tuned to achieve an adequate productive level from internal resources, while at the same time maintaining an ecological equilibrium in the environment. It may be helpful to outline some of the major types of farming in the Third World with these relationships in mind.

SHIFTING AGRICULTURE

Shifting agriculture, once much more widespread, comprises a variety of practices, mainly in areas of tropical rainforest, but also in some savanna lands. It is sometimes known as 'swidden agriculture' or 'slash-and-burn' but there are also many local names: *conuco* in Venezuela, *roça* in Brazil, *chitemene* in Zambia, *milpa* in Central America, *ladang* in Indonesia, for example. The essential feature is the temporary cultivation (a few years) of clearings made in the forest, which are then allowed to revert to secondary vegetation for a substantial period, while new clearings are successively opened up. The ratio between the period of cropping and the length of the fallow period during which the forest is allowed to regenerate varies a great deal. In the rainforests of West Africa and South-East Asia one or two years of crops may be followed by 8 to 15 or more years of fallow; in semi-deciduous and dry forest zones and some savanna areas, 2 to 4 years of crops can be followed by 6 to 12 or more years of fallow. But there is a great deal of regional and local variation, ranging from *ad hoc* and irregular movement of individual farmers from one clearing to another to complex arrangements of clearing and fallow in long period cycles which may last up to 45 years.

The associated settlement may be stable, located within the area involved in the clearing cycle, but it may also shift to new sites more conveniently located in relation to a new cycle of clearings. A move of every 10 years or so has been noted in the Rio Negro valley in the Amazon basin; once every 5 years in the Philippines; but stable settlement within a defined area of movement of clearings appears to be fairly common.

Clearings are almost invariably made by hand methods, though mechanical handsaws are increasingly being used in Latin America; the larger tree stumps are left, and branches and forest debris are normally burnt, especially where there is a drier season, but in some areas of African savanna lands, for example, in Tanzania, and in western Colombia, cut vegetation is left or prepared as a mulch. Crops may be planted directly in the ash or the ground prepared by hoe or digging-stick. In Zambia branches are brought from other parts of the woodland to add to the ash content of a clearing.

It has frequently been observed that the system is adapted to a forest ecology and the fragility of tropical soils. Plant nutrients are concentrated in the vegetation itself rather than in the soils from which nutrients tend to be rapidly leached by heavy rainfall in combination with high temperatures. Clearing of the forest vegetation breaks the normal cycling of plant nutrients; the ash resulting from the burning of branches and debris reduces soil acidity and makes some minerals immediately available for crop production, but fertility tends to fall off rapidly and yields in the third year of cultivation are often only half of what is obtained in the first year. The decline in fertility, and therefore of crop yields, is the main reason for the abandonment of a clearing and the creation of a new one, but it has also been noted (in Venezuela, for example) that the growth of weeds may make the opening of a new clearing less laborious than continued cultivation of the old one.

Cropping systems are often complex, and the initial impression may be one of chaos. Crops apparently planted quite haphazardly are often, in fact, very carefully sited. Intercropping of different species is normal, and sites are chosen with a precise eye for differences in the levels or drainage conditions on the cleared land. The variety of crops fulfils a number of functions: it ensures a varied diet and a phasing through the year of harvests and of labour demands; it helps to reduce risks from pests and diseases; it also ensures a complete ground cover at various levels of height in such a way as to reduce the impact of rainfall (and indeed to emulate to some extent the layered structure of natural vegetation) and thus to reduce the risk of soil erosion. Special crops may be grown around the settlement itself, frequently with manuring from household wastes, and fruit trees are planted near permanent settlements. Crops grown are adjusted to local conditions: root crops such as cassava (manioc), yams, coco-yams, sweet potatoes; grain crops such as maize, millets, hill-rice or even padi; pulses and fruits such as bananas or plantains. Two points in relation to cropping systems may be noted. Firstly, shifting cultivation systems, often regarded as static and traditional, have assimilated staple crops of alien origin: maize and cassava from the New World have become, over the years, accepted into many African systems of shifting cultivation, for example. Secondly, crops for subsistence are usually combined with some production for sale, sometimes of vegetables and fruits for urban consumption, sometimes of tree crops producing cocoa, coffee, rubber, or palm-oil for wider markets.

Shifting agriculture, along the lines described above, is to be found in Central America and in the Amazon basin, and not only among remote Indian tribes, for forms of shifting cultivation are a normal practice of peasant colonists in the forests of western Amazonia – Colombia, Peru, Ecuador, and in the *campo cerrado* and the rainforests of Brazil. It is still widely practised in the rainforests of Central Africa and in much of West and East Africa in forests and tree-savannas; it is rarer in South-East Asia, but occurs in the Philippines, parts of Malaysia and the Outer Islands of Indonesia. It has been seen as an adequate response to the problem of maintaining soil fertility, under the difficult conditions posed by climate and soil in the humid tropics, by a sparse population at a fairly low level of technology. Under optimum conditions, it yields both subsistence and cash crops while allowing the regeneration of the forest vegetation that is necessary for the recuperation of soil fertility and it has proved adaptable to the assimilation of new crops both for subsistence and for income. Furthermore, it has been shown that shifting cultivation is a system that yields an adequate subsistence for a low investment of labour. Investigations of widely dispersed areas suggest labour inputs of the order of 120 to 200 days' labour a year per hectare of cultivated crops.

In the lower Amazon, for example, the commercial production of manioc flour based on shifting cultivation has been regarded as a system producing high output for a low input of human energy. Yet it should also be said that shifting agriculture is not always seen as a means by which regeneration of secondary tree vegetation ensures the recuperation of soil fertility and thus the long-term maintenance of a cropping system. Peasant colonists in western Amazonia, for example, are often inclined to see the clearing of forests and shifting cultivation of crops as an intermediate stage leading to the creation of pastures on which commercially oriented cattle production can be developed. The pastures, which represent an ecological deterioration from one point of view, are seen as the desired aim of peasant colonists seeking a marketable product.

Furthermore, in a changing world, shifting cultivation poses two difficult problems: one concerned with modernization and the other concerned with the growth of population. The first problem is bound up with the nature of shifting cultivation itself. Clearings are usually made by hand methods, occasionally with the use of mechanical handsaws, but mechanized clearing is expensive and far beyond the means of most peasant farmers. Cultivation of cleared land is by hoe or digging stick and the presence of tree stumps, roots, etc. precludes the use of other means of cultivation. Weeding of intercropped fields must be done by hand. There are clear limits to the area that *can* be cultivated by hand, and intensification of production by the use of mechanized clearing and the plough is difficult, expensive and potentially dangerous ecologically.

The second problem is related to the capacity of shifting cultivation to accommodate an expanding population. Growth of population implies a progressive shortening of the fallow period, which may prevent the recuperation of soil fertility, leading to a long-term decline in yields. The proportion of fallow may be progressively reduced to as little as 50 per cent of the area available; settlement tends to become fixed, with a distinction between intensively cultivated land near the settlement given preference in the application of animal or green manures, and fallow systems at a distance from the settlement. As cultivated land occupies more of the available land, larger areas may be cultivated at a greater cost in

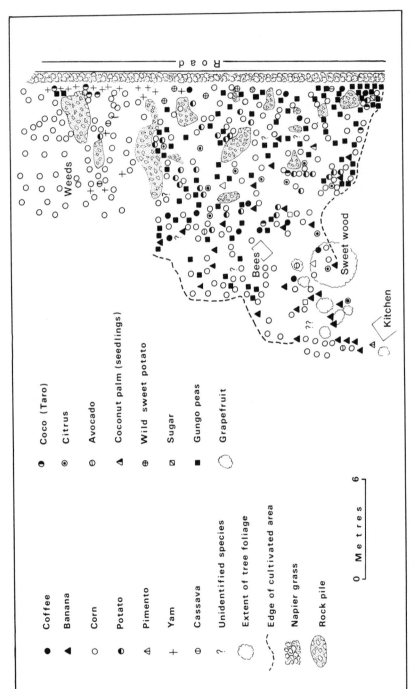

Figure 4.4 Mixed cropping on a small farm in the Devon area, Jamaica. Population pressure on land has reduced the possibilities of shifting cultivation, but the plots of small farmers demonstrate the complex inter-planting of cash and subsistence crops and fodder.

Source: Innis, 1961: 20.

Legend:

- ● Coffee
- ▲ Banana
- ○ Corn
- ◑ Potato
- ◁ Pimento
- + Yam
- ⊖ Cassava
- ? Unidentified species
- Extent of tree foliage
- Edge of cultivated area
- Napier grass
- Rock pile

- ◐ Coco (Taro)
- ◉ Citrus
- ⊕ Avocado
- ▲ Coconut palm (seedlings)
- ⊕ Wild sweet potato
- ◪ Sugar
- ■ Gungo peas
- ◯ Grapefruit

0 Metres 6

Road

Weeds

Bees

Sweet wood

Kitchen

labour, but with declining yields per hectare of cropped land. A low-level equilibrium of soil fertility may be reached which can still, however, support a larger total output than a similar area under true shifting cultivation, but with a greater expenditure of labour. Many areas in West and East Africa and the Caribbean which were formerly in shifting cultivation are now characterized by bush-fallow farming with relatively short fallow periods, low yields and permanent settlement (figure 4.4).

WET-RICE FARMING

In marked contrast to shifting cultivation, wet-rice farming has for many centuries been able to support very high densities of population in humid-tropical and subtropical areas, particularly in monsoon Asia. In many of these areas wet-rice farming is also associated with a landscape in which the hand of man is dominant: carefully levelled plots, surrounded by low water-retaining banks or bunds, banks of terraced slopes and, above all, detailed and unremitting attention to the control of water. And with a few exceptions, it is an agriculture conducted by peasant farmers at a relatively low level of technology but which incorporates not only intensive labour but also a high level of traditional skills.

The basic outlines of rice cultivation are well-known. In South-East Asia, for example, land is flooded, then cultivated by ploughs drawn by oxen or water buffaloes. Soils are puddled and the surface smoothed ready for planting. Seedling rice is commonly grown in nurseries and transplanted into the wet soils by hand. Later the fields are drained and the ripened crop harvested, most often by hand. One rice crop a year is the normal practice, but much depends upon the availability of water, the length of the growing season and the amount of labour available. Three crops in two years have been noted in Sumatra, where rainfall is abundant throughout the year. Two rice crops a year require a careful scheduling of labour, and again depend upon the availability of water and pressure of population on the land, and are characteristic of parts of south China, for example. Even three crops a year can be grown with rapidly maturing varieties, very intensive cultivation and favourable conditions of climate and water supply. In most areas, however, rice is associated with other crops, planted in rotation in order to maximize returns from the land available in the light of water supplies and climate.

Multiple cropping, in the sense that more than one crop a year is produced, is normal in rice-growing areas, rice alternating with other cereal crops, root crops such as sweet potatoes, vegetables, cotton or sugar. In Taiwan, for example, intensive rotation is closely geared to the availability of rainfall and irrigation water in a 3-year system: rice is grown with the benefit of summer rains and seasonal irrigation, and is followed by unirrigated sweet potatoes and wheat during the winter and spring. In the second summer, the same land is devoted to green manure crops, groundnuts and soya, relying on rainfall rather than irrigation water, followed by sugar for 15 months.

Plate 4.2 Rice cultivation, Java, Indonesia.
An elaborately manicured landscape of intensive rice cultivation, developed on rich soils of volcanic origin, and supporting population densities in excess of 1000 per square kilometre.

Intercropping of various types, involving the growth of more than one crop at the same time, is also indicative of the intensity of land use. A new crop of vegetables or sugar may be planted as the previous crop is still ripening; short-period crops such as vegetables may be planted at the same time as crops that mature and ripen more slowly, so that the quick-maturing crops yield a harvest before the long-period crop is mature.

There are, therefore, many variations in cropping systems and in their intensity. In general, they are finely adjusted to seasonal variations of climate, to the availability of labour through the year, and above all to the availability of water and the degree to which it can be controlled. The farming structure as a whole depends, obviously, on the maintenance of fertility at an adequate level to support the heavy demands made upon it by multiple cropping.

The preoccupation of rice farmers in south and central China with the need to maintain soil fertility by recycling all possible wastes of vegetable and animal origin back to the land, has long been known and commented on by geographers. This includes the composting of vegetable wastes; the incorporation of pig-raising into the process, by which vegetable wastes are first 'converted' into meat, then into manure for the rice-fields; the use of human excreta (with consequent health risks); and the production of green crops for ploughing-in. Writers have noted a 'migration of fertility' in China to the neighbourhood of towns where wastes from foodstuffs, animals and people tend to be concentrated and can enhance the productivity of nearby agricultural land. Upland vegetation may be raided to make composts for the benefit of irrigated land, and the contrasts in China between carefully attended irrigated lands and the neglect and erosion of the uplands (at least until recent years) has more than once been noted.

Even where such painstaking husbandry is not practised, however, wet-rice cultivation permits the maintenance of adequate fertility without necessary recourse to fallow years. Irrigation itself brings silt and soil nutrients to the cultivated fields; the presence of blue-green algae on flooded rice beds and wet soils fixes nitrogen in a form that becomes available to plants. Irrigated rice requires an impermeable soil, and impermeability is increased by the puddling of water-logged soils so that few mineral nutrients are lost by leaching; and the repeated flooding and working of soils for rice cultivation tends to lead to neutral pH soil values which facilitate the availability to the plants of soil nutrients. Finally, the care with which water control must be exercized reduces soil erosion to minimal levels. Yet it is also evident that rice yields respond well to the application of natural manures, as traditional Chinese experience shows, and also to the application of mineral fertilizers.

The labour requirements of wet-rice cultivation are much higher than those of shifting cultivation, even though agricultural operations are normally assisted by animal power for the ploughing and preparation of the soil. But it is also true that the returns from an increase in intensity of labour (weeding, transplantation, application of compost and green manures, detailed water control and maintenance of irrigation channels, etc.) tend to be higher than in other forms of tropical agriculture. The point at which additional labour produces little or no additional return in yields occurs at a very much higher intensity of labour than in other systems. Thus rice cultivation can at once support, and give employment to, very high densities of rural population, as it does in much of India, south and central China, Java, the Tonkin delta and other parts of South-East Asia.

Wet-rice cultivation, therefore, unlike shifting agriculture, has provided a system capable of the continued maintenance of high densities of population. It requires high levels of skill and of labour inputs. It can be, and often is, combined with non-irrigated agriculture on surrounding upland areas for the production either of annual or permanent crops. On peasant holdings in Malaysia it is often combined with the production of rubber; in Java, with coffee. Indeed, the relative security of the rice harvest (given good irrigation and water control) permits farmers to cultivate rather more speculative, income-producing crops on adjacent lands. Rice cultivation has spread widely from its original heartland in monsoon Asia and is being adopted increasingly in West Africa, for example, in coastal areas of Sierra Leone, and in Nigeria. Rice cultivation has increased greatly in the last 30 or 40 years in Latin America, notably in Brazil, Peru and Ecuador, and has long been established in coastal Guyana. In general, production of rice in Latin America has tended to be commercially oriented from an early stage.

Finally, and again unlike shifting agriculture, wet-rice cultivation is flexible in terms of its capacity for improvement of output under modern conditions. Improved strains of rice, simple forms of mechanization, and increased inputs of mineral or organic fertilizer promise increased yields of rice both per hectare and per man hour without necessarily completely overturning the social fabric built around agricultural operations. But above all, the provision of improved irrigation and water control seems to offer the greatest scope for increased output, welfare and security, though the planning and execution of such projects are outside the control of peasant farmers themselves (see chapter 5).

MONTANE AGRICULTURE

One of the major characteristics of traditional peasant farming is its use of a multiplicity of ecological niches in order to grow a wide variety of products at different altitudinal levels. The use of different ecological niches is quite often to be seen at a microlevel in shifting agriculture, where slight differences in level, slope or location of cleared land in relation to settlement are sought out for the planting of different crops. It is to be seen in many wet-rice areas where intensive rice cultivation on level land or on terraces is combined with the use of unirrigated uplands for rain-fed crops or permanent tree crops. But it is in truly mountainous areas that there is the clearest zoning of crop systems with respect to altitude, slope, aspect and water supply. Patterns of exploitation and the institutional arrangements adopted to exploit the maximum range of environmental resources differ with respect to scale. Such systems are characteristic of mountain areas throughout the tropics – for example, in the Himalayas or the Rift Valley of East Africa – but they are perhaps best developed in the Andes.

The Tarma valley in central Peru, focused on the small town of that name at an altitude of 3000 metres, contains level land on the valley floor and moderately sloping land, carefully terraced from before the Spanish conquest in the sixteenth century, and traditionally the location for intensive, irrigated production of maize and beans, the nitrogen-fixing qualities of leguminous plants making possible continuous cultivation. Irrigated alfalfa or lucerne, introduced by the Spaniards, later helped to supply fodder for mule trains operating along the length of the valley and beyond, and also helped to maintain fertility for the production of maize and wheat (also introduced by the Spaniards). On the fairly steep slopes of the valley sides, and on moderate slopes above, root crops and especially potatoes could be grown without irrigation up to 4200 metres and barley up to 3900 metres, with a characteristic pattern of temporary cropping for a few years followed by long grass-fallow periods. The third element in the pattern as a whole was the grazing of common pasture land at these and at even higher altitudes, sheep (introduced by the Spaniards) tending to replace the indigenous herds of llama. Individual peasant farmers in the villages around Tarma normally had access, therefore, to irrigated valley-bottom land, temporary plots of land for rain-fed production of temperate crops, and to common pastures. Improved access by road has tended to increase the intensity of production for external markets, and the highly valued irrigated land is now frequently used for the production of fresh vegetables and flowers for the Lima market, and fertility is maintained at a high level by the careful use of animal manures.

Differing ecological conditions, similar in range and character to those outlined above, may be found within a single community, and even within the property of a single peasant farmer. But at a larger scale, much greater distances may separate communities located predominantly within a single ecological level, so that traditional exchange systems have operated by barter or by conventional monetized values, for the exchange of potatoes, other root crops and animal products such as meat or wool from the high-level communities; for maize, wheat, beans and fruits from the valley communities.

A similar distinction underlies the patterns of exchange in the high *puna* of southern Peru. This is high plateau country over 4200 metres above sea-level dominated by the tundra-like vegetation that gives the *puna* its name. Pastoral Indian communities are structured around the herding of llama and alpaca in areas well above the limits of arable cultivation, but their pastoral economy has long been symbiotically linked with agricultural communities at lower altitudes with which they exchanged llama meat and alpaca and llama wool for maize, potatoes and other agricultural products. The whole constituted a multi-community subsistence unit in which exchange was regulated on a barter system, and later by monetary payments. With the expansion of an international market for alpaca wool in the nineteenth century, the raising of alpaca was stimulated, but the alpaca trade was, and still is, handled by itinerant merchants rather than by the traditional mechanisms of the rural market – the proceeds of alpaca sales are regarded as supplementary cash that may be reasonably spent, not on essential foodstuffs, but on fiestas and other expenditures of a similar kind.

Before the colonial period highland communities with their major nucleus at one altitudinal level quite often controlled outlying settlements at other levels in order to provide themselves with supplies of maize, coca or other products. In modern times individual families from the highlands have settled in the humid montane forests of the lower eastern Andes below 2500 metres above sea-level, maintaining links with the highlands through family networks. Eastern settlement is occasionally the product of deliberate efforts by a highland community to acquire rights over land in the eastern regions. Production and exchange are organized on commercial lines rather than by barter, but a distinction may be drawn between a system of commerce among peasant producers which is more or less internal to the zone of contact between the highlands and the montane forest lands, and the system of larger-scale commerce by which products such as coffee, bananas, and beef are exported from the eastern slopes of the Andes to national urban and international markets.

Quite apart from various forms of large-scale agriculture to be discussed in the next chapter, there are other characteristic patterns of farming in the Third World: pastoral farming in various forms in the savanna lands of Africa and

Latin America; rain-fed crop–fallow systems involving grain crops such as millets, wheat, sorghum and pulses in north China, northern India and Latin America; irrigated agriculture for crops other than rice. But the discussion of shifting agriculture, wet-rice and montane farming in the Andes serves to illustrate a number of important issues in relation to Third World peasant agriculture.

The common characteristic of the peasant systems outlined above is the use of local resources in such a way as to support the rural community by the production of foodstuffs both for internal consumption and for sale or exchange, and also to maintain the productive capacity of local resources for future generations. The *primary* aim of production has traditionally been for subsistence, either at the level of the domestic household or at the level of the rural community as a whole. But most peasant societies must also produce an additional surplus for sale, exchange or for the payment of rents and taxes. The balance between production for subsistence and production for sale is, however, changing steadily in most Third World countries. Secondly, the peasant systems outlined above rely *primarily* on inputs drawn from the internal resources of the community: energy in the form of human labour or animal power; materials for agricultural implements (though metal for ploughs, hoes, sickles, etc. may have to be bought); and above all the maintenance of soil fertility by fallowing, regeneration of the forest, or by application of green manures.

It is also necessary to stress that rural communities and peasant households are not simply agricultural units. They are also concerned with many other activities which in the advanced industrial world have become specialized industries. To a greater or lesser extent, depending on the degree to which local economies have become commercialized, peasant households may be involved in food-processing (most often by the women), the domestic production of textiles or clothing, household and agricultural implements. They may carry out much of the work involved in house construction, using predominantly local materials and with the help of specialized craftsmen such as carpenters. Agriculture is an essential part of the rural way of life, but it is generally a part and not the whole. What in the Western world are separate activities and specializations are often, in the Third World, the concern of communities involved in other activities besides agriculture, entailing intricate use of time and labour throughout the year, but always closely geared to the insistent demands of agriculture and climatic seasonality.

The domestic household is the basic unit around which these multiple activities usually revolve, but the rural community has an identity and cohesion to a much greater degree than in the advanced industrial world. It is usually, as is traditionally the case in Western Europe, a unit for religious celebrations, and for the organization of festivals and ceremonial rites; it may have formal or customary procedures for the appointment of communal officials. But there are other communal functions which serve to integrate the community. Land, or rights to the use of the land, may be vested in the community as a whole, and even where individual peasant holdings are carefully and jealously demarcated, land may be held in common for the grazing of animals, or the extraction of wood for fuel and house construction. On land irrigated by traditional means, the allocation of water and the maintenance of canals and ditches is often a collective responsibility. The repair and construction of tracks and local roads, the building and maintenance of communal structures (the communal meeting place, washing places, even football fields) may also be communal functions. Communal needs of this kind may sometimes be met simply by forms of local taxation, but in the central Andes, for example, they have traditionally been met by a levy of labour on the peasant membership of the community. All contribute their labour on appointed days to lay out a new plaza or mend irrigation ditches, and the occasion is made festive by the provision of food and drink.

Individual peasant households, similarly, may be able to call on the labour of their remoter kin or neighbours in the community for work beyond the scope of the family itself – for the construction of a new house, clearing of forest, or harvesting, for example. But the provision of help sets up an obligation for reciprocal assistance at some later date, and these obligations are carefully calculated according to such factors as the degree of kinship and social distances of the parties concerned.

The cohesion of rural communities varies enormously in the Third World of course, but in general they are the units that give a sense of participation, stability and even permanence, and in some ways encapsulate many aspects of a regional or national culture. Rural communities are integrated generally by kinship networks, patronage, the celebration of religious observance and local feast days, and by the organization of local government; they may also be physically integrated as nucleated village settlements. They are also given identity in other ways: by the existence of communal property, usually of land, control over irrigation water, rules governing the use of land, and also by the networks of communal labour obligations and reciprocal labour arrangements. Agricultural operations are characteristically deeply embedded in the whole fabric of rural society, and it is important, therefore, to recognize that agricultural changes adopted in the process of modernization frequently imply consequential social change in rural society as a whole (see chapter 5).

Adaptation to change

The idea that peasant farmers of the Third World are inherently conservative and resistant to change seems, increasingly, to be a myth. Even with a limited technology, peasant societies have shown a capacity to adapt to the growth of population, the introduction of new crops and the pressures of international commerce, though it is evident that there are limits to the extent to which adaptation is possible within the traditional framework of dependence on locally available resources. As population has expanded, shifting cultivation in parts of West Africa has given way to bush–fallow systems that produce a greater output from a given area of land at the expense of greater labour cost, even though yields per hectare of *cultivated* land have fallen. In the Far East, complex systems of terracing and careful water control have extended the cultivable area for rice, and have enabled larger populations to be supported. In Indonesia the replication of the tiered structure of rainforest on a small scale by the cultivation of food crops at different levels (sometimes known as 'agricultural involution') makes the maximum use of small plots of land. Over the centuries peasant farmers have readily adopted new crops, not only for cash income (cocoa in Ghana, coffee and cotton in Uganda, palm oil, rubber and coffee in Java and Malaysia, for example) but also for subsistence. A massive and largely unrecorded interchange of crops slowly took place from the sixteenth century onwards between the Old and the New Worlds: cassava (manioc), maize, tomatoes, potatoes and fruits such as avocado pear, pawpaw and pineapples and cocoa were transplanted from the New World to the Old; wheat, barley, coffee, citrus fruits, sheep, cattle and other domesticated animals moved from the Old World to the New.

Peasant farmers are not blindly resistant to change; nor can it be said that they are, in general, profit-maximizing entrepreneurs. Peasant strategies have been seen as 'satisficing' in the sense that they aim at an adequate return for effort rather than a maximum return at all costs. They may, in short, be prepared to trade off potential income for extra effort against the leisure that must thereby be forgone, and leisure is still highly valued in many parts of the Third World. But it is also important to recognize two other factors affecting peasant attitudes towards change. One is that the peasant household is not only concerned with a strategy for the use of its land, but also with a strategy to make the best use of the labour available to it. The best use of labour from the point of view of the peasant household may not necessarily coincide with the best use of land from the point of view of external observers, particularly where temporary labour off the peasant farm offers a higher return than the use of that labour on the farm. Secondly, peasant strategies towards agricultural change can often be best understood in the context of risk avoidance, or the minimization of risk. Farmers in the Third World face natural hazards of drought, pests and plant diseases, unseasonable rainfall, hail and frost; they have often to face an unpredictable and unstable market for saleable produce; and sometimes the instability and unpredictability of government and government policy. To face natural and man-made hazards they have little or no reserves of land or capital, and what is at stake may be survival itself for the peasant and his family. Risk avoidance is the only sensible strategy for the peasant under these circumstances, and changes can only be risked if he perceives a virtual certainty of a successful outcome.

Rural societies in the Third World have certainly adapted to change in the past, but what is different in the recent past has been the rate and scale of change, and the strength of the pressures for change. These pressures are complex and often subtle and indirect, but it seems possible to identify two major categories: the consequences of rapid population growth, and the pressures for transition from subsistence farming to commercialized production.

RESPONSES TO THE RAPID GROWTH OF POPULATION

Rates of population growth in much of the Third World have accelerated rapidly in the recent past (see chapter 3). Rates of growth of population of 2.5 to 3.5 per cent per year have outstripped the capacity of many rural communities to support it by traditional methods of intensification relying on local resources. It was noted above (table 4.1) that much of the increase in agricultural output in the 1970s came from an expansion in area cultivated, but in many areas, notably in South Asia and the Far East, the limits of land cultivation by traditional methods have long ago been reached and further extension requires heavy investment by governments in large-scale projects of irrigation, land reclamation and road building, or in land reforms that may make land available to peasant farmers.

Meanwhile, in the absence of government help, peasant communities take up whatever spare land they can, frequently by cultivating marginal and submarginal land or by grazing too many stock on natural pastures. The results are all too evident in many areas: soil exhaustion, accelerated soil erosion, degraded secondary vegetation and over-grazed and exhausted pastures. A recent report on population and development in Kenya observes, for example, 'The harmful effects of population pressure on Kenya's farmland is currently taking many forms. . . . Part of the marginal (low, dry) land is becoming arid because overpopulation is leading to improper cultivation. Squatter migrants on marginal land often harmfully exploit natural resources, both by destroying forests and by using poor farming techniques' (World Bank, 1980: 55). In the densely populated provinces of Kenya bordering on Lake Victoria, about half of the small farm households are estimated as being below the poverty line and land hunger has forced people to seek opportunities in these marginal lands and take economic and environmental risks.

In intensely cultivated areas, the most obvious consequence of the growth of population has been the fragmentation of holdings as a result of the division of land among the children of successively larger generations. In Peru, for example, a holding of 5–6 hectares of arable land in the mountains, or 3 hectares of irrigated coastal land is regarded as necessary to provide an average peasant household with an adequate level of living (in terms of standards customary for the region). But between 1961 and 1972 the number of holdings of less than 1 hectare increased by more than a half from 318,945 to 483,350, and the number of holdings of less than 5 hectares increased by just less than a half from 725,452 to 1,083,775. Other countries can show equally depressing indications of the fragmentation of smallholdings to levels below that which can satisfy family needs even at a very intensive level of farming. In Java, in 1973, for example, 57.5 per cent of all holdings were of less than 0.5 hectare and 20 per cent were less than 0.2 hectare; and in India (1970/1), 33 per cent of holdings were less than 0.5 hectare.

Even allowing for the occasional existence of communal pasture or woodland with which individual farmers may supplement their resources, such figures as these indicate the scale of the problem. The land is forced to produce as much as possible by intensive labour, but on such tiny plots there are rarely savings which can be used to invest in seed, expensive fertilizers, pesticides or more efficient methods of cultivation. The small cultivators are so often too numerous and too scattered to be reached by agencies that offer credit and technical advice (which is often inappropriate), even if the political will exists to reach them. Little more can be grown than will feed some of the family most of the time, and seasonal hazards of climate or flood and the failure of crops spell disaster.

Since scarce land must be dedicated to the major priority of keeping the family alive, and since there is insufficient land to occupy the peasant and his family, cash income must be secured by the sale of labour, usually by migration to large estates, plantations, or to towns. The implications of migration, either on a temporary or seasonal basis, or by the permanent migration of one or more family members, are very varied indeed. Seasonal migration has long been a custom where there is a slack agricultural period. Demands for temporary labour may sometimes fit this structure if it can be combined with a slack season for agricultural operations; but the demand for seasonal labour may not be so conveniently arranged. The carefully evolved scheduling of labour in the traditional society may be profoundly disrupted by the need to migrate for part of the year. Traditional cultivation practices may be abandoned, including such vital tasks as weeding and hoeing. In the Amazon basin, need for seasonal labour to gather rubber led to an abandonment of maize cultivation on fertile flood plains because of the rigorous timetable maize cultivation involved, and it was replaced by cultivation of manioc on poorer terrace soils, which was less productive but allowed much greater flexibility in planting and harvesting.

The migration of labour on a temporary or seasonal basis brings cash income back to the villages; more permanent migration to the towns may yield remittances from the migrant. The household is deprived of the labour of its active youth, but tiny and uneconomic holdings, inefficiently cultivated, are maintained by the injection of remittances. There are other consequences. Migration to the towns, offering some possibility of release from the grinding poverty of rural life on inadequate plots, becomes a major target for the small farmer so that the family plot is seen as a subsistence base but no more, and ambitions for the young focus on educating them for urban life rather than an agricultural future. The family holding, in a sense, is seen as an insurance against economic disaster and a guarantee of survival of a sort, but not as a primary source of income. And this role should not be forgotten in countries where health services, social services, social security and unemployment benefits do not reach the countryside or most of the urban poor. It is certainly a factor to be taken seriously into account when considering the arguments for and against policies aiming at the consolidation of plots into viable holdings in the interests of agricultural efficiency.

SUBSISTENCE TO COMMERCIAL PRODUCTION

In the modern world, very many pressures are brought to bear on traditional peasant society to increase the share of their output that is devoted to commercial markets, but it is necessary to precede a discussion of these pressures by a brief clarification of what is implied by subsistence farming. Essentially, it implies that subsistence farmers produce a substantial part of their own food requirements, but it does not preclude the production of a surplus for sale or barter, the proceeds of which may yield a cash income, or income with which to pay rents or taxes. The difference between subsistence and commercial farmers may thus be seen simply as a matter of the degree to which they participate in the market, but it can be argued that there is an important and critical threshold at the point where a farmer ceases to base his strategy of production on the need to provide food for his household and relies on the market not only for the sale of the bulk of his produce but also for the purchase of the greater part of his household's food requirements.

Systems of rural exchange
The development of rural systems of exchange in the Third World is not, there-fore, incompatible with the idea of subsistence production. However well-adjusted subsistence production may be, there are times of famine and times of plenty according to vagaries of climate or the health and fortunes of the peasant family. Deficits and surpluses occur from year to year, but may be resolved by the exchange of gifts, though like the exchange of labour discussed above the provision of gifts implies a reciprocal responsibility. The gift is in fact an insurance policy, and implicitly recognized as such by a recipient who can accept charity without loss of face. Further extensions of this principle are the gift-making ceremonies that reinforce ties at all levels, cementing marriage bonds (dowry), placating a potential enemy, winning political support, gaining prestige, impressing a rival. The gift has become part of the political, social and economic system of many Third World countries, all of whose roots are strongly rural. Although it often has an economic purpose, it is not in itself an economic act. It is this essentially social and political character of transactions that permeates all rural-exchange relations so that no interchange is purely economic.

Barter is the next stage in the establishment of rural-exchange systems. A family with a surplus of beans and a deficit in rice looks for a family with more rice than it needs and a failed bean crop. The exchange that results is the subject of a transaction where values are precisely defined by a process of barter. The question of how many beans are equal to one basinful of rice can only be estab-lished by negotiation. This negotiation is an essential part of many rural trans-actions in a Third World rural system, and often has a social function – it becomes an intellectual exercise, a game of skill for the purpose of fixing value. Here the reader will recognize a transition point to the next stage in the process. Value can best be established at places where items for exchange can be com-pared. Where many items are to be exchanged the process can best be rationalized by a meeting held in one place. The rural market place is a central agreed point for collective bargaining and bartering and the fixing of value. It is also a place for the exchange of information, gossip and ideas, for organizing social events, settling quarrels and making political deals. The introduction of money into the economy

Plate 4.3 Vegetable market, Rabaul, New Britain, Papua New Guinea.
Rural markets such as this provide an outlet for the surplus production of peasant farmers.

has not altered the essential character of gift, barter, and exchange relations in the market place·in rural-dominated social systems. All forms of activity are endorsed in open interchange – gifts are used to cement buyer–customer relations, all goods are bargained for as a means of constantly adjusting value in response to hourly changes in supply and demand.

A good deal has been written about the development of rural markets beyond this early stage. Their full development has been related to a particular stage in the growth of a local and regional economy when population densities reach a certain level, and when an urban system is emerging to 'fill out' the range of commodities circulating in the rural areas. Then rural markets become part of the set of trade relations that allows brokers from the towns to draw on local produce. Traditionally, it is in the larger rural markets that rural items can be bulked by wholesalers for shipment to town, and it is here too that town-manufactured and bulked items can be broken down by traders for sale to a rural population (figure 4.5).

The system that develops is complicated and uncontrolled – except by its own internal mechanisms. The rules that govern the spacing and timing of rural markets operate according to local systems of social, economic and political organization. The distances between markets are governed by the time taken by a sufficient number of customers and traders to travel on foot or by horse or donkey to reach the scheduled market place. Spacing and size are also conditioned by the

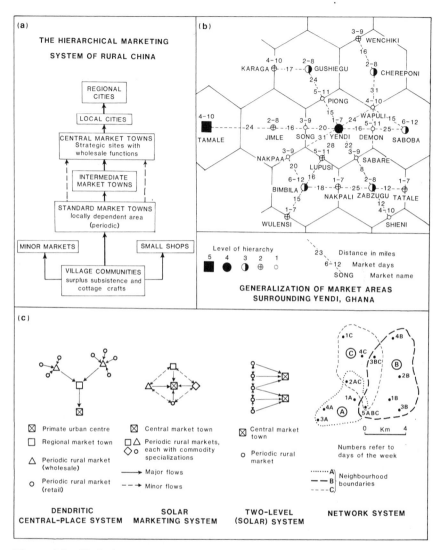

Figure 4.5 Marketing systems.
(a) shows a hierarchical marketing system, in which permanent markets in the larger towns serve the needs of periodic markets operating on specific days. (b) is a stylization of the market system of Tamale in Ghana, and reveals that a synchronization of time and space allows each market a large enough number of traders and customers to justify regular trading activities. (c) shows there are several ways in which a maximum number of interactions can be achieved between periodic and permanent markets.

Source: Skinner, 1964; Mckim, 1972; Hollier, 1981.

circulation habits of traders. Some larger markets are held each day of the week, but others are held periodically according to a schedule of calendar days in 3, 4, 6 or 10 day cycles. Whether a market is held periodically or daily depends on the range of goods exchanged and the distance people are prepared to travel to acquire them – a factor related to the density and wealth of the population. Clearly, then, not all regions are blessed with a rich network of rural markets. In some regions the range of produce and the density of population is insufficient to sustain a network at all. In other areas the social structure has not encouraged this form of exchange relations. Gradually, however, one of the results of the development process has been to diminish the importance of this feature of rural society. As systems become increasingly urbanized the inefficiencies and uncontrolled unpredictability of rural markets make them 'uneconomic'. New cash crops bypass the markets altogether through government-controlled marketing agencies that control prices according to national and international, rather than local-commodity, pricing structures. A pessimistic view is that as more and more traders and producers rationalize production and marketing in this way, rural markets and their rich web of social functions and connections may become as much a relict feature of the rural landscape as they are in more developed countries. Modern systems of organization are too well orchestrated to be able to absorb the lively, self-regulating anarchy of the rural market place.

From a local to a national economy
Particularly in the former colonial territories of Africa and Asia, political independence has been followed by a strenuous drive towards the building of integrated nation states both in an economic and political sense. In Latin America, economies formerly dominated by export sectors and the élites associated with them have followed policies aimed at internal development. These shifts have implied industrialization, investment in energy production, the creation of a national network of communications in place of export-oriented links, investment in education, the widening of the political franchise, the provision of subsidized credit, and rapid urbanization. Rural communities which were formerly no more than marginally affected by the need to produce cash crops are increasingly involved in a wider, national society. Urban expansion has created growing internal markets for foodstuffs; industrialization has created new markets for raw materials; rural education and improved communications (including radio networks) have stimulated a wider consciousness of economic opportunities and also a 'revolution of rising expectations' in terms of material welfare; subsidized rural credit has tempted farmers to produce primarily for the market rather than for subsistence. For isolated rural communities the stimulus towards commercial production and towards social change may come in many other ways than by the careful calculation of potential profits, through, for example, the completion of a new road, the return of migrants with new skills and experience, the presence of an influential teacher in the village, the mobilization of the community against the depredations of a neighbouring landowner, and also, of course, through the direct action of government agencies.

Road-building and the improvement of communications are rightly seen as prerequisites for the extension of markets. There are many examples of the rapid expansion of production for the market following or being reinforced by the building of ports, roads and railways. Unused resources may be called into play for the production of foodstuffs and raw materials for urban or international markets – production of rubber and palm oil by peasant farmers in Malaya, for example, or the extension of rice production in northern Peru along the Northern Transandean Highway in the 1960s. Lower costs of transport for the marketing of surplus produce should, in principle, stimulate concentration of effort on those products for which the community may have a relative advantage, and thus lead to greater income and welfare. But there is a negative side to this equation. It becomes possible, and cheaper, to *import* goods into rural communities which were formerly self-sufficient. In historical terms, cheap imported manufactured goods (textiles, clothing, plastic goods) have in many places replaced indigenous, traditionally produced goods of homespun fibres, wood or pottery. In one sense, these imports represent a net gain in terms of standards of material welfare. But they also remove many of the non-agricultural functions of the rural population and help to create a rural underemployment problem. But improved communications also bring in imported foodstuffs which may have a greater prestige value than the traditional diet. One of the effects of road-building in some Andean communities has been to bring in rice and imported wheat products at the expense of locally produced potatoes, barley and maize. In the forested eastern slopes of the Andes one remote and old-settled community virtually abandoned its own domestic production of rice for imported products following the construction of a new road – and promptly turned to the destruction of forest to extract its marketable timber.

SOCIAL IMPLICATIONS OF ECONOMIC AND DEMOGRAPHIC CHANGE

Many traditional farming structures are based on the exploitation of a variety of ecological niches that allow for the production of a varied and complementary pattern of consumption goods, either at the level of the individual household or of the rural community or a group of communities. The exchange of complementary goods took place by negotiated barter or conventional money valuations, and at traditionally organized rural markets. Concentration of production on commercially viable crops frequently distorts or destroys this complementarity, for example maize may be sold in the national market at prices higher than those traditionally offered to producers of barley and potatoes; locally produced wheat and barley may be replaced by cheaper imported wheat products. The results of such changes may well lead to a rising total *cash* income to the community, but it is often not equally distributed. The innovators in the community or those fortunate enough to hold or to acquire the appropriate land (for example, irrigated land for maize cultivation in the example mentioned above) may receive substantial rewards for their efforts, but those with land suitable only for wheat and barley (to continue the analogy) are likely to be impoverished by the shift to commercial production. Others may be impoverished by the loss of non-agricultural occupations or by the fragmentation of holdings as a result of population growth. One consequence of production for the market, then, tends to be the creation of economic inequalities in the village communities, which are often accentuated as the fortunate gain access to credit facilities, improved methods of cultivation and take on some middleman functions. (To be in a position to acquire a lorry and participate in the commercialization of agricultural production is commonly an ambition of the rising farmer in the Mantaro valley of Peru, for example.)

Many studies of rural communities suggest that economic and demographic changes in the recent past have led to a greater degree of inequality within village communities, and that greater inequality has in turn strained, and even caused the disintegration of the communities themselves. Inequality in wealth and land ownership threatens traditional reciprocal labour arrangements and often presents a threat to traditional controls over the use of communal agricultural resources, since the relatively well-to-do are often able to pre-empt a major share of communal grazing, for example, or appropriate for their own use land formerly allocated equally to members of the community for temporary cultivation. At the same time, returned migrants, the better educated and the young innovators are often inclined to challenge the traditional order of seniority in the administration of the community.

It is suggested above that in the transition from subsistence agriculture to commercialized farming and a totally monetized economy, there is a threshold to be crossed at the point where the peasant strategy of decision-making shifts from the need to assure his own food supply to a desire to maximize cash income from the sale of crops and stock. The peasant must know that it is possible to sell his own produce for a satisfactory price, and also that there is a *reliable* supply of essential goods for him to buy. It is a step which presumes a fairly advanced commercialization of the economy. But the crossing of this threshold also carries with it other implications. It implies the replacement of a varied, risk-spreading range of crops by a high degree of specialization on those products which yield the highest cash income. Specialization carries with it a greater degree of vulnerability to climatic hazards as well as to the price fluctuations on the commercial market. In short, specialization may bring with it a greater degree of efficiency, higher total output and greater incomes, but at the price of greater vulnerability.

There is another sense, too, in which an important threshold is crossed at the point where the decision is taken to concentrate almost exclusively on production for the market, and it is also of profound importance. Agricultural inputs of stock, implements, seed and fertilizer are drawn, in predominantly subsistence societies, from locally derived sources: stock from the natural increase of locally bred animals; implements from simple and often home-produced raw materials with a little imported metal; seed from the previous harvest; and fertilizer from domestically produced organic materials, either as animal manure or vegetable waste by way of the rotation of leguminous crops. But to cross the threshold to commercial agriculture it becomes necessary to widen the field from which agricultural inputs are drawn if yields and quality are to be adequate for a national or international market. Seed and manufactured fertilizer must be purchased; agricultural implements bought rather than made; improved breeds of stock introduced. And in the absence of sufficient accumulated capital, the farmer must rely on external sources of credit in order to effect improvements. In turn this increases his vulnerability – to the banks for credit, as well as to ruling market prices, and the vagaries of weather. It is an important and difficult threshold to cross, and one that can only be crossed if the farmer can perceive a substantial and predictable benefit to compensate for the risks involved. To participate wholeheartedly in the national, commercial economy is to enter a world of new risks associated with price fluctuations, credit, rates of interest, and changes of government policy; and in many cases, the necessary conditions of political and economic stability at the national level do not exist.

The discussion so far has focused on peasant farming, still the most important sector of Third World agriculture, and the adaptation of peasant societies to change, but two important issues remain to be discussed: the role of large-scale enterprises and the role of government, directly or indirectly, in affecting the conditions of agricultural production. These two topics form the subject matter of the next chapter.

5 RURAL DEVELOPMENT: MODERNIZATION, REVOLUTION OR ADAPTATION?

In the last chapter attention was drawn to the ways in which peasant societies of the Third World are the product of a long process of adjustment to a frequently hazardous physical environment – a situation often made more difficult by social, economic and political instabilities. It was suggested that the systems of production that evolved in these circumstances were based on family and community, kin group and village; they also involved bargaining and bartering in an open rural market rather than fixed-price transactions between factors and farmers. It is precisely in these ways that peasants everywhere developed the ability to balance the risk of producing a surplus for local trade against the security of providing for their own subsistence, so that strategies are neither subsistence-oriented nor commercially oriented but a mix of the two, and are geared to survival rather than towards rapid increases in productivity. The speed of innovation in such communities has often been seen as needlessly slow by outsiders interested in creating regular surpluses from rural areas. Indeed the whole history of what is called rural development can be represented as the attempt by increasingly well-organized entrepreneurs, or government agents, to make rural areas more productive.

Many peasants may see 'rural development' as the effort of 'outsiders', whether capitalist or socialist, exploitative or well intentioned, to devise increasingly sophisticated methods for subverting, circumventing, transforming or accommodating peasant structures in the interests of enlarging landholdings, improving yields or introducing new crops. Some writers have regarded these interventions, now underpinned by modern science and high technology, as the only basis for the modernization of rural societies. Others have pointed to the ways in which business interests reinforced by governments have used such interventions to transform the peasant into a wage labourer within an urban-oriented production system, or at worst to focus wealth and power in fewer and fewer hands, and in this way to increase rather than reduce social and economic differences between rich and poor. Clearly such arguments extend beyond the field of rural development, but it is in presenting an overview of the changes in rural areas that such different views about the nature of the development process come sharply into focus.

Among the outsiders there are, on the one hand, the forces of free enterprise: first the landlord, then the merchant and moneylender, and more recently the representative of the international business consortium. On the other hand there are the forces of bureaucracy: first the tax collectors and the district administrators, then the representatives of national political parties, and finally the international aid advisers. All these agents have been interested, to a greater or lesser extent, in increasing the surplus from peasant landholdings or in 'releasing' land and labour for more productive use than traditional practice allowed. Whether this is seen as marshalling the productive energies of the system or extracting surplus production is very much a question of interpretation and of local circumstances, for the peasant the result is often much the same.

Landlord and peasant

Inequalities in access to land have long characterized the ownership of agricultural land. Figure 5.1 summarizes the distribution of landholding in four selected countries in a way which emphasizes the inequalities of access to land. Thus in Brazil, 20 per cent of all agricultural units are less than 2.0 hectares, occupying only 0.3 per cent of agricultural land, while 0.1 per cent of agricultural units are over 5000 hectares in size, occupying 20 per cent of all agricultural land. Other Latin American countries display similar landholding characteristics, with a dichotomy between a smallholding peasantry and massive rural estates. Indian statistics relating to land ownership show the same pattern of inequality, though the sizes of holdings involved are much smaller, and the fact that 37 per cent of farmers have less than 0.2 hectares is an indication of rural poverty on a very large scale. Indonesia's profile is also expressive of the extent to which there is pressure on the land, especially in Java, where half the holdings are less than 0.4 hectares and three-quarters less than one hectare. But, at the other extreme, some 1800 estates, devoted to the production of palm-oil, rubber and other tropical crops, occupy 2.2 million hectares in Indonesia, mainly in the more sparsely populated Outer Islands, and especially in Sumatra. Finally, the landholding profile for Kenya is even more indicative of a history of dualism in agricultural development, with its recognized division between registered smallholdings on the one hand, and a relatively small number of large farms occupying a half of the agricultural land.

Large holdings of land have been accumulated in a variety of ways and with very different points of departure both in time and space. They have often involved the withdrawal of land from communal usage and the subordination of a peasant population. They have also been created in virgin territory, requiring the import of labour from elsewhere, and representing new additions to the area of cultivated land. At all events, policies of agricultural development have long been focused on the large estates and medium-scale farms as the easiest and most rapid

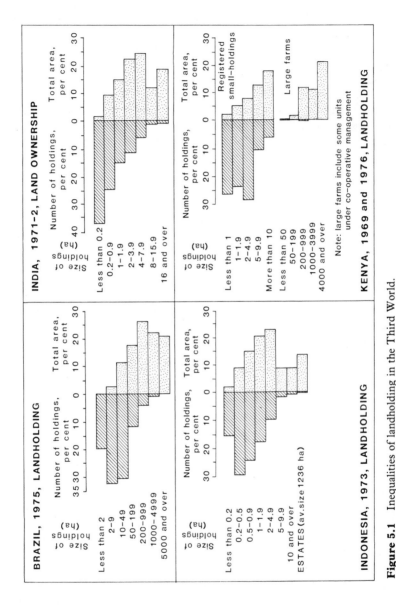

Figure 5.1 Inequalities of landholding in the Third World.
The figures for India relate only to land ownership; those for the other three countries may include tenure holdings.

Source of data: Land Tenure Centre, 1979.

way of encouraging the adoption of modern agricultural techniques. Economies of scale are possible; credit is more easily available; and the scale of resources available implies a minimization of the risks which plague the small farmer. Medium and large-scale farms can and do introduce new agricultural techniques and more efficient methods of production, including mechanization. In South-East Asia it has been the larger farmers who have enthusiastically embraced the Green Revolution, with its heavy demands on careful managerial control of inputs and capital investment, and have reaped high yields as a result. In Mexico, the expansion of agricultural production in the north is associated with the innovative capacity of large or medium-scale farmers, and although small farmers (*ejidatarios*) have willingly adopted the cultivation of higher yielding hybrid strains of maize for the market, they have been more reluctant than medium-scale farmers to adopt the cultivation of sorghum, for which there is little subsistence demand. Medium or large-scale farmers such as the coffee producers of Brazil, the beef-cattle producers of the Argentine or the white farmers of Kenya and Zimbabwe, have been ready to adopt technical innovations in the production of export crops which can compete on the world market.

But a great deal depends on the ways in which the medium and large-scale holdings are operated. It is by no means necessarily the case that largeholdings are more productive or efficient, even in their use of labour, than family-size farms. It has been frequently observed that large-scale holdings in Africa and Latin America are, in general, less intensively used than small peasant farms. There are many examples in Latin America and Africa of estates held in extensive pasture employing very few labourers and herdsmen, side by side with over-populated and intensively used small farms. It can be argued that the high profitability of extensive pastoral estates is not compatible with the social function that land should perform in providing employment and food for over-populated rural areas.

Moreover, the possession of land may still carry with it a social prestige and a degree of social control over a subservient rural population which may relegate high profitability to a secondary role. More importantly, the owners of large estates in parts of Latin America, for example, have fairly consistently followed a thoroughly rational policy of investing capital where it can secure the highest return. But this has often meant that capital accumulated by extensive farming on large estates or from rents from tenant farmers, has been invested, not in agricultural improvements, but rather in urban real estate, urban construction, and more recently in the shares of multinational companies. Savings accumulated in the countryside of the Peruvian sierra, the Kenya Highlands or the Ganges plain, are channelled into the urban and industrial sector directly by individuals, and indirectly by state taxes, and even find their way into industrial development in the advanced industrial world.

Finally, the medium and large estates are by no means always directly operated by their owners, but frequently parcelled out into tenant farms operated under a variety of conditions. Under some of the most common forms of tenancy systems operated in the Third World, the cycle of low productivity, low returns and poverty reaches its lowest ebb.

Landlord and tenant systems

The subordination of peasant farmers by powerful groups and the creation of a landlord class dedicated to the creation and extraction of surplus by rents, tribute and taxation was a feature of preindustrial societies throughout much of Europe and Asia. Feudal arrangements and relationships were gradually eroded in Western Europe and overthrown by revolution in the USSR and Eastern Europe. In China, North Vietnam, North Korea, Kampuchea and Ethiopia, similar systems have been replaced by similarly violent revolutions. But in the other areas of the Middle East, the Indian subcontinent and South-East Asia the structure of landlord and moneylender, merchant and tenant farmer still remains strong, and in some ways the currents of economic development often strengthen these class differences.

More drastic changes were superimposed on indigenous societies by the appropriation of land by privileged non-indigenous groups with the consent, or under the protection, of a colonial administration or an emergent state. Usually, though not by any means universally, these were large estates, sometimes incorporating indigenous communities, sometimes created from hitherto unused land resources in order to produce new crops for export or to supply an urban sector. The Latin American *hacienda* represents one such group of large estates, and its origins go back to the sixteenth and seventeenth centuries. Other examples are the rubber estates of Malaya, palm-oil concessions in Sumatra or Zaire, and banana estates in Central America. The large farms carved out by white settlers in Kenya or Zimbabwe form another later development of the same kind. Large estates required labour for their operation which was not always easily forthcoming. Slavery and the import of indentured labour were two of the historical solutions which set up a train of international migration. The imposition of taxation and the extension of large estates to erode or to incorporate traditional communal territory forced indigenous societies to seek access to land by tenancies or by providing wage-paid labour.

Various forms of tenancy have evolved. Labour-service tenancies tend to be associated with relatively backward farming systems on large estates, particularly in Latin America, South-East Asia and the Middle East. For the large estate owner they represent a means of securing income from the land with a minimum of cash expenditure. The tenants supply labour for the cultivation of the landowner's crops and rearing of his stock in return for the right to cultivate a plot of land. Sums paid out in wages tend to be minimal. Tenants must focus their attention essentially on the production of subsistence crops for their own support. The tenant is tied to the landowner's enterprise in such a way that the improvement of agricultural methods becomes very difficult. The condition of the tenant is a subservient one, and in many Latin American countries where this form of tenure survived until recently it has become accepted that the abolition of this kind of tenure is a *sine qua non* of social and economic development. Labour-service tenancies provide a mechanism for internal subsistence within the estate economy which is oriented externally to the production of a surplus only for the estate owner.

Share-cropping tenancies are very varied in detail. The essential feature is that the harvest is shared in some fixed proportion between landlord and tenant. In some cases the landowner provides the land and no more, in other cases the landlord may provide seed, implements, fertilizer or agricultural credit for the share-croppers to secure the necessary inputs. The share-cropping tenant has a greater scope for decision making on his holding than the labour-service tenant, but only within the narrow limits imposed by the landowner, who frequently dictates what crops shall be grown and how they shall be cultivated. At times of relative scarcity of labour, share-cropping was sometimes a way in which landowners could ensure the exploitation of their holdings by providing the wherewithal for prospective landless farmers. The agricultural exploitation of the Argentine pampas and the conversion of natural pastures into agricultural land producing wheat and then alfalfa for stock rearing was geared to a system of temporary share-cropping leases offered to immigrant farmers who were charged to clear the land, sow it with arable crops for a few years, lay it down to alfalfa, and then leave. Very often, the expansion of share-cropping tenures has been associated with the production of commercial crops, and particularly crops for which methods of cultivation are relatively straightforward to produce a standardized product. The expansion of cotton cultivation on the Peruvian coast from the late nineteenth century was accomplished primarily in this way. The production of rice in coastal Ecuador has been similarly based.

Under a share-cropping system the landowner is able to extract an income without directly participating in production himself. In this it is quite different from the labour-service estate in which the labour services are directed precisely to the land directly operated by the landowner. The landowner secures income from the sale of his share of the crop and frequently is able to purchase the share remaining to the cultivator at a relatively low price. The middleman role of the landowner under share-cropping systems is therefore important, and in addition he is some-times in a position to gain from the differential rates of interest on credit supplied to him from the banks and which he then supplies to his tenants. Share-cropping systems offer a means by which the area under cultivation can be expanded rapidly for the production of commercial crops, and under conditions in which the tenants bear much of the risks. But it also makes it difficult to adapt rapidly to changing economic circumstances. It is this last characteristic which led to another significant type of involvement in increasing surpluses: the plantation.

The plantation, agribusiness and the family farm

Direct intervention by business enterprises concerned with increasing the reliability and regularity of supply of tropical produce has been a major feature of agricultural development in most tropical countries of the Third World. Different in kind if not in result to the 'landlord' system, the plantation served the less directly personal interests of a family firm – a management enterprise rather than a landed estate. The reasons for this development are bound up with the changing relationship between Europe and North America and the Third World.

First of all, from about 1880 the volume of trade increased very rapidly with rising standards of living, the growth of population and the increasing complexity of the industrial world. The demand for imports of agricultural produce took on a new dimension in quantity and variety – cotton, rubber, coffee, tea, and temperate farm products, including meat and wool. Secondly, improvements in transport now made a major impact both in maritime trade (steam navigation, the screw propeller, steel, refrigeration) and in inland trade and transport by rail. Thirdly, direct foreign investment in colonial territories had been necessary to establish railways, port facilities and public utilities, but from 1880 there was also an increasing tendency for foreign capital to invest directly in the production of tropical foodstuffs and raw materials. After the emancipation of the slaves in the Americas, plantations could no longer be defined in terms of slavery, but rather in terms of technical management, foreign ownership and large-scale monocultural production for export. More land, labour and capital were needed, and if capital was imported, or accumulated, by the ploughing back of profits, land had to be acquired; often, it is true, by clearing unused land, but equally often at the expense of an indigenous peasantry. Labour was recruited from various sources and by various means: from a displaced peasantry; by the levying of poll taxes which forced migrant labour out of their traditional societies to seek cash for the payment of taxation; or by a new form of international migration to replace the role of West and Central Africa as the supplier of slaves. Instances of this process are the Chinese migration to Peru and Malaya, and Indian migrations to Burma, Malaya, East and South Africa and even to the Caribbean. Fourthly, the protection of investment or the establishment of a 'safe' environment for investment, together with politically inspired imperial designs, led to a vast extension of colonial empires in Africa and South-East Asia by the British, Dutch, French and Germans.

It could be argued that not all European involvement led to open exploitation. Some private family firms have long engaged in encouraging the growth of cash crops from the traditional base. This kind of relatively benign initiative led to the development of cocoa production in Ghana and palm-oil production in Nigeria. Some tea and coffee production has always been associated with peasant producers rather than with large estates. But while developed countries of the world still rely on the Third World for supplies of what are non-essential luxury commodities, like bananas, coffee, tea, chocolate, sugar and tobacco, it has become more and more difficult to earn foreign exchange through the sale of such commodities using traditional plantation or tenancy methods of production. Despite increases of more than a third in the tonnage of such cash crops since the early 1960s, the real income earned from such crops scarcely increases at all.

Raising the prices of luxury crops like coffee and cocoa merely means that fewer people buy them, and do so less regularly.

In these circumstances, advisers are forced to suggest increasingly cost-effective methods of increasing the productivity of these essential foreign-exchange earning cash crops. In the face of this problem, those state economic planners who see development very much in terms of an increased surplus which can contribute to Gross National Product (GNP) or a reduction of balance of payments deficits are ready to accept the most economically rational of all development strategies: the introduction of large-scale commercial enterprises owned or part-owned by major multinational companies. The way towards this is already well developed. Plantation farming is a system which first developed to increase and regularize supplies of items to cater for escalating demand, particularly for beverage crops, from a rapidly industrializing Western Europe and North America. This natural extension of the plantation system has provided the Third World with its most successful examples of increased agricultural output.

Since the first plantation owners in the sixteenth century acquired large acreages in the West and East Indies and in South America for the monoculture of sugar and other crops, the methods of business organization and the technologies of production have both been transformed. Instead of relatively small family businesses, large international consortia, often with only a secondary interest in agriculture, increasingly finance, control and organize the production of most tropical crops. Large firms with a base in international finance even come close to controlling the economies of several small and not so small countries, manipulating the political conditions to serve their need for economic stability. Even where a measure of local control over the decision process is exerted by governments who have nationalized foreign assets of the kind described above, the demand for profitability in the face of increasing costs and falling production margins allows free rein to the processes of economic rationalization which lead back to the expertise of large business enterprises. In common with modern agriculture everywhere, increasing the scale of operation by mechanization and high technology has been seen as the most effective way to increase profits both by the business firms involved and by host governments who are persuaded by the apparent financial safety of investment of this kind. High technology eventually reduces involvement of local people either as a labour force or as managers, and is an inevitable consequence of this form of development. Even governments take a secondary role in these operations. Faced by so much technology and the sophistications of high finance, governments are often content merely to take their share of the profits. Indeed, it is ironic that so much foreign exchange acquired in this way is used to buy foodstuffs for the richer element of an urban population who have grown used to the products of temperate agriculture, such as whisky, beer, brandy, wheat and dairy products and packaged foods, the consumption of which is a mark of status and prestige. The creation of large agribusiness enterprises may temporarily ease the balance of payments problem of a new country, but creates a level of economic dependency which may not be in the long-term interests of sound economic management.

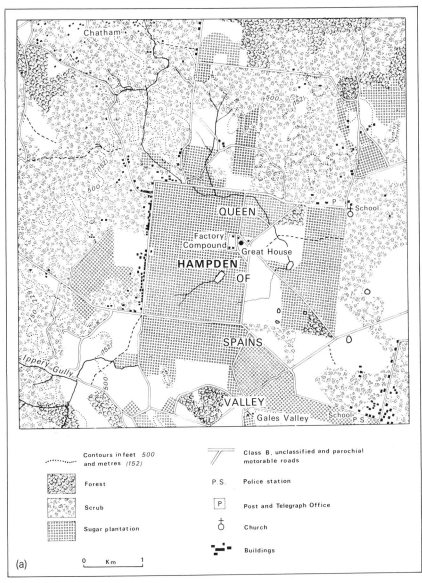

Figure 5.2(a) and (b)   Sugar plantations in Jamaica.
(a) Shows the pattern of monoculture on a sugar plantation. Cane dominates the use of land.
The nucleus of the estate is the great house, built in the eighteenth century, and the sugar
mill and ancillary buildings. The labour force, much of it employed only seasonally, lives in
the village on the edge of the plantation. (b) Shows the continuing importance of sugar
plantations in Jamaica. In recent years there has been some consolidation of plantations and
rationalization of sugar processing.

Source: Clarke, 1974: 47 and 71.

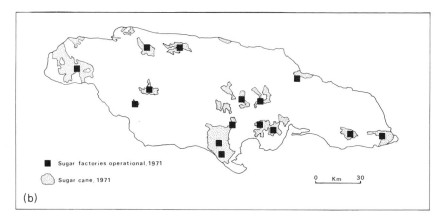

(b)

New techniques

A second and apparently successful route to increased agricultural output has been the creation and introduction of improved plant and animal strains. Such improvement, by empirical methods, has been part of Western agricultural tradition since the eighteenth century, but the major modern breakthrough occurred in the early 1960s, and by the time Norman Borlaug had won his Nobel Prize for work on developing higher yielding varieties of rice and wheat in 1970, the Green Revolution was being heralded as the means by which poor farmers could first secure their own subsistence and produce a surplus for sale to the burgeoning towns. Its greatest impact as a philosophy of transformation has been on farming in the Indian subcontinent and in South-East Asia, where production of basic cereal crops has certainly increased dramatically since 1970 (see table 4.1). But the new crops have brought with them a series of side effects which make their benefits less than total. First there were the economic problems generated by the need for rapid dissemination of the new varieties. As indicated in chapter 4, peasant farmers are rational conservatives. They will not abandon tried and tested methods of a traditional kind for some new and (for them) untested alternative. The only way governments could launch the seeds of new plant strains on the market was to offer massive subsidies and a system of guaranteed prices well above world market figures (Mexico 33 per cent; India and Pakistan 100 per cent). At the same time the improved strains often tasted different and were not so rich in protein, so their market price was further depressed in competition with local grain. In order to sell at all, Green Revolution grain is often discount priced and the real subsidy is therefore even higher than it appears. Moreover, assistance to farmers has not been uniform. The more 'progressive' landlords and farmers are often those with spare capital and a larger land area at their disposal for new investment. In countries such as India and Pakistan, where landlord and tenant systems operate, poor tenants are often evicted to make way for the improvements in irrigation and mechanization that new grain varieties demand. It is not merely the landless tenants who are affected. New seeds increase yields only if they are supported by large quantities of fertiliser, pesticides and water. This extends the need for loans. For the small farmer faced with annual interest rates well in excess of 20 per cent, the new technology becomes too expensive. While richer neighbours compete to increase acreages for mechanization, the higher land rents which result increase the incentive for the small farmer to sell land to raise capital for improvement of this kind. Eventually he is squeezed out altogether and forced to seek employment either as a wage labourer on a neighbouring successful farm or in the town. With the pressure to substitute mechanization for labour it is often only the second course which is open to peasant families, who then swell the ranks of the urban unemployed.

Apart from the social cost of these improvements in total production, the Green Revolution has engendered further economic and ecological problems. The use of high-technology agriculture also increases dependence on external supplies of fuel, fertilizer and pesticides. Large petrochemical companies provide all three support elements and in this way the economy of the developing country becomes

Plate 5.1   Improvements in the pastoral economy, Ceará, North-East Brazil.
Cross-bred cattle, combining the resistant qualities of Asian zebu cattle with the productive qualities of European Friesian stock have been introduced to replace low-grade scrub cattle. Use is also being made of fodder crops instead of traditional uncontrolled grazing of poor natural vegetation.

increasingly dependent on the international vicissitudes of the oil industry and its suppliers. The world economy is not yet sufficiently sophisticated to cushion the developed world, let alone Third World countries, from the effects of inflation problems and variable oil prices. In ecological terms, moreover, the impact of high technology and sophisticated agronomy is perhaps even more insidious. Most local strains of cereals which new varieties replace have been bred by trial and error over a millennium. They may yield fewer calories but they often have a higher protein content and are more resistant to disease. Epidemic plant diseases are much more likely to attack weaker imported varieties. The only way this problem can be tackled is by yet further imports of pesticides. In 1967 the US Science Advisory Committee estimated that if the Third World was to double its food production by 1985, to feed rising populations, there would have to be a sixfold increase in the application of modern agricultural pesticides. It is now argued that the only way to halt this vicious spiral towards high-cost vulnerability lies in the re-appraisal and incorporation of locally resistant plant species and local peasant knowledge concerning the effective environments for extension of cross-breeds.

Direct intervention: the state and the peasantry

Intervention by the state has taken a number of other forms short of revolutionary transformation. These depend to a large extent on its political stance and on its degree of commitment to internal pressure groups. The most important movements have been towards agricultural colonization and land reform.

Agricultural colonization involves, simply, the extension of farm settlement on a fairly large scale into new land. It is a process that took place on a massive scale in the nineteenth and early twentieth centuries: in the settlement of Canada and Australia, in the great frontier movement across the USA and in the expansion of Russian settlement into Siberia; although the Third World also had its share of the grand movements of colonization. Expansion on a smaller scale occurred almost everywhere in the Third World for the production of export crops to satisfy the demands of industrial countries or to provide new land for internal population expansion. Even up to the 1950s, at least in Latin America, much of the expansion in agricultural production took place as a result of the extension of the cultivated areas rather than because of intensification of production on existing cultivated land.

To a substantial degree these historical movements of expansion took place with a minimum of guidance from the state or from colonial governments. Governments provided a framework of land law within which land was made available to pioneer settlers; immigration was encouraged by various means; and although much of the necessary investment in the building of railways was by private enterprise, government was concerned to exercise a degree of control. But in general terms the expansion of agricultural settlement has slowed down in the last 30 years, in spite of the rapidly increasing populations of the Third World countries. In part this slackening of settlement is due simply to the fact that good, accessible land has already been occupied, and what remains tends to be either of marginal quality, relatively inaccessible to national or international markets, or requires heavy investment in the provision of irrigation facilities or draining before it can be effectively used. Furthermore, the worldwide shift in the relative terms of trade between agricultural and industrial products has tended to make agricultural colonization less profitable than it was in the late nineteenth century; migration to the towns is frequently seen to be more desirable from an economic and social point of view than a hard and risky existence on the pioneer fringe. In some countries the climate of opinion is unfavourable to the uncontrolled expansion of large estates with private capital to clear and exploit new land (though this is notably not true of Brazil since 1964), so that public policy requires that new frontier settlement should be undertaken by medium or small-scale farmers who lack the necessary capital and must therefore be subsidized by the state.

Nevertheless, although much of the modern pattern of agricultural colonization is underwritten and planned by government, 'spontaneous' colonization still occurs where suitable land is available for the expansion of peasant farming. In Latin America it is likely that the majority of new settlement in the western margins of the Amazon basin and to the south of the Andean ranges in Venezuela has taken place as a result of the piecemeal infiltration of peasant farmers to clear and settle new land. In southern Peru, for example, the drift of peasant settlement towards Tambopata from the department of Puno or eastwards from the Mantaro valley has been accomplished with a fairly close and continuing integration between the old highland settlements and the new clearings in the montane forest. Kinship networks link the old and the new; there is an exchange of products between the two as trading links are established; and there is sometimes an integration of labour needs between the two settlements, which may in fact be a 100 miles apart. Much of this kind of settlement is simply by occupation on a squatter basis, and although the pioneer settlers may be evicted by nominal owners, as they have been in eastern Bolivia, they live in hopes of official recognition of their right to occupy the land they cultivate.

A notorious process of settlement has often followed the building of roads in South America east of the Andes. Road-building is accompanied on the one hand by a flurry of ownership claims and land speculation in the offices of the capital city, and on the other hand by a drift of squatter settlements along the line of the road itself. Squatters clear and cultivate the land, only to be evicted if the legal owner sees a possibility of profitable exploitation after 'his' land has been cleared at no cost to himself, and the squatter must either move on, or remain as a tenant or wage-paid labourer. Nowadays, legislation often requires that claims of owner-ship must be followed up by effective occupation within a few years, limits the size of holdings, and sometimes gives rights of title to those who clear and culti-vate new land, but it is difficult to say how far these requirements are actually met. As Hennessy has pointed out, the Latin American frontier is far from being the nursery of democratic nationalism, independence and rugged individualism – the qualities Frederick Jackson Turner claimed for the frontier in the USA – it is more like a pioneer fringe of poverty, refuge, instability and lawlessness, in which, all too often, the inequalities of power, income and wealth between the *latifundio* and the *minifundio*, characteristic of the old lands, are being recreated in the new: as appears to be the case, for example, in much of the Brazilian interior and in eastern and northern Bolivia.

Planned colonization, organized by governments, is intended to conduct the settlement of new land in a rational, orderly manner that will provide economic opportunities for small or medium-scale farmers. The degree of planning and the scale of investment varies enormously. At a minimum level, it involves the building of roads, land survey and the control of settlement by the allocation of plots. It may involve, in arid or semi-arid lands, the provision of irrigation facilities which represent a very heavy investment. More elaborate schemes involve the integrated planning of new settlement patterns with new villages and urban nuclei. They vary considerably in the financial assistance given to new settlers: the preliminary clearing and preparation of land, the construction of housing, the provision of essential needs until the first crops can yield an income, the provision of health services and schools, electricity and supplies of drinking water, the provision of implements, seed, etc. They vary, too, in the extent to which potential settlers are selected as suitable and well-equipped for their task. Some colonization schemes have proved quite excessively costly; many have been less successful than their planners had hoped.

The aims of colonization schemes have often been mixed or vague and, indeed, incompatible. They may be summarized, perhaps, in the following terms:

(i) To secure an expansion of national agricultural output, either to supply an internal market, to substitute domestic production for imports, or to provide agricultural exports. Colonization schemes in Malaysia associated with the Federal Land Development authority in the state of Pahang, for example, are aimed primarily at increasing domestic food production, particularly of rice. In Latin America much of the expansion of settlement in the montana of Peru has, in the past, been directed towards increasing the production of coffee. From the late nineteenth century concessions of land awarded, for example, to the Peruvian Railway Company in the Perené area, and then later to an Italian consortium, were intended to expand coffee production.

(ii) To consolidate an unpopulated or sparsely populated frontier zone by the building of roads and the establishment of settlement colonies. As a motive for settlement policies, this aspect clearly has military-strategic overtones which are not by any means always explicit in settlement plans. But the military-strategic motivation, based on the principle that occupation of territory is the most important validation of political frontiers, seems to underlie a good deal of thinking about colonization in Latin America, at least. Venezuelan policy has at times stressed the importance of stimulating new settlement along its borders with Colombia, Brazil and Guyana; Peruvian policy has focused on eastern settlement on the northern border with Ecuador, and the building of the Northern Transandean Highway was, in fact, put into the hands of the army in the 1960s; the establishment of settlements by veteran soldiers is a policy that has been pursued in eastern Peru and in eastern Bolivia. And it is hard to resist the conclusion that the Brazilian policy of road-building in the Amazon basin has been stimulated by the desire to achieve rapid access to the frontier zones of the west and to occupy them with Brazilian settlers.

(iii) To relieve the problem of overcrowding and of pressure on the land in older settled regions. Many planned or semi-planned colonization schemes include the relief of an over-crowded peasantry among the primary reasons for adopting a colonization policy. It has been the motivation for massive resettlement programmes from Java to Sumatra, and for the colonization schemes in Amazonia to relieve pressure in north-eastern Brazil. Projects for resettlement accompanied by heavy investment in new irrigation in Venezuela to the south of the Andes were also intended to provide land for small-scale farming.

In areas of very high population densities in the highlands of east-central Africa, in Burundi, Rwanda and the extreme south-west of Uganda, there were schemes started by the Belgian and British colonial authorities in the 1950s which were continued into independence to provide more localized additions to the area that could be used by peasant farmers, by improving drainage from the previously swampy valley bottoms in areas of considerable drainage reversal associated with rift-valley formation, and by improving water supply on the floor to the western Rift Valley itself. The schemes on the Rift-Valley floor in particular involved permanent migration from higher altitudes to formally organized *paysannats* in Burundi, and also into the Belgian Congo before 1960.

(iv) But there is a further, and rather less obvious, motivation for modern colonization schemes that stems from political motives. In the old settled regions of much of Latin America, the inequalities of landownership – the dichotomy between large estates and large numbers of smallholdings and dependent tenant farms – have long been the target for programmes of land reform which aim to break up the large estates and redistribute the land to peasant farmers. The colonization of new land, however, seems to offer a strategy which may relieve the pressure of an increasingly vociferous peasantry for more land, yet at the same time leave the large estates intact. Pressures for land reform have thus been diverted towards colonization programmes in an attempt to maintain the status quo while maintaining an attitude superficially sympathetic to the ideals of land reform. This undoubtedly appears to have been the case in the application of the Venezuelan agrarian reform and that of Colombia.

Problems and inconsistencies arise where the aims of colonization programmes are, in fact, incompatible. Aims of military-strategic character are likely to emphasize, in many cases, the building of communication links to and along political frontier regions, or the establishment of colonies in remote areas, and may have little chance of commercial success in view of the high costs of transport to accessible markets. The expansion of agricultural output, whether for home or export markets, implies emphasis on efficiency and modernization that is likely to conflict with social policies aimed at resettling small or medium-scale farmers, and in reality involves an expansion of large-scale estates run on extensive and capitalistic lines at the expense of the peasantry. In eastern Bolivia and Brazil, colonization has involved the recreation, in a new setting, of the social inequalities of the old settled regions. Even where settlement projects have rejected the creation of large estates in favour of an organized policy of peasant settlement on medium-sized holdings, there is a potential conflict of policy aims. Peasant resettlement on new land, subsidized by the provision of transport, tools, housing and sometimes preliminary clearing of the forest or large-scale irrigation, is an expensive process. Investment may be justified by the anticipated expansion in commercialized agricultural output, and by the anticipated role of planned settlements as the nuclei of later spontaneous growth. But successful planning also involves a careful selection of potential colonists according to age, ability, skills and motivation. This in turn reduces the likelihood that colonization schemes will benefit peasant groups who are the hardest pressed in the old settled lands in terms of their access to adequate land; and where the natural increase of rural populations is of the order of 2 per cent or more per year, as it frequently is in the Third World, the likelihood of relieving population pressure by planned colonization schemes is a fairly remote possibility. In the Peruvian Andes, for example, there are about a million peasant families with inadequate land to support themselves. By natural increase alone the population will increase at the rate of about 30,000 a year. Even at a very low cost of resettlement at £2000 per family on planned colonization schemes this would require an impossibly high investment of £60 million a year just to maintain rural conditions in the Andes as they now are.

The agricultural colonization of new land is still important and necessary to expand food production. The frontiers of settlement are being pushed back in areas of rainforest in South America and Africa; irrigation schemes are making new settlement possible in the savanna lands of areas like Venezuela and Colombia. But it is important (many would say essential) that the new lands that are being opened up should be occupied with careful consideration both of the ecological consequences, and of the kinds of social relations that are to be built in the new zones of settlement.

The Transamazonica project
Brazil's Transamazonica highway project exemplifies many of these objectives (figure 5.3). Originally the scheme was a rapid response to the impact of a severe drought in north-east Brazil in 1970. The basic idea was to move excess people from the hazardous conditions of the drought-prone north-eastern sertão to the

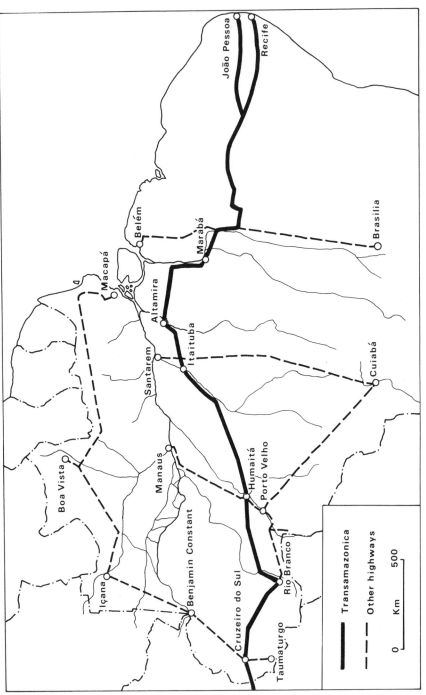

Figure 5.3 The Transamazonica highway and related highways in Brazilian Amazonia.

empty lands of Amazonia. This would ease the problem of population pressure in the sertão and help to fill the demographic vacuum of Amazonia. Migrants were initially to help with the construction of the 5000 km highway and later form the labour force to settle along it in organized colonies. The scheme was, on paper at least, neatly planned, with a careful layout of landholdings and a regular hierarchy of settlement nuclei which would provide a range of educational, medical, agricultural and other services. In a broader context it was hoped that the highway would open up new resources. It was also a confirmation of Brazil's possession of the region, against possible encroachment by other countries.

Originally the scheme was to absorb 70,000 families by 1974, but it did not approach this number. The reasons for this lack of success are various. It was hastily planned, without precise knowledge of the conditions of the rainforest environment. One of the consequences of Brazilian activities in Amazonia in the 1970s is a much better knowledge of the region, but initially basic information about environmental conditions was inadequate, and there were insufficient technicians, such as pedologists and agronomists, to provide assistance and advice. Because of this imperfect knowledge, colonization schemes planned on the drawing board faced various obstacles when they came to be implemented on the ground. The migrants themselves were perhaps not entirely suitable. They were mainly farm labourers from a dry-land environment who now found themselves as smallholders in the tropical rainforest. Broader checks to the implementation of the schemes were changing priorities on the part of the government, and opposition to it on the grounds of its likely environmental consequences in terms of deforestation and soil despoliation. In addition, the post-1973 oil crisis cast doubts on the logic of developing a major highway network (for the Transamazonica was to be the spine of a series of highways) when Brazil was heavily dependent on imported oil. The envisaged scale of the scheme has not, therefore, been realized, and the pattern of land use has been modified to one in which much larger holdings, often owned by companies from São Paulo or abroad, are used for extensive pastoralism.

A good deal of criticism has been levelled at this scheme because of its potential impact on the rainforest environment, but it is probable that major damage may be done, not by organized colonists and large-scale pastoralists, but by thousands of uncontrolled migrants who have moved in along the highways, becoming squatters and cutting clearings in the forest. In the territory of Rondônia, opened up by the Cuiabá–Pôrto Velho road during the 1970s, population increased from 113,000 to 503,000 between 1970 and 1980. In some areas the population doubled every 2 years. An agricultural census in 1975 recorded that the area being farmed had doubled in 5 years, and that figure is almost certainly an underestimate as land occupation was rapid and uncontrolled on this dynamic frontier.

LAND REFORM AND AGRARIAN REFORM

Pressures from very different directions have converged towards demands for land reform and agrarian reform. Land reform, in its strictest sense, implies the reorganization of landholding and tenurial structures, and this has usually been taken to mean one or both of two things: (a) the expropriation, with or sometimes without compensation, of privately owned large estates, and their reorganization in such a way as to benefit a small-scale peasantry or a landless rural labour force; and (b) the consolidation of excessively small or fragmented holdings into a size adequate to support a peasant family. Agrarian reform should, in principle, involve a redistribution of land, but in addition also implies the provision of an infrastructure such as roads, rural electricity, agricultural extension services and cheap rural credit. This distinction between land reform and agrarian reform is one which has had important implications for the way in which rural change has been conducted.

The formulation and execution of land-reform policies are a function of government, and two basic considerations underlie most of the political arguments for land reform: social justice and economic efficiency. These considerations are differentially mediated through political needs and pressures in such a way that there are two distinctive contexts in which land reform takes place: as a more-or-less 'reformist' development within a capitalistic frame of reference or, by contrast, as part of a radical socialist transformation of society involving a more generalized movement towards public ownership. The majority of land reforms have taken place within a reformist context and this deserves primary attention.

The impoverishment of many sectors of rural society as a result of expansion of population and pressure on land resources, or as a result of encroachment of landowners on peasant communities or the exploitation of tenants and labourers, has met with a rising groundswell of increasingly vociferous and articulated protest from peasant populations anxious to maintain or to improve their status. Since the 1950s rural protest has taken many forms as rural populations have become politically more mobilized: rising participation in the political process with increasing literacy and voting power; the creation of rural trade unions incorporating the peasantry as well as landless labour; and occasionally rural guerrilla movements which have seemed to present a threat to the status quo. On the other hand, the political power of traditional or colonial landed oligarchies has been threatened increasingly by new groups representing the new forces of commerce, industrialization and the bureaucracies associated with the extension of the role of the state. For these rising, predominantly urban-middle-class groups, land reform of a fairly moderate kind may be seen as a way of reducing oligarchic power and of increasing the internal market for domestically produced industrial goods.

In economic terms, the case for 'reformist' land reform has rested on two major propositions. First, the gross social and economic inequalities stemming from the concentration of landownership are frequently, though not invariably, associated with an inefficient use of resources. Small peasant farms are characterized by an excessive use of labour and a minimal use of capital on restricted land resources, large estates by the under-use of capital and labour. Land ownership may be a matter of prestige or a hedge against inflation rather than the major source of income; tenancy arrangements may be a positive deterrent to the introduction of new technologies. A more egalitarian rural society would release energies of self-reliance and individual enterprise currently stultified either by the lack of adequate land or by exploitative tenancies. Second, inequalities of rural incomes currently mean that the purchasing power of the vast majority of the rural population is minimal, while that of the fortunate few tends to lead to the consumption of high-quality imported manufactures. By this argument, greater equalities of income in the countryside as a result of the redistribution of land would lead to a greater internal demand for the products of a modest kind (such as clothing, shoes and fairly simple consumer durables for the home) which are within the capacity of national industries to satisfy.

The mechanisms of land reform must involve certain processes: arrangements for the expropriation of land (the criteria for expropriation may be laid down in terms of size, efficiency of operation and the characteristics of tenancy arrangements); and the financial compensation, if any, to be given to former owners. Who is to benefit among the rural population, and on what terms? Are the reformed estates to be divided among beneficiaries or to be made the basis of co-operative or collective institutions? What residual rights does the state continue to exercise over the reformed sector? All of these questions are important and are answered in different ways within the context of the social and political aims of those who formulate or execute the reforms. For example, good financial terms for compensation may lead some landowners to welcome the opportunity to dispose of unwanted land in order to secure cash to invest in non-agricultural activities, as sometimes seems to have been the case in Venezuela and Chile between 1965 and 1969. The restriction of the right of entry to former estate tenants and wage-paid labourers may lead to the creation of new frictions between the new beneficiaries and the old peasantry nearby. The question of whether the reformed estates should be subdivided into individual peasant holdings or organized into co-operatives is another issue on which land-reform programmes have been much divided. Finally, not all land reforms have been executed with vigour and efficiency; political pressures change, and the execution of land-reform laws has often been partial or hesitant, and at times has been diverted towards what is effectively the colonization of new land, or to programmes of assisted rural credit (Colombia), or to little more than the validation of squatters' rights. And in a number of cases, for example, Peru after 1963, Chile in the 1960s, the prospects of successful land-reform programmes were vitiated by a massive decapitalization of estates as a result of the threat of land reform.

In Africa the problems associated with land reform have been confined to those countries which had settler populations in the colonial era. Algerian land tenure has been subject to a socialist transformation that has had a major impact on the landscape. In Kenya, on the other hand, the decolonization of the former White Highlands, centred round the Million Acre Resettlement Scheme of the 1960s, served the political aim of providing peasant farmers and landless people in the former reserves with the opportunity to acquire the freehold of former white land, often subdivided into small family plots. However, about 80 per cent of the land that changed hands was bought by Kenyan individuals or companies, and farmed in much the same commercial extensive fashion as before independence. Output has not fallen greatly, but great political advantage has been derived from the fairly limited redistribution. More fundamental reforms have taken place in the reserves themselves since the 1950s, particularly in the Kikuyu areas north of Nairobi where there was considerable land consolidation and granting of formal title to the customary land, and substantial improvement in the income and productivity of some of the larger beneficiaries of the reform; but, for the first time, a significant landless population was created.

From the early 1960s great hopes were entertained of land-reform programmes as a basis from which agricultural production may be raised and a stable and relatively prosperous peasantry might be created. On the whole, these hopes have not so far been fulfilled. Critics point to figures for agricultural production that show a decline of output following reform (for example, in Bolivia, Peru and Mexico). But it is sometimes difficult to disentangle the effects of massive decapitalization of agriculture immediately preceding a reform from the effects that follow reform, and it has also been said that figures for agricultural production fail to show that peasants were, in fact, eating more of what they produced after the reform. In some cases the expropriation of specialized plantations was followed by a withdrawal of technical expertise (for example, in the sugar plantations of Cuba after 1960 and in Peru after 1969). More seriously, perhaps, and of longer term significance, is the fact that land-reform programmes have revealed only too clearly that even when a substantial proportion of large estates has been expropriated, there is still just not enough land to provide existing peasant families with adequate holdings to support themselves at a modest level of living. This has certainly been the case in Peru. Furthermore, land reform of itself cannot produce an overnight expansion of production; it is, after all, no more than a redistribution of property rights. Land reform giving land to a peasant population also requires support in terms of the availability of rural credit, the provision of technical advice and, above all, a potential market for the produce; and this may imply not only the provision of roads, but also the reorganization of marketing systems for agricultural products and a realistic pricing policy. The beneficiaries of land reform have frequently found themselves with a higher income as a result of it, even though the number of beneficiaries may have been limited. A major consequence of land reform has, whether for good or ill, been to generally increase the role of the state in the agricultural sector. Even where lands have been divided into peasant holdings, the state has retained residual rights relating to the future disposition of beneficiaries' holdings (for example, by requiring that they should not be subdivided on inheritance or by retaining legal title to the land). Thus the state is in a position to control the provision of rural credit or even to lay down conditions as to the use of land. Where reform has been followed by the creation of co-operatives, it is frequently possible, even more directly, to control agricultural planning and thus to orient development towards national needs or to introduce 'modernizing' policies.

In many rural societies the pressures of exploitation and expropriation have periodically exploded into rebellion. For centuries rebellions have fizzed and foundered partly through lack of organization and partly in the face of the well-disciplined forces of the establishment. Although the Russian Revolution involved the radical transformation of rural economic and social structures, it was not in the first place a rural revolution. The most distinctively rural revolutionary movements have taken place in the less-developed countries of the world since the Second World War. The inspiration for them all came from China. The tactics of guerrilla warfare – winning the hearts and minds of rural populations and establishing local alternative government and re-education programmes during the armed struggle – have been used as a model for similar revolutions not only for China's neighbours, Korea, Vietnam and Cambodia, but for Cuba and Libya, Algeria, Angola, Mozambique, Zimbabwe and Ethiopia, and more peacefully, Tanzania. The reasons why some areas pass through this form of social and economic change when others do not is to do with the particular chemistry of oppression on the one hand, and leadership on the other. What is of more concern is the structure of land appropriation which they have involved. It is in the nature of socialist revolution to re-allocate land to private individuals only as a short-term policy. In all the countries of socialist government the state plays a major role in organizing and controlling the means of production. Yet the problems of reconciling the need for increased productivity with personal satisfaction and initiative and both with a policy of public control, is one with which no Marxist government has fully come to terms.

Agrarian reform in China
The case of China is particularly instructive. During and immediately after the revolution land was redistributed by depriving rich peasants and rewarding the landless. The effect of this policy was to dispossess the marginally more successful and to allow the previously landless labourers scarcely enough land to meet subsistence needs. In this process the average peasant landholding was increased by only one-twelfth of an hectare in the densely populated areas of the riverine basins. In the politically and socially disturbed post-revolutionary period it gradually became clear that only a programme of major works and social reorganization could cope with the massive inefficiencies of Chinese agricultural systems. So limited attempts to create mutual aid teams of ten families and to foster group co-operative initiatives in the villages during the fifties, were swept aside by the major social economic and administrative reorganization of the Great Leap Forward of 1958–9. In the first place this was a grass-roots movement. Twenty-seven collectives in the province of Hunan, south of Peking, grouped themselves together into the first large commune, put all land into public ownership and set about an impressive programme of public works including land drainage, canal and reservoir construction. The well-established Chinese propaganda machine gave the commune a good deal of publicity. A visit from Chairman Mao was followed by ecstatic approval for the initiative and within 6 months the whole of

the Chinese rural population was incorporated into large rural communes with an average population of 20,000 and with an administrative hierarchy that ran from the worker-brigade of two families to the central commune committee.

The commune has remained the main functional and organizational unit in China implementing an impressive set of agricultural improvements, reducing the risk of natural disasters by major improvements in water control, extending the area of cultivation into previously unused or degraded land and initiating rural social services and industrial developments. During the last twenty years attempts have been made to force the Chinese peasant into a mould that removes all individual initiative and replaces private desire by collective will. Through it all, and despite the Cultural Revolution, the peasant family has clung tenaciously to the need for a 'private' plot of earth on which to raise domestic produce and (at times of more benevolent central government) to raise farm animals and grow vegetables for market in the small private sector.

Most other attempts to collectivize agriculture totally have also foundered because of the individual's desire to retain a private plot and its produce. Tanzania, for example, has found that its socialist transformation has worked best in poorer areas in the south and has met considerable opposition in the north where cash crop farming is well-established and private initiative flourishes. China is now finding its way towards a compromise. The basic structures of socialist organization of the means of production are retained but, increasingly, a free rein is allowed to small-scale private enterprise for intensively produced horticultural crops and animal husbandry. Whether this emerges as a contradiction within the system, causing further modification of the socialist ethic, or as a necessary and beneficial compromise, remains to be seen. The continued political experiment will be watched with interest by many other neo-socialist states in the Third World.

Transforming peasant agriculture and society from within: the aid agencies

It has been argued above that the basis for a good deal of what passes for rural development in the Third World has been the extension of commercial enterprise and the creation of larger and more efficient forms of business or bureaucratic organization; that such developments involve the peasant as wage labourer, share-cropping tenant or as a token-receiving 'comrade worker'. Such systems remain exploitative, demeaning and unsatisfying. At the same time, the increasing size and political significance of urban populations in Third World countries makes it imperative that the productivity of land should be improved and that export crops be produced. The world scale of this problem has generated a response from relief agencies and the UN, and their role as intermediaries between the peasant and the state, and the peasant and commercial exploitation, will now be examined.

Faced with the prospect of large-scale famines, international agencies have disbursed increasingly large sums of aid in the direction of improving agricultural productivity in the Third World. Although we are often reminded that this represents only a small fraction of the wealth generated and spent in the north, these are substantial programmes of assistance. Working through independent governments, rural-development aid has been of various kinds:

(i) Large-scale schemes designed to serve national budgeting strategies for import substitution: similar in style and conception to plantation farming, they can immediately transform the peasant into a wage labourer.

(ii) The provision of demonstration farming units designed to form the focus of an innovation process.

(iii) The 'model farm' approach.

(iv) The provision of credit for acceptably innovative farmers.

(v) The creation of marketing facilities for specific cash crops designed to bypass middlemen and give 'better' prices.

A number of variants of all these approaches exist to incorporate some regional differences in political and social systems. In one area the tenant farmer is the focus of attention, in another a settlement scheme attempts to replicate the 'community spirit' of a tribal village. Sometimes there are experiments which copy exactly the style of the European idea of a village settlement. One thing they have in common: very few survive more than a few years. The Third World is littered with examples of failed schemes and can show very few 'successful' ones that have any hope of a self-sustaining future. Everywhere the short-term local successes have meant increased reliance on just the same kind of external supply factors that dominate European farm-management systems. In this case, however, fuel, pesticides and fertilizers, tractors, harvesters and plant-breeding technology are all imported at high cost and with no security of supply. Every developing country has its piles of rusting machinery, the relics of ambitious schemes to mechanize peasant agriculture.

Even if the spare-part problem could be overcome, the sheer scale of the operation to reach a largely illiterate population in *all* rural areas makes nonsense of this attempt to transfer modes of production without taking full account of the social formation. The most propitious result from this sort of enterprise is to raise the living standards of a few families and in this way exacerbate rural class differences, which are already beginning to appear in many rural areas, as advantaged families who are enjoying the benefits of wage remissions from migrant workers inflate the prices for local foodstuffs, especially in times of shortage.

Some of the interchanges between the rich and poor regions of the world are overtly or covertly exploitative and can be more easily criticized as such, but many more are the products of ignorance or conservatism. For example, at each scale of investment of advice and aid, from local water supplies to regional-planning policy, far too much foreign expertise has been used to serve in circumstances in which the experience and wisdom was inappropriate. Far too few have been flexible enough to see why the assistance they bring is ineffective, and few bear any ultimate responsibility for mistakes that are made. It is perhaps inevitable that foreign advisers, from the economist at one end of the scale to the agronomist at the other, should bring with them the knowledge and experience based on the way in which food surpluses are created in the Northern hemisphere, and many inexperienced Third World governments, whose administrators were trained in the ways of thinking of the North, have not always had the strength or insight to resist the blandishments of those who see this process of development as replicable.

Food surpluses in developed countries were created at a particular stage in the development of the world economy and the history of capitalism. Industrialization absorbed labour from the rural areas, and the efficiency of the remaining rural population was improved by the rationalization of landholding, which allowed farmers to increase the scale of their external inputs. This they did through mechanization, by the application of new agronomic research, the development of efficient advisory and marketing services, and the extended use of artificial fertilizers and pesticides.

More recently, the increasing efficiency of farming in the developed world has been maintained against potential Third World competition by the increasingly sophisticated deployment of central-government subsidy and support mechanisms that are the products of national and international trading policies. It is expertise from a highly complex system, evolved over the last 200 years in Europe and North America, that is now on 'package' offer to the Third World. So it is not surprising that many schemes for improvement have been based on premises or assumptions that may have some validity in Iowa or East Anglia but bear little relation to circumstances in Bangladesh or Sierra Leone. Despite a continued catalogue of failure, the approach of international aid agencies to rural development persistently follows the assumptions that allowed the abstraction of surplus in the later phases of capitalist development. It is as though each bad experience is thrown away and the channel of information blocked for the next user. Now at last it would seem that the Third World is reaching some kind of watershed; a crisis of confidence has been reached in which many strategies for development have been tested and found wanting, while the prospect of greater inequality and resultant social economic and political instability increases.

It might be suggested that the purely *economic* approach to rural development that permeates most rural-development initiatives in the Third World, even those which are less overtly directed to creating surplus as a sole objective, has been overly myopic. Real rural development involves more than agricultural productivity. It implies a much greater commitment to the effective provision of a wide range of social services: housing, schools, health centres, electricity, sanitation, water supply. It is the failure to bring effective improvements in this area which is the most important aspect of the crisis now affecting rural areas of the Third World. Rural development may be more broadly defined as 'the effort to increase social justice and to improve the whole quality of rural life in such a way as not to threaten the ecological basis for subsistence'. Within such a definition it is important to focus attention not on the rich and poor *in general*, that is, at the macro scale, for it is just this which in the past has led planners to focus on national rather than local problems. Looking more carefully at the growing gap between the haves and have-nots within the rural areas of poor countries and even within actual rural communities, it is clear that increasing levels of discrepancy between the income earners and the destitute have not been eased by those whose main concern is economic efficiency and the creation of surplus; nor by those who are willing to identify 'success' or 'failure' within such narrow terms.

Increasing inequality has been identified by Michael Lipton (1977) as an urban–rural problem. He argues that although poor countries have managed to increase their output of wealth considerably since 1945, the poorest rural people have grown poorer. Comparisons between Europe and Japan in their early stages of development and Third World countries today, he suggests, are inappropriate because modern programmes of public investment, aid policies, education and pricing systems all push rural and urban incomes further and further apart. This imbalance is difficult to change because the urban sector contains most of the 'articulate organized power'. While there is clearly some truth in these generalizations, Lipton presents too simplistic a view of Third World economic landscapes, which involve rich and poor rural areas as well as rich towns and a poor countryside. It also takes no real account of the migrants who move from one milieu to another and send cash to rural members of their families. The true position is obviously more complex and varies from one region to another, but perhaps these broad generalizations serve the purpose of focusing attention on under-privileged and weakened sectors.

The generally poor record of rural-development agencies in attempts to reduce disparities between richer and poorer can be attributed also to the circumstances endemic in all Third World countries. The morale of those who do not join the migration streams but live most of their lives in rural areas is increasingly low. If we examine the situation of a poor peasant cultivator whether he be in Ecuador or Somalia, Sumatra or India, certain conditions do not vary. Against a depleted or depleting stock of environmental resources he is generally expected to raise sufficient livestock and grow enough crops to cater for the subsistence needs of his family. Failure to do so can mean starvation. At the same time there is pressure to produce a surplus of cheap staple cereals to feed the increasing numbers of indigent poor who now live in the cities of the Third World. If he is particularly privileged he may be a member of a scheme or co-operative, able to grow an exotic cash crop that has national export potential, and he may have an effective marketing system to channel his produce and pay him reasonable prices for its production. The chief beneficiaries will still be the richer rural families who can corner most of the production and those urban dwellers who benefit from any spillover effects from its sale in terms of better services. Few of the returns from cash-crop farming reach the poorest sector of the rural population either directly in the form of cash or indirectly and more importantly in the form of better social services. Only the wealthiest peasants, with access to land and labour, can accumulate any reserves of capital to pay for education and the chance to migrate to a better social and economic environment.

Yet at the same time all people in rural areas are made increasingly aware of the possibility of an improvement in their condition. In fact they are encouraged to increase their output against a background of media information and evidence concerning the quality of urban life. Moreover, the wage-employed migrant temporarily returning to the village, brings back not only information but also the tangible symbols of relative affluence – the evidence of an easier life style in the form of better clothes or even a cheap watch or a transistor radio. It is the 'pull' factor as well as the 'push' of poverty that impels more and more of the young and more enterprising to leave for the higher income rural areas close to the towns and the rural economy and society begins to disintegrate. Weeding and bird scaring is neglected, rotation practices are abandoned, reciprocal systems of labour exchange fall into disuse and the downward spiral of environmental deterioration and social decay is completed when marginal settlements are left to the old, the infirm and the indifferent. It is this process that development planners have generally done little to halt, and it is a sad fact that many of the communities on the margins of production are sustained indirectly only by the remissions of urban workers. Their only hope for advancement is that this can continue for long enough so that the increasing number of urban dwellers who retain their rural identity can make sufficient investment to lead to some kind of general local improvement in conditions of housing or sanitation, and that more will be tempted to stay. There are those who may see this circular process as eventually bringing some kind of revival to rural areas. Many urban dwellers still retain their rural social and economic links and it is at least a positive and hopeful feature of difference between the developed and 'underdeveloped' world that this is still so even for third or fourth-generation migrants.

Clearly, in order to approach the problem of increasing the quality of life in rural areas in such a way that the demographic situation changes and populations begin to stabilize, it is necessary to approach the rural community *as a whole* – not as a separate entity but as part of a system that now almost inevitably includes migrant wage labourers in varying proportions – and to ask very different questions from those that relate only to the increase of agricultural production. How can the well-being of a whole community be best improved? With so much rural–urban interaction, what *is* a rural community? How can the linkages with urban areas be better orchestrated to improve the conditions of those who stay in or return to rural areas? Can state intervention be anything but ham-fisted, ill-directed and inept? Are there political structures that sustain local self-help and initiative rather than destroy or subvert them? Is there a realistic role for international aid agencies in the development of rural areas, or is this work inevitably either cosmetic (to satisfy consciences or retain influence) or short-term and remedial following a major disaster?

In other words, how far can the many mistakes made be translated into lessons learnt so that the approach to the problems of rural improvement in the next decade can benefit from the dismal experience of three ineffective decades of rural development planning in the Third World?

During the last ten years or so a number of writers have drawn inspiration, on the one hand from the disillusion felt among social scientists and businessmen alike for the long-term effectiveness of the large-scale enterprise, and on the other from the recent interest in low-technology solutions to world energy problems, to look afresh at the interrelationships between man and his environment. It has become increasingly apparent that many rural areas enjoying the benefits of modern economic farming have also had to sustain some kind of environmental deterioration. This experience opens the way to a set of potential solutions to the problem of rural decline in the Third World.

This new low-key approach has several characteristics. It identifies alternative technological solutions that rely as far as possible on local expertise and local raw materials; it concentrates on small-scale enterprises; it represents a very low-level approach to advice, which is primarily based on the local wisdoms and the indigenous society and economy, and it encourages self-respect and self-reliance. The approach now has the weight of an important central organization designed to promote it – the Intermediate Technology Group – and has been reinforced by a trend in recent thinking and research towards re-evaluation of self-sufficient styles of life.

The main drive towards finding what is now called 'appropriate technology' has come from India, where Schumacher (1974) first developed his ideas of an alternative to high technology. Appropriate technology programmes have sprung up in a number of different parts of India (Bombay, Lucknow, Bangalore, Ranchi) initiating work on the use of solar energy and bio-gas for heat and power generation, the use of local building materials instead of imported cement and steel, hand pumps, small-scale rural industries making soap, for example from local fats and oils, sodium silicate from rice husks, plastics from castor oil, cellulose fibre from groundnut shells. Similar attempts to introduce improved hand or treadle spinning and sewing-machines, which are a labour-intensive alternative to the factory system, have been extended in Uttar Pradesh in north India. Similar developments are to be found in a number of other countries: Pakistan, Tanzania, Kenya, Ghana and Colombia. Most projects aim to introduce low-cost labour-intensive small industries, with workshops of no more than fifteen or twenty people, to areas where labour is cheap and plentiful. This movement is now enjoying the support of international aid agencies, including the International Labour Office, the Commonwealth Fund for Technical Co-operation, and most recently (1978) the Appropriate Technology International based in Washington, has an aid investment of US$5 million. Their work as a co-ordinator and initiator of programmes is measured by the range of countries receiving their support: more than a dozen in the first year.

It is possible to argue that investment in aid of this kind is still pitifully small, but in many ways diffusion of ideas and of an approach is not a question of vast financial backing but of communication and education.

6 MINING, ENERGY AND MANUFACTURING

Mining

Minerals have been a significant element in shaping the relationship between the developed and less-developed countries. Journeys in the Age of Discovery were in part motivated by the desire to find gold, silver and gemstones. In Latin America the finding of such riches helped to shape the pattern and process of colonial development. In the nineteenth century similar considerations contributed to the scramble for Africa, influencing both the economic and political geography of that continent.

Minerals continue to provide an important potential resource for the Third World, both as a base for industrialization and as a source of export earnings. Currently the developed capitalist countries consume over two-thirds of world mineral output, and depend on imports for 60 per cent of their needs. A significant proportion of these imports comes from the Third World, for these countries produce one-third of global mineral output, consume less than 10 per cent of the total, and provide half the needs of the First World.

The Third World is, then, an important source of minerals and has about 38 per cent of the world's estimated mineral reserves. However, these are not distributed equally and the area has greater reserves of some minerals than others. For example, it has over half of the known reserves of phosphate, tin, fluorspar, cobalt, copper, tin and nickel, but its reserves of zinc, manganese or tungsten are much less significant. Table 6.1 shows how certain countries are important sources of some of the world's minerals, and how a few of them are heavily dependent on earnings from the export of such minerals. Figure 6.1 includes earnings from mineral fuels, but for countries such as Bolivia, Chile, Jamaica, Zambia and Zaire metallic minerals provide over half of their export earnings.

Despite the wealth and diversity of minerals known to be in the Third World their full potential may not yet have been realized. There is still a basic lack of knowledge of the geology of these countries, and of the detailed distribution and scale of their mineral deposits. Furthermore, the mining industry has some

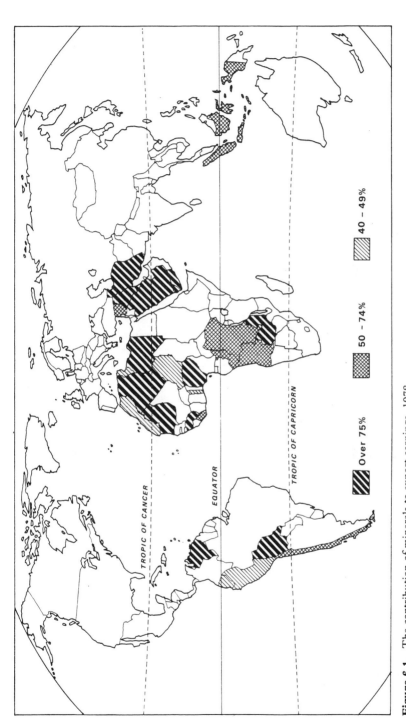

Figure 6.1 The contribution of minerals to export earnings, 1978.
The significance of minerals in the trading patterns of many Third World countries is clearly evident, whether from petroleum or metallic and non-metallic minerals.

Source of data: World Bank, 1981, 150–1.

Over 75% 50 – 74% 40 – 49%

Table 6.1 Contribution of the Third World to output of some minerals, 1978.

Mineral	Country	Percentage of world production, 1978	Rank in world
Bauxite	Guinea	14.3	2
	Jamaica	14.0	3
Copper	Chile	13.0	3
Iron	Brazil	8.5	4
Phosphate	Morocco	15.4	3
Tin	Malaysia	31.5	1
	Bolivia	15.5	2
	Thailand	15.2	3

Source of data: UN Statistical Yearbook, 1979/80, 1981.

distinctive and awkward characteristics when compared to other economic activities. Mineral deposits are 'fixed' in nature – they have specific locations, they are finite in size, and the minerals have fixed physical and chemical properties. They are non-renewable – once the mineral has been exploited it cannot be re-used (except for a small degree of recycling). Some minerals are widely available, or 'ubiquitous', such as sand, gravel and brick clay, and because of this they have low values per unit and are generally worked close to their markets. Others are more localized in occurrence, and their relative scarcity increases their price and means that they can bear the costs of transport over longer distances. In addition some minerals occur in remote locations so that their exploitation requires substantial investment and is a high-risk activity.

The exploitation of minerals has been seen as a potentially important contribution to the development of Third World countries. Besides the contribution made to export earnings, mineral development may attract foreign capital, provide infrastructure, create jobs, provide new skills for the labour force and generate demands for local goods and services. Yet mines have finite lives; the returns may be short-lived. For many of the more important minerals production is on a large scale and is heavily mechanized, so that the industry is capital-intensive rather than labour-intensive. Considerable use may also be made of skilled expatriate labour rather than local sources.

Critics also argue that much of the profit from mining goes to the parent mining company, often in foreign countries, rather than remaining in the source country. The fact that much of the world mining industry has been controlled by a few companies, and that much of the exploitation of Third World minerals has been by such companies, has generated considerable hostility. Part of this domination reflects the increasing scale of activity, with considerable economies of scale, high levels of infrastructural provision and use of advanced technology. Because of these trends and the high-cost risks involved in the exploration and preliminary development of minerals, large companies have acquired prominence through their ability to raise the necessary capital and spread the risks involved. In the 1960s eight firms accounted for 60 per cent of the world's refined lead output, and six firms dominated aluminium production. Within some individual countries control was even more pronounced. In Chile two US companies controlled 90 per cent of copper production, in Peru three such companies dominated the industry; and in Zambia two foreign companies controlled the output – while most of the production of bauxite in the Caribbean was carried out by North American firms. Returns from mineral extraction may not therefore have been maximized by the producing country, but it is possible that had the minerals not been exploited by foreign companies they would not have been exploited at all, since indigenous capital was unavailable to secure their development. In a number of countries foreign mining companies have been nationalized or required to participate in joint ventures with government or private local capital. But multinational companies and foreign importers may have other mineral sources to exploit, so that securing control of a resource may not ensure its development or determine the scale at which it is utilized.

Increasingly in the 1970s many Third World countries have sought to increase their control over the exploitation of their mineral resources – for political and economic reasons, to reduce environmental damage or to improve the working conditions of miners. By 1977, for example, majority-owned government concerns had taken control of copper production in Chile, Zaire and Zambia, and in the Jamaican bauxite industry joint ventures between government and foreign companies had been created.

Mineral working has also created more detailed problems for some Third World countries. The remote location of many minerals has given rise to developments of a limited nature in isolated locations, with the creation of mining camps, often with foreign staff and advanced technologies, in otherwise undeveloped or backward areas. The infrastructure that has been developed in the form of railways, ports, power stations and education facilities has been primarily in the interests of foreign countries and only incidentally in those of the host country. Although there has been some 'spin-off' in the creation of demands for local food and equipment, much has been imported. It is also the case that earnings from mineral exports have not been wisely used, with concentrations of investment around the already more-developed core areas of the country, or in conspicuous consumption, rather than in securing development more widely.

By no means all of the known mineral reserves of the Third World have been exploited. Alternative choices are open to mining companies and consumers, so that cost considerations are important. Most minerals are commodities of high bulk and low value so that transport costs and difficulties of access have confined exploitation for export to areas reasonably close to the sea or navigable waterways. In consequence much of the mineral production takes place within 300–500 km of the coast and only with reductions in cost consequent upon transport improvements will more remote resources be exploited.

A major concern for the producing countries is that they do not derive full benefit from the linkage effects to be obtained from their minerals, as many of these accrue abroad. In addition to the purchase of foreign mining equipment, much of the smelting and processing of ores is carried on abroad, so that considerable income and foreign exchange is 'lost'. There are various considerations in the location of smelting facilities, and a number of major mineral exports from the Third World, such as tin, bauxite and copper, pose particular smelting problems, which may be more easily tackled in more-advanced countries. Considerable raw-material inputs, in excess of the production of a single mine or country, may be required to sustain an efficient smelter; while small units of production may make for high costs of production. Considerable fuel demands may also be significant, particularly in coal-deficient countries. In addition it is in the more-developed countries that the principal markets for the finished metals and metal goods are found. Transport costs and freight policies are such that it may be cheaper to export ore, even with a high proportion of impurities, than to ship metal.

There is evidence that only about one-third of the mineral output of less-developed countries is processed locally and this pattern has changed little since the 1950s. None the less some Third World countries are beginning to establish processing plants and ship at least part of their ores as concentrates or refined metal. More than 75 per cent of copper mined in the developing world is now being processed into metal before export, and there is more local processing of tin; however a considerable part of iron-ore production is still exported as crude ore.

Aluminium represents a good example of the factors involved, in that its production requires the processing of bauxite to yield alumina, which is further processed to give aluminium. Some 2–3 tons of bauxite yield one ton of alumina, and 2 tons of alumina give one of aluminium, so that there is considerable weight loss in the production process. Before 1939 much of the world's bauxite and all of its aluminium came from the developed world, but increasingly the Third World has become a major source of bauxite, and about one-quarter of production comes from Guyana, Surinam and Jamaica. In consequence these producing countries have been able to exert some pressure to secure a degree of processing capacity close to the mines. The high cost of transporting bauxite made this attractive to the aluminium companies and Jamaica secured an alumina plant in 1952. Even so, up to 1970, 80 per cent of Jamaica's bauxite was exported unprocessed, but this earned less than half as much per ton as the bauxite exported as alumina; besides these higher earnings, alumina production generates additional demands for labour, equipment and supplies. In recent years Jamaica has granted bauxite-mining concessions only if alumina is to be produced and it is hoped that eventually over half the island's bauxite will be processed before export.

The further processing of alumina to aluminium requires large power inputs and to date the majority of the world's aluminium smelters have been located at cheap power sites in the developed world. In addition technical complexities in the smelting process make for economies of scale, such that large units of production are required. Local demand for aluminium in the Caribbean could not sustain such plants, but the three bauxite producers hope to develop reduction plants to produce aluminium for export, despite the tariff barriers of the USA and the EEC that protect their domestic producers.

To date exploitation of the minerals of the developing world has been primarily in the interests of the consuming nations of the developed world, which do not necessarily accord with the best interests of the producing nations. Decisions to exploit particular deposits, the pattern of investment, the nature of the extraction and beneficiation of minerals, and the apportionment of earnings, have not always been consistent with the development needs and objectives of the Third World.

Energy

Advances in the use of energy sources such as water power, steam and coal played a vital role in the Industrial Revolution in Europe; and it has come to be accepted that provision of energy is an important factor in the development process. There is certainly a good correlation between levels of energy consumption and economic output, with the industrialized countries having levels of consumption greatly in excess of those of the developing world. One source (Dunkerley, et al. 1981: 10) suggests that the industrialized countries use nine times as much energy per capita as the non-communist developing countries.

In broad terms it can be shown that levels of energy consumption in the Third World are less than in the First; that there is still a heavy dependence on primitive energy sources; and that conventional energy sources are unevenly distributed. In the developed world energy is derived mainly from coal, oil, gas and electricity from fossil fuel, water and nuclear sources. It is easy to overlook the fact that in the less-developed world considerable inputs of energy still come from the muscle power of men and animals, and that seemingly crude energy sources such as wood, charcoal, vegetable waste and dung are important. Since these are simple and do not enter into commerce it is likely that their use is underestimated, but it is probable that such materials provide one-third of China's energy, half that of India, and in some countries, such as Chad, Upper Volta, Nepal and Haiti, over 90 per cent. Such fuels are inefficient energy sources, their collection is often time consuming as they are gathered from field and forest, and their use may be detrimental to the environment. Clearance of woodland for firewood encourages soil deterioration and erosion, and the use of dung deprives the land of scarce fertilizer.

In the use of more conventional energy sources, since most Third World countries began to promote economic development after the Second World War when energy prices were relatively stable and crude oil was abundant and inexpensive (at US $2 per barrel), they developed energy strategies largely dependent on cheap oil, and paid only limited attention to other sources. In consequence the bulk of their energy needs was met mainly by imported oil and traditional fuels. Even in 1977 these two sources provided an estimated three-quarters of the energy consumption of the non-communist Third World countries. Reflecting the economic progress of the Third World, its share of world commercial energy consumption rose from 9.5 per cent in 1955 to 20.3 per

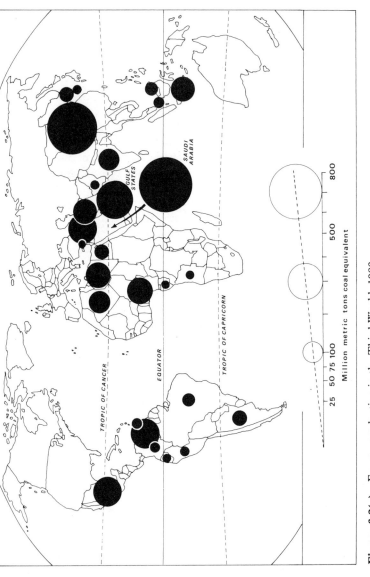

Figure 6.2(a)　Energy production in the Third World, 1980.
The production of energy from various sources – oil, gas, coal, etc. is converted to a common standard, in this case coal equivalent. On this map countries with an output of less than 10 million tons coal equivalent are excluded, revealing the limited energy output of much of Africa, and the significance of the few major oil producers.

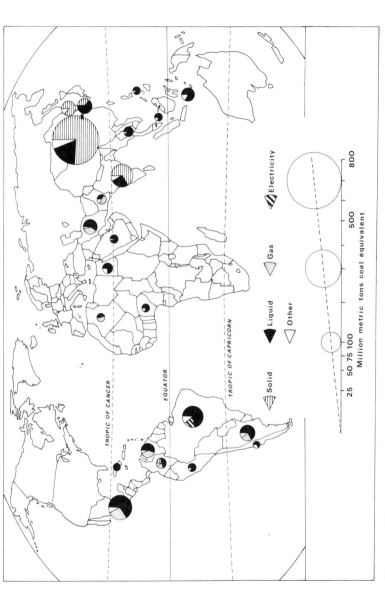

Figure 6.2(b)   Energy consumption in the Third World, 1980.
Comparison with figure 6.2a, drawn to the same scale, again reveals the limited use of energy in Africa, but also indicates that a number of Third World countries produce considerably more energy (mainly petroleum) than they consume. Relatively few have a balance between production and consumption, and only in China, India and North and South Korea are solid fuels of significance.

Source of data: UN Statistical Yearbook 1979/80, 1981: 786–809.

cent in 1978. Within that expansion oil was of growing importance, increasing its contribution to Third World commercial energy consumption from 24 to 42 per cent between 1960 and 1978.

The quadrupling of world oil prices in 1973–4 by the OPEC countries had a major impact on those countries without oil resources of their own. They were faced with substantial increases in their energy bills and the need to borrow abroad to pay for the oil necessary to sustain the rate of economic growth, or else accept a slow-down in that growth rate. In addition they were stimulated to search for their own sources of oil or alternate forms of energy.

As in the case of mineral reserves, the Third World is seemingly well endowed with energy sources. Third World countries provide 80 per cent of world energy exports but consume only 25 per cent of the world's usage. However, the distribution of these reserves is uneven (figure 6.2). The Third World is rich in petroleum resources, but these are concentrated in distribution. The OPEC countries and Mexico together provide over 80 per cent of the world's oil exports, and OPEC has about 80 per cent of the non-communist world's oil reserves. With limited exceptions, the Third World is poorly endowed with known coal sources, but has significant potential reserves of hydraulic energy.

OIL

The growing dependence on petroleum by both the developed and developing countries after 1945 was a consequence of the discovery of abundant oil resources in the Middle East, greatly in excess of demand, with resulting low prices, coupled with the utility of oil as a high-quality energy source which is easily transported and stored and which can be processed to yield a variety of fuels and industrial raw materials. In the 1970s increasing demands in excess of the discovery of new reserves, OPEC policy and the revolution in Iran all prompted an escalation in price. For those countries with substantial oil reserves the benefits were considerable. It increased their wealth significantly, so that some at least now form a distinctive category of countries, the capital surplus oil exporters, with the highest per capita GNP levels – in the case of Kuwait, Qatar and the United Arab Emirates in excess of US $15,000 in 1979. Such prosperity sustained considerable conspicuous consumption, financed major development projects and provided funds for investment in the developed world and aid to the less-fortunate Third World countries. Although the USSR and USA are respectively the first and third largest oil producers (1978 figures), the other principal producers are all within the Third World or the capital surplus oil exporters group.

The impact of the discovery of oil coupled with these price rises has clearly had a profound effect on some countries in the Third World. In the case of Nigeria, the discovery of oil in 1956 was a considerable stimulus to the country's economic advance. By 1980 oil was providing 95 per cent of export earnings, 80 per cent of government revenue and over one-third of GDP. In addition to the countries with oil surpluses to export, China, Argentina, Peru, Colombia, Tunisia and Egypt are approximately self-sufficient in oil. The other Third World countries are to varying degrees dependent on oil imports. The 'oil crisis' prompted an increased search for domestic oil sources so that some existing producers increased their known reserves, and others, including Benin, Chad, Ivory Coast, Guatemala, Vietnam and Papua New Guinea, have found oil in commercial quantities. Natural gas, associated with oil fields or in independent deposits, is also likely to be an important energy source for OPEC, other producers and for export.

COAL

In contrast to the considerable, if ill-distributed, oil reserves of the Third World, its share of known coal deposits is limited. Most of the world's known coalfields are in temperate latitudes, and the USSR, USA and Australia have three-quarters of the known reserves. Production within the Third World is principally in those countries where coalfields were developed before the era of cheap oil – in China, India, Zimbabwe and Korea. In 1978 China and India were ranked respectively first and sixth as world coal producers, contributing almost 28 per cent of world output. Few other Third World countries are so well endowed and their coal production is often small and of poor quality. It is possible, however, that the availability of cheap oil has discouraged careful searches for coal deposits and new sources may be found. Recent evidence suggests an increase in the known reserves of Colombia, Brazil, Bangladesh, Indonesia, Nigeria, Zimbabwe and Botswana.

HYDRO-ELECTRICITY

Hydro-electricity power offers considerable possibilities for energy provision in the Third World. Reserves of water power are considerable but utilization to date is limited, only an estimated 4 per cent of the total available. Furthermore, this figure varies regionally from 1.5 per cent in Africa, 6 per cent in Latin America and 7.5 per cent in Asia. There are clearly variations in the distribution of reserves, in response to climatic conditions and the pattern of river flow. However, the fact that water power is a renewable resource, and that there is very considerable untapped potential within the Third World, makes it likely that there will be substantial increase in the production of energy from this source. In addition the construction of dams can bring other benefits in the form of flood control, improved navigation and the provision of water for irrigation.

In 1980 Brazil, China and India ranked respectively fifth, sixth and twelfth in the world in terms of their installed hydro-electric power capacity. As table 6.2 indicates, the amount of electric power available varies enormously within the Third World, from major producers such as India and Brazil to those, such as Mali and Niger, among the world's poorest countries, with no significant power-generating capacity. The contribution made by hydro-electricity also varies considerably,

Table 6.2 Installed electric-power capacity and percentage derived from hydro-electric sources, 1980.

	Installed capacity ('000 kw)	Per cent from hydro sources
Uganda	163	96
Ghana	900	88
Brazil	31,735	86
Colombia	4,860	65
Malawi	106	63
Egypt	4,500	57
India	33,675	37
Venezuela	9,113	32
China	67,000	31
Nigeria	1,900	31
Iran	5,300	16
Mali	42	14
Iraq	1,200	5
Kuwait	2,810	0
United Arab Emirates	1,090	0
Niger	23	0
United Kingdom	69,363	3
USA	630,782	12

Source of data: UN Statistical Yearbook 1979/80, 1981: 810–24.

from countries with heavy dependence on this source, to those where the availability of coal or, as in the case of the OPEC countries, oil, provides the basis for thermal power generation. In some cases a single dam site, such as those at Aswan (Egypt), Akosombo (Ghana) and Owen Falls (Uganda), may make a considerable contribution to the total power capacity. In some cases Third World countries have developed hydro-electric projects that rank among the largest in the world, such as Liuchia in China, with a capacity of 1,225,000 kw, and Itaipu in Brazil/Paraguay with a planned capacity in 1988 of 12,600,000 kw.

OTHER ENERGY SOURCES

Largely as a result of the oil crisis there has been a search for other sources of energy, both conventional and unconventional. The price of petroleum has encouraged an interest in oil shales, of which countries such as Brazil and Zaire are known to have substantial deposits; however, technology for their exploration remains experimental. The possibility exists of the development of nuclear power plants in the Third World, by transferring developed-world technology, but their economic viability is uncertain, and they pose questions of both safety and security. In 1980 only Argentina, India, Korea and Pakistan were producing nuclear power.

Exploitation of wind and solar energy, despite the seeming promise of the latter

Plate 6.1   Alternative energy source, India.
A biogas plant constructed to supply a small rural community near Lucknow.

in the tropics, is also still at a preliminary stage, and they, and other sources such as tidal power, probably require considerably more development in the advanced nations before they can be used in the Third World. Successful exploitation of geothermal energy in the developed world, by the USSR, USA, Iceland and New Zealand, suggests that this may be a useful source for some Third World countries, particularly those located on the volcanically active parts of the world. These include the circum-Pacific 'circle of fire' of western south America and islands in the Pacific, along with areas in East Africa and the Indian subcontinent.

Increasing attention is also being paid to biomass energy sources, from the forests, biological wastes and energy crops. Greater and more efficient use might be made of the remaining forests in the Third World or of planted woodlands. Crop residues and urban waste could be put to effective use − there has already been some progress in the use of crops to provide energy sources. In Brazil alcohol obtained from sugar cane has been used to ease the impact of rising oil prices, being mixed with petrol or used alone in cars with adapted engines. Other plants are also being investigated as potential energy sources.

ENERGY SOURCES AND THE LOCATION OF ECONOMIC ACTIVITIES

In the Industrial Revolution coal was a significant influence on the location of new economic developments in Europe and North America. These ties have weakened with the development of other forms of energy, more efficient transport for the movement of fuel and power, and particularly the availability of electricity – which can be transmitted over considerable distances – thus diminishing the locational 'pull' of energy sources.

For those countries with significant coal deposits, these have exerted some influence on the location of coal-using industries, such as metal working, and for thermal-power generation. For those countries with oil resources, these have provided the foci for refining activities, and in some cases for the development of petrochemical industries. However, oil is a more mobile energy source, capable of relatively low-cost transfer by road, ship or pipeline to the point of consumption. The development of electricity has also afforded greater freedom of location. However, early power stations were frequently located adjacent to existing markets, that is, in the major cities, which were supplied by diesel, thermal or oil-fired power stations or hydro-electricity brought short distances from small dams. The increasing size of power stations and efficiency in transmission have extended the availability of electricity, but the larger cities still tend to be the best served, and much of the rural Third World remains without access to electricity for light and power. In Latin America Peter Odell (1978) has demonstrated that over 90 per cent of the continent's electricity-generating capacity in the mid-1960s was located close to only forty-nine centres, mainly capital cities and coastal towns.

Similar patterns of concentration exist in other parts of the Third World, and although transmission grids and rural electrification schemes are beginning to push into the countryside, there are still considerable deficiencies, as well as scope for the development of other forms of rural energy sources. Traditional sources are diminishing, and in addition to trying to use these more efficiently, new intermediate technologies might be utilized to provide power. Even improvements in wood-burning stoves or use of charcoal rather than wood might make more effective use of available timber reserves and diminish the consequences of deforestation. It may be possible to exploit scaled-down developments in the technologies using solar, wind and hydraulic power, but much of the research to date has been in the interests of large-scale, developed world users, rather than villages and peasants. The use of dung or vegetable wastes to produce biogas appears to offer possibilities as a rural energy source, and in India a substantial programme of this kind has been developed. In the near future conventional power sources are likely to remain concentrated adjacent to the principal cities and markets of the Third World; there is likely to be some diffusion outwards of this provision, but it is possible that alternative small-scale technologies may provide output appropriate to the needs and level of development of the rural population.

Industrialization

WHY INDUSTRIALIZE?

For much of the period since 1945 the countries of the Third World have given considerable attention to the expansion of manufacturing industry. A crucial problem for these countries is the provision of jobs. Many of them are faced with rapidly increasing populations (see chapter 3), there is substantial unemployment and underemployment in the rural areas, and it has been argued that modernization in agriculture could result in further shedding of labour. In consequence, therefore, of high rates of natural growth of population and lack of rural employment, there has been a search for alternative employment opportunities, both in a broad sense by development planners and, more specifically, by individuals in search of jobs.

One seemingly obvious possibility was the provision of jobs in manufacturing industry. Most of the countries of the more-developed world have experienced or benefited from an industrial revolution, and their degree of industrialization is one feature that distinguishes them from less-developed countries. The World Bank makes a basic distinction between the low and middle-income countries on the one hand and what it calls the 'industrialized' countries, the centrally planned economies and the oil-rich countries, on the other. In 1978 manufacturing contributed 37 per cent of GDP in the industrialized countries, 34 per cent in the middle-income group and only 24 per cent in low-income countries. It is true that the tertiary sector now makes a larger contribution to GDP than manufacturing in the industrialized countries, but taken together the essentially urban-based secondary and tertiary sectors contribute 96 per cent of their GDP; only 4 per cent comes from the primary sector (figure 6.3).

Another indicator, relevant to the demographic rather than the economic dimension of development, is that in 1970, 85 per cent of the labour force in the low-income group and 51 per cent of that of the middle-income countries was employed in agriculture. By contrast 39 per cent of the labour force in centrally planned economies and only 11 per cent of that of industrialized countries was in agriculture. Given these patterns, there has been an understandable tendency on the part of Third World countries seeking to develop to equate industrialization with development.

A further influence has been the example of the USSR. Whether one accepts the Rostovian analysis or not, most of the countries that have taken off and become industrialized, did so before 1914. The American economist Peter Drucker (1971) suggests that since then the only industrial areas to emerge, Canada, Mexico and Australia, are in effect extensions of the old industrial regions. The only possible exceptions are south-east Brazil and the USSR. In the development strategy of the latter after 1917, very high priority was given to the industrial sector. It was believed that if the USSR was to survive economically and politically, it must rapidly develop a substantial and self-sufficient industrial sector. In consequence heavy emphasis was placed on industrialization in Soviet planning, at the expense of agriculture. Between 1918–70 over one-third of all capital investment was in industry, as against 15 per cent in agriculture. Particular emphasis was given to creating a large complex of heavy industry, to which consumer industries might be added at a later date. From the USSR's First Plan, in 1928, until the early 1950s, over 80 per cent of industrial investment went into basic industries, such as steel and chemicals.

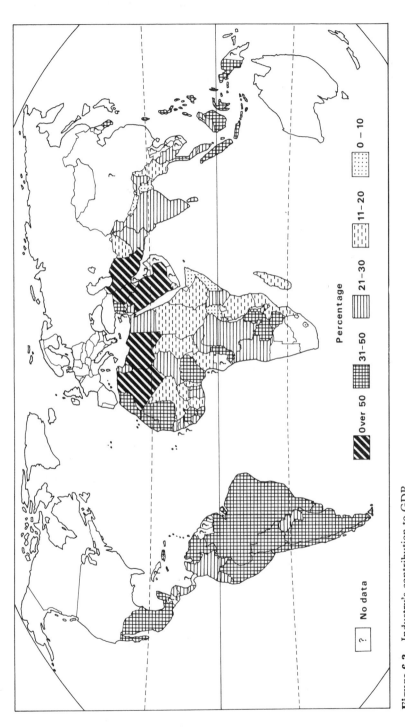

Figure 6.3 Industry's contribution to GDP.
Industry here includes not only manufacturing, but also mining, construction and water, gas and electricity supply, and thus indicates the importance of mining in some otherwise little-industrialized countries.

Source of data: World Bank, 1978.

Percentage

Over 50   31–50   21–30   11–20   0–10

No data   ?

In addition to the general example of the developed and industrialized countries, and the Soviet strategy, several more specific arguments favouring industrialization have been advanced. A basic one might be called the 'demonstration effect', outlined above, which rests on the belief that high levels of industrialization are a key factor in producing the higher levels of economic well-being of advanced countries; so that in order to advance, Third World countries must try and emulate this industrialization.

Closely linked to this view is the realization that there are large numbers of people unemployed or underemployed in the rural areas and in agriculture. It is claimed that industrialization will provide jobs for such people, and also make agriculture more productive by removing the surplus labour. In addition it is also claimed that industry will provide new inputs such as machinery and fertilizer to increase productivity; while the industrial workforce of the towns will provide larger markets and better prices for farm output of food and raw materials. Industry will also be a more secure base for economic advance, as it is less subject to variations in output, such as those that affect agriculture because of climatic vagaries.

Supporters of industrialization also claim that Third World countries need to diversify their economies away from dependence on agriculture and the export of primary produce. Such dependence makes their economies vulnerable to fluctuations in demand and price of world markets, over which they have little control. Some evidence suggests that export earnings for the generally limited range of primary products on which Third World countries depend, have been falling relative to the prices of the manufactured goods they import.

Manufacturing might also have a number of spin-offs and spread effects benefiting the rest of the economy. There will be backward and forward linkages to sectors such as transport, energy, finance and commerce. Industry will be a focus of dynamism and change, and is seen as a source of 'modern' attitudes in contrast to the tradition and conservatism believed to characterize the agricultural/rural sector.

In addition to its basic role of creating new jobs, industrialization might have other effects on the population. The industrialization process has generally been associated with urbanization. The agglomeration of people into towns and cities makes it easier and cheaper to provide them with basic services of education, health care, electricity and water supply than if they remain dispersed in the countryside. The experience of the now-developed world also suggests, by analogy, that urbanization will lead to a fall in birth rates and population-growth rates.

Third World countries also seek to industrialize for essentially political reasons: to demonstrate that they are independent, not only politically but also economically, of former colonial powers. Factories can be important status symbols, for politicians and for people, of such independence. They symbolize 'progress'. More practically, industrialization may provide economic security in times of war or political instability.

CHECKS TO INDUSTRIALIZATION

Given the apparent benefits of industrialization, why does a low level of industrial development remain one of the defining characteristics of the Third World? Why are Third World countries under-industrialized?

A range of constraints to industrialization is apparent. A major one is the legacy of colonial rule. Much of the Third World was colonized by European countries – Britain, France, Belgium and Germany – which had experienced an industrial revolution and were important producers of manufactured goods in the nineteenth century. They saw their colonies as sources of tropical produce and raw materials for industry, and as markets for the export of manufactured goods. In such circumstances it was not in their interests to encourage indigenous industries which might compete with such exports. France, for example, saw the natural function of her colonies as that of a market reserved by right for the mother-country's industry. In Brazil, even after independence from Portugal, some politicians argued that the country's proper role in the world economy was to export primary produce in return for imported manufactures.

Closely linked to the colonial legacy are the Third World countries' deficient infrastructures, necessary for industrialization. Much of the available energy and transport provision, for example, was created by colonial powers and foreign investors, in their own interests, primarily to extract raw materials, and not in the interests of the industrial-development strategies of independent nations. Thus infrastructural provision may be inadequate, and what there is may be inappropriate for the needs of industrialization. Moreover, the provision of new infrastructure is often expensive and involves what is known as 'lumpy' investment; that is, it cannot be provided gradually but must be a total project which, initially at least, may provide capacity in excess of demand (for example in a railway, road or power station). Provision of such utilities is frequently spatially concentrated, so that some areas are more favoured than others.

To provide factories or infrastructure a developing country needs capital, and capital shortage is again almost a definition of underdevelopment. Third World countries are poor, with little surplus for saving. Capital has, however, to be sought by savings from limited resources, taxation, foreign loans and investment, and government provision. Not only is capital for investment limited, but the cost of providing an industrial job is high, and given the advanced technology currently available is probably more expensive than during the industrialization of European countries.

Some general characteristics of Third World populations also limit their potential as industrial labour forces. High levels of illiteracy and low general educational levels are barriers to the use of modern machinery and technology. Poor health is a factor in absenteeism and labour instability, while traditional life styles may make adjustment to factory routine difficult. The training of labour in basic and industrial skills incurs extra cost for the industrialization process.

In addition to general difficulties with the labour force, Third World countries lack the entrepreneurial skill for large-scale industries. Capital and labour must be combined with management skills to organize, plan and cope with the decision making and risk taking involved in industrialization. Countries seeking to industrialize are short of such skills and have only limited opportunities for their acquisition.

A crucial problem for many Third World countries is the limited size of their market. Despite images of teeming people, many of the less-industrialized countries have small populations; in 1976 sixty out of ninety-eight low and middle-income countries had less than 10 million inhabitants. Markets are not only small but also, of course, poor. In 1976 the per capita GNP of the low-income group was US $150, only 2.4 per cent of that of the industrialized countries; that of the middle-income group was US $750 per capita, 12.1 per cent of the level of the latter. Furthermore, income distribution in such countries is often highly skewed, so that many people may have little or no money to spend on manufactured goods. Such limitations prevent industrial firms from taking full advantage of economies of scale associated with manufacturing, and give rise to high costs of production and under-use of installed capacity.

In an effort to create wider markets Third World countries have sought to establish regional groupings such as the Latin American Free Trade Area or the East African Common Market. While these may create larger markets they also face some problems. Unequal levels of development of member states may impose a need to protect the weakest. There is often difficulty in agreeing on the distribution of the benefits of integration, while the amount of trade between member states is frequently limited, since their economies are competitive rather than complementary.

The East African Common Market was established in 1967 by Kenya, Uganda and Tanzania, though there had been trade, customs and other common-service agreements in the colonial period, especially since 1948. However, ideological differences between all three countries from the late 1960s exacerbated the problems caused by their unequal development, with Kenya not only having a more balanced economic structure at the beginning but also registering a mean annual GDP growth rate of 7.5 per cent, 1967–77, compared with only 6.3 per cent and 2.0 per cent in Tanzania and Uganda respectively. New industries to serve the community were being established disproportionately in Kenya and her trading surplus with community partners increased five-fold between 1961 and 1976, consisting mostly of manufactured goods, and Kenya's share of all trade between the countries rose from 63 per cent in 1961 to 83 per cent in 1976. The benefits of the agreement were unevenly distributed and redistributive mechanisms were not sufficiently strong to counter the accumulation in Kenya. A decade of continuous argument over the distribution and extent of benefit was brought to an end in 1977 with the formal ending of the Treaties of Co-operation.

Third World countries have also sought greater markets for their industrial goods in developed countries, particularly for those goods where they have some comparative advantage. Countries such as Hong Kong, South Korea and Taiwan have achieved some success in this export-oriented industrialization, but they and other industrializing countries face considerable hostility from the older industrialized countries anxious to protect their own industries.

Global concern for environmental pollution may also have implications for Third World industrialization. The underdevelopment of industry limits the scale of industrial pollution, though some Third World cities have significant pollution problems. It has been argued that the relocation of polluting industries to the Third World offers some potential for their industrialization, but this clearly carries with it an environmental cost. International desire to reduce global pollution might inhibit Third World efforts to industrialize, while efforts to reduce pollution usually involve higher-cost production processes.

It is often claimed that the inadequacy of its resource endowment is a major barrier to Third World industrialization. It is perhaps better argued that while individual Third World countries may be deficient in particular resources, in total the Third World is not resource-deficient. It should also be noted that the resource endowment of the Third World is imperfectly known. Comprehensive surveys of geology, hydrology, soil and land-use potential are still lacking but, despite this imperfect knowledge, the Third World has been, and remains, an important source of resources for the more-developed countries. The exploitation of land and mines was a significant factor in the colonial penetration of the region, when it became an important source of tropical crops and precious metals. It continues to fulfil this role, with the addition of more basic minerals such as iron ore, bauxite, tin and petroleum. Much of the developed world is heavily dependent on the developing world for resource inputs into its economy. In this respect, then, the Third World is resource rich. However *within* the Third World resource distribution is uneven and some countries are poorly endowed.

THE ORIGINS OF MANUFACTURING IN THE THIRD WORLD

Because Third World countries are generally characterized as underdeveloped or agricultural there is a tendency to assume that they have little or no industry. Obviously this is not so. Some have a degree of industrialization in consequence of the initial processing of their agriculture and mineral exports, and this is not necessarily recent, for in the early colonial exploitation of Africa and Latin America some export commodities were subjected to rudimentary and preliminary processing.

Furthermore, indigenous, pre-colonial populations had developed significant craft industries. Before the Age of Discovery native craftsmen were producing textiles, metal goods, pottery and similar items. European settlers imported manufactures from Europe, but also relied on local production of food, clothing and housing materials, and were involved in processing commodities for export. In the nineteenth century the impact of the European Industrial Revolution tended to undermine artisan industries of the Third World. For example, craft textiles produced in India were an important trade item in the East in the seventeenth and early eighteenth centuries, but were then severely hit by competition from Lancashire machine-made cottons. Even so, a factory-scale textile industry emerged in India in the mid-nineteenth century, based on local raw materials of cotton and jute and on local markets. By 1900 India had 160,000 workers in cotton factories.

Similar conditions elsewhere in the Third World, where local raw materials and markets sustained production, encouraged spontaneous and modern industrialization. Non-durable consumer-goods industries, such as textiles, clothes and foodstuffs, and those producing low-value, high-bulk goods such as building materials, where even inefficient producers could compete against imports, were important pioneers. The mechanization of agricultural processing activities, for example coffee in Brazil and Colombia, and the development of railways led to the establishment of repair shops and then simple engineering plants. Such developments did not occur throughout the Third World. There was probably greater progress in Latin America and Asia than in Africa. Although much of the activity was concerned with consumer non-durable goods, there were some early developments in heavier industries: Brazil and India, for example, had established modern ironworks before 1890.

Artisan industries, export processing and consumer industries linked to local resources and markets, were the pioneers of manufacturing activity in the Third World. The period since 1914 has seen increasing interest and progress in Third World industrialization. The two World Wars indicated their dependence on imported manufactures, and the consequent difficulties when supplies are cut off. The inter-war depression, with the slump in the trade and prices of primary exports, revealed the danger of dependence on such an economic structure, and encouraged independent countries to try and diversify their economies. For other countries achievement of political independence after 1945 carried with it a desire for economic independence. Emerging 'development economics' in the late 1940s also tended to the view that the 'solution' to the problem of 'backward' countries lay in industrialization.

For all these reasons most Third World countries therefore sought to industrialize. In this process various alternative strategies have to be considered. What should be the balance between 'heavy' and 'light' industries? What should be the relative roles of private, state and foreign investment? Should the technology used be capital or labour intensive? And so on. Such choices are not necessarily mutually exclusive; they may be appropriate to different sectors or stages of the industrialization process.

THE IMPLEMENTATION OF INDUSTRIALIZATION

Import substitution
Third World countries formerly imported many of their manufactured goods in return for primary-produce exports. Increasingly, they have sought greater self-sufficiency by producing their own manufactured goods, often behind some form

of tariff protection. In the import-substitution process, light industries such as food, drink and tobacco, textiles and clothing tended to be the first to be substituted. These tend to be technologically simple, requiring relatively few engineering skills and do not demand high levels of capital investment, both of which are scarce. Markets already exist, and as these are consumer goods, demand is direct. Many Third World countries chose this relatively 'easy' strategy, leaving more complex industrialization until later. In Argentina, Brazil and Mexico import substitution was an important element in their early industrialization.

Heavy industry
Following the Soviet model, some countries have given high priority to developing basic industries. Post-independence India provides a classic example of this strategy. Its large population implied a very large demand for consumer goods. In order to provide these a considerable input of capital goods was required. For many Third World countries these would have been imported, but it was argued that Indian demand was sufficiently large to sustain internal production, and that it was unlikely, anyway, that Indian exports could be expanded sufficiently in order to pay for large amounts of capital goods over a long period. Consequently India's second Five-Year Plan, 1956–61, gave very high priority to developing capital-intensive basic industries such as steel, chemicals, coal and petroleum. Mining and manufacturing were to receive 20 per cent of planned investment compared with 7.6 per cent under the First Plan. In pursuing this strategy India was aided by good resource endowments of coal and iron ore in the Damodar valley, and by technical assistance from various developed countries.

State participation
In the industrialization process in developing countries the state has often played a major role. Where resources for development are scarce, central government is often the only agency capable of marshalling the savings and taxation, or securing the foreign investment or aid necessary for industrial investment. The state makes decisions on the allocation of resources (see below, chapter 9) between sectors of the economy or within industry. It may stimulate industrialization through financial aid or tariff protection, or may involve itself directly in certain industries, which are politically or strategically sensitive, or where private capital is reluctant to invest.

In Chile the Corporación de Fomento de la Producción (CORFO) was established in 1939 as a government agency to foster economic development. It was responsible for formulating an electrification plan for Chile, for developing the petroleum and refining industry, for establishing the Huachipato steelworks, and sugar-beet and paper factories, and formed a model for later development agencies in other Latin American countries. In India the state distinguished between three broad categories of industry. After 1956 further developments in strategic and basic industries such as munitions, steel, heavy machinery and coal, which were seen as the foundations of the industrial structure, were to be the exclusive responsibility of the state. A second category consisted of industries that would become progressively state owned, with government taking the initiative in establishing new plants, but supplemented by the private sector. It included industries such as ferro-alloys, machine tools, fertilizers and synthetic rubber. Remaining industries were left essentially to the private sector.

Foreign investment
Investment by colonial powers was significant in the early exploitation of the Third World. In the nineteenth century there was a substantial amount of private foreign investment in plantations, mining, urban services and infrastructure. In the present century there has often been considerable hostility to foreign invest- ment, but it remains significant, particularly in certain industrial sectors, through the activities of the multinational corporations. These large firms, usually with their headquarters in the USA or Europe, are responsible, through their subsidi- aries, for the production of a wide range of goods – vehicles, chemicals, pharma- ceuticals, electrical goods – in Third World countries. Many multinational companies have annual sales volumes greater than the GNPs of most Third World countries. In 1977 only Brazil, Mexico and India had GNPs greater than the annual sales of General Motors, the world's largest industrial company.

It is estimated that about 33 per cent of the total investment of multinational companies is in the Third World, and of that about 28 per cent is in the manufactur- ing sector. Such companies are important sources (and not only for Third World

Plate 6.2   Tea factory, Kericho, Kenya.
Factories to process agricultural products for export were part of the early industrialization of the Third World. This factory belonged to Brooke Bond-Liebig, a multinational company with its headquarters in Britain, but with extensive interests in tea and other plantation crops in Africa and South Asia. The factory is now owned by a Kenyan-based subsidiary, in which Brooke Bond retains a controlling interest.

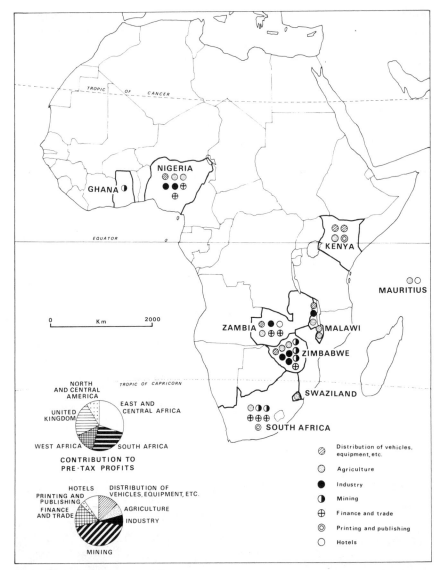

Figure 6.4 The Lonrho company in Africa.

Source of data: Lonrho, 1980.

countries) of industrial output, investment, skills, technology and employment. On the other hand, they have been criticized for the overwhelming control they exercise in some industries, and because their strategy is dictated by the global policy of the parent company, which is not necessarily compatible with that of the host Third World country. They are also criticized for producing goods aimed only at a limited section of the market, for discouraging domestic producers, and inhibiting ˙development of domestic skills and entrepreneurship. It is often claimed that they avoid full taxation on their profits, and that they interfere in the economic and political affairs of host countries. Because they are involved in high-technology industries they tend to have relatively limited impact on employment.

The activities of the Lonrho company indicate the scale and diversity of the operations of a multinational corporation. The company has major economic interests in five continents and over forty countries. These include not only manufacturing industries but also agriculture, tourism and finance. As figure 6.4 illustrates, Lonrho's activities in Africa contribute almost two-thirds of company profits. The company's interests are largely concentrated in former British territories, and include activities as diverse as food processing, tanning, metal refining, printing, manufacture of vehicles and agricultural machinery, textile production, brewing and soft-drink bottling.

ACHIEVEMENTS AND PROBLEMS

As a result of their efforts to industrialize, Third World countries have achieved high rates of growth in manufacturing in recent years. In the period 1938–50 the rate was about 3.5 per cent a year; over the period 1950–70 it averaged 6.6 per cent. During the 1960s and 1970s industry was the fastest growing sector, though the rate between 1970–6 was slower than in the previous decade, a reflection of the general slow-down in the world economy. During this period the industrial sector of low-income countries grew at 4.5 per cent a year, and that of middle-income countries at 7.2 per cent. This compares with growth rates in industrialized capitalist countries of only 3.2 per cent.

Industrialization also secured some of the change desired in the economic structure of Third World countries, increasing its share of GDP and reducing dependence on agriculture and primary-produce exports (see table 6.3). Over the period 1960–76 manufacturing contributed about 33 per cent of the increase in the exports of developing countries, a further 40 per cent coming from fuel exports.

Table 6.3 Distribution of GDP, 1960 and 1979 (per cent).

	Agriculture		Industry		Services	
	1960	1979	1960	1979	1960	1979
Low-income countries	51	34	17	36	32	30
Middle-income countries	22	14	30	38	47	48
Capitalist industrialized countries	6	4	40	37	54	59

Source of data: World Bank, 1981: 138–9.

The patterns, of course, vary in detail. Most countries in South America derive over 30 per cent of their GDP from industry, but it is only in ten African countries, mainly those with rich oil or mineral deposits, that industry's contribution reaches this level. Asian countries fall into two major groups. There are a few – Bangladesh, Burma, Nepal and Afghanistan – where the contribution is small, below 15 per cent; for most of the remainder it is between 25 and 33 per cent of GDP.

In following import-substitution industrialization programmes, Third World countries have become more self-sufficient in manufactured goods, though to varying degrees. In 1975 Argentina produced 75 per cent of the manufactured goods it consumed, Colombia 84 per cent and Korea 71 per cent. (It should be noted that these figures are a rough guide, derived by taking the industrial output of a country, subtracting its exports of manufactures and adding imported manufactures, and then calculating the percentage of domestic contribution to total industrial consumption.) A majority of Third World countries opted for some form of import-substitution industrialization. As we have seen above, these industries were the easiest and least risky to develop. Demand already existed and output could be more easily geared to existing markets, whereas export-oriented industries required the securing of external markets. Internal markets in many countries were too small and poor to sustain intermediate and basic industries, though it was hoped that economic progress would make it possible to develop these later as income levels, demand and skills improved. In consequence the industrial structure of many Third World countries remains dominated by light or non-durable consumer goods industries producing everyday necessities: food, drink, tobacco, textiles, clothing, wood, furniture, building materials and printing. The development of other sectors is limited when compared with industrialized countries (table 6.4).

Few Third World countries have progressed much beyond the stage of import-substitution industrialization. This reflects the very low initial level of their industrialization, the difficulties of achieving transformation to a more diverse

Table 6.4   The structure of manufacturing (percentage of total).

		Non-durable goods	Intermediate goods	Durable consumer and basic goods
UK	1951	37.8	25.7	36.5
	1970	30.5	29.2	40.3
Latin America	1950	65.5	23.3	11.2
	1974	40.3	34.1	25.6
Egypt	1970	55.5	29.6	14.9
Republic of Korea	1970	52.1	34.2	13.7
India	1970	41.5	33.5	25.0
Argentina, Brazil, Mexico	1974	36.2	35.2	28.6

and dynamic industrial structure, and the constraints of resources, capital and markets. Available data for twenty-five African countries indicate that light industries linked to food, textiles, wood working and paper provided over two-thirds of industrial employment and value added. In countries such as Sudan, Ghana, Togo and Kenya these industries and processing activities linked to export crops such as palm-oil, cacao and sugar dominate the industrial structure. In a few exceptional cases particular resource endowments sustain rather different structures – metal processing in Zaire and oil refining and petrochemical industries in Libya and Algeria.

In Latin America there are rather greater contrasts. Traditional light industries provide over four-fifths of the industrial output of Bolivia, Peru and Paraguay, but Argentina, Brazil and Mexico have made considerable progress beyond the import-substitution phase. Light industries contribute less than one-half of Mexican production and below one-third of that of Brazil and Argentina. The latter two countries have made most progress in developing intermediate and capital-goods industries, and the latter sector, which includes metallurgy, engineering, electrical goods and vehicles, provides over one-third of their industrial output.

Some measure of these patterns is illustrated in figures 6.5, 6.6 and 6.7, which show that while many Third World countries have developed industries producing cotton textiles, few have steel or automobile industries. The cotton industry depends mainly on local raw materials – markets capable of sustaining some production exist, as a necessity, even in small poor countries – and technology is relatively simple and levels of capital investment low, such that local capital can sustain the development of cotton mills. At the other extreme a steel mill requires a substantial market, complex technology and large capital investment. In consequence few Third World countries have developed significant steel industries, though some have attempted to do so for prestige or symbolic reasons. Because of the high investment required, and because of the perceived strategic role of steel, state capital is important in many of the existing steelworks in the Third World. The automobile industry has similar needs for technology and investment, but is generally characterized by the intrusion of multinational capital into the Third World, since many of the vehicle plants belong to firms such as Ford, General Motors, Fiat, Volkswagen and Toyota. Vehicle-assembly production represents an intermediate stage, in which components are imported from developed countries and assembled, because local markets are inadequate to sustain domestic manufacture.

A further characteristic of Third World industrialization is the generally small scale of units of production. This reflects the survival of significant segments of artisan industries with few employees and little mechanization; the limited size of markets which sustain only smaller units of production; and the dominance of light industries, which tend to be smaller in scale than plants required in basic and intermediate industries. Available data for a group of African countries show a range from an average of forty-nine workers per plant in the wood-working

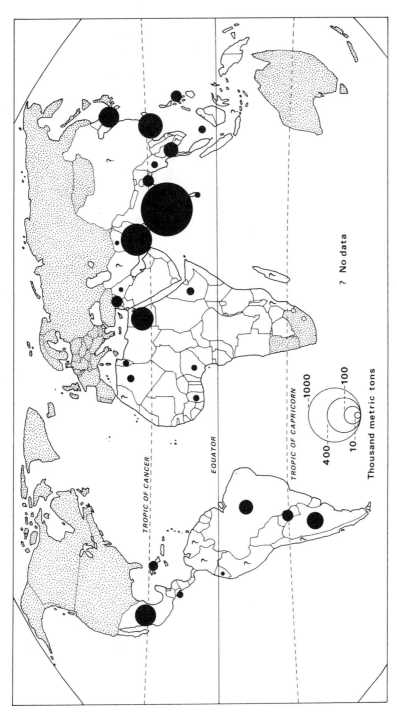

Figure 6.5 Production of cotton yarn, 1975. Some small producers are not shown.

Source of data: UN Statistical Yearbook, 1978: 257–8.

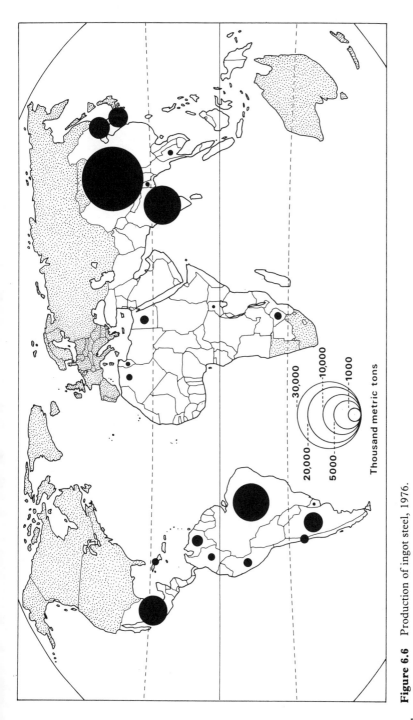

Figure 6.6 Production of ingot steel, 1976.
Source of data: UN Statistical Yearbook, 1978: 330.

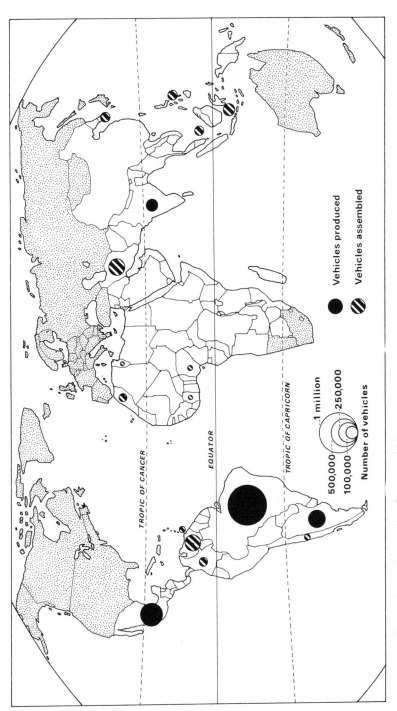

Figure 6.7 Production and assembly of motor vehicles, 1976. Assembled vehicles are produced from components imported from the developed world and put together, sometimes incorporating locally produced parts, in the Third World.

Source of data: UN Statistical Yearbook, 1978: 351:3.

Table 6.5   The structure of industry in Brazil, 1975 (per cent).

Number of workers per plant	Factories	Employment	Value added by manufacture
1–9	47.4	7.9	4.7
10–99	45.6	37.0	30.7
100–499	6.2	35.8	40.4
over 500	0.7	19.3	24.1

Source: Calculated from IBGE, 1982: 190.

industry to 412 in basic metal-working. Even these figures may undervalue the significance of small plants, for many industrial censuses exclude firms employing less than a certain number of workers. Table 6.5 indicates this pattern in Brazil in 1975. Small units of production provide the largest proportion of factories, but make lower contributions to employment and value added. Conversely a few large plants dominate the latter two categories. Some idea of the contrast between industries can be gained from the structure of the food and vehicle industries in Brazil (table 6.6). The contrast in factory structure is perhaps not as great as might be expected, for the census definition of vehicle manufacture in Brazil includes not only shipyards, locomotive workshops and car factories, but also repair shops, cart makers and other small-scale activities. However, the contribution of larger plants is apparent in their share of the labour force.

In spite of the progress in industrialization, in terms of high rates of industrial growth, changing economic structure and trends to self-sufficiency, the Third World remains of limited significance on a world scale. In 1977 the developing countries contributed 9 per cent of world manufacturing output. A target of 25 per cent share has been set for 2000 A D, but even if this were achieved, it would be measured against an estimated 75 per cent share of world population.

Exports of manufactured goods have made some contribution in reducing the dependence on primary products. In 1960 almost half of the less-developed countries were dependent on a single commodity for over half their export

Table 6.6   The structure of food processing and vehicle industries in Brazil, 1975 (per cent).

	Factories		Employment	
	Food	Vehicles	Food	Vehicles
Factories employing under 100 persons	96.8	87.5	55.7	26.0
Factories employing more than 100 persons	3.2	12.5	44.3	74.0

Source: Calculated from IBGE, 1981: 192 and 196.

earnings; now less than one-fifth are so dependent. Over the period 1960–75 manufactures were the fastest growing export sector at a rate of 12 per cent a year. Over the same period food exports grew at 2.8 per cent and minerals at 4.8 per cent a year. In 1975 manufactures contributed 26 per cent of Third World exports, energy sources 40 per cent and agricultural produce 34 per cent.

Despite these changes, manufacturing exports remain markedly concentrated in source and specific in character. About 45 per cent of these exports come from four middle-income countries. A further 35 per cent come from a further eight countries, leaving only 20 per cent generated by the rest of the Third World. Of the leading twelve exporters only seven – Korea, Hong Kong, Brazil, Mexico, China, India and Singapore – are part of the Third World. Some countries that had previously established manufacturing exports, such as India, have experienced little benefit from recent expansion of Third World industrial exports, while others, particularly in sub-Saharan Africa, make little contribution to the trade. The pattern of exports is dominated by textiles, clothing and footwear, though recently more complex products, such as machinery and electrical goods, have increased in importance. A crucial problem for Third World countries trying to develop export-oriented industries is the hostility of developed countries to their products because of the threat they pose to domestic producers. This opposition derives from the recent slow growth of the industrialized countries and consequent high rates of unemployment; and from the concentration of exports in a few commodities, such that the generally cheaper Third World manufactures threaten further unemployment in particular industries. Developed countries have sought to check imports by quotas, price controls and subsidies to domestic producers.

The pattern of industrialization

The spatial distribution of manufacturing industry in the Third World shows a marked degree of concentration at various levels. As has been indicated above, manufacturing makes a varying contribution to the GDP of the countries of the Third World. As a broad generalization Latin America has made most progress in industrialization, Africa least, with Asia occupying an intermediate position. In terms of employment, Asia has the largest share of the region's industrial workers, a reflection of the large contribution of India and Indonesia.

At a second level, within the main continental areas, spatial concentration is again notable. In Africa (excluding Angola, Mozambique, Zimbabwe and South Africa) the northern countries of Morocco, Algeria, Tunisia, Libya, Egypt and Sudan, with about 25 per cent of the population, contribute almost 50 per cent of the value added by manufacturing. In contrast, central Africa, with 14 per cent of the population, provides only 10 per cent of value added. In the early 1970s Egypt and Nigeria contributed 40 per cent of the value added, and eight other countries a further 36 per cent, leaving only 24 per cent from the remaining thirty-one independent countries.

Similarly, in Latin America, Argentina, Brazil and Mexico contributed 77.8 per cent of manufacturing output in 1974. Chile, Colombia, Peru and Venezuela contributed a further 15.8 per cent, leaving only 6.4 per cent from the remaining countries. The three major countries had increased their share from 72.4 per cent in 1950, at the expense of the other countries.

Spatial concentration is also apparent at a third level, within individual countries. In India about 70 per cent of all industrial employment and about 80 per cent of large-scale industries are located in only six of the country's twenty-three states. Maharashtra and West Bengal alone account for 38 per cent of industrial employment and 48 per cent of value added. Conversely the seven least-industrialized states have less than 1 per cent of industrial jobs and contribute less than 0.6 per cent of value added.

In Latin America not only is industry concentrated in three countries but it is markedly concentrated within those countries. Three zones – La Plata–Buenos Aires–Rosario in Argentina, Rio de Janeiro–São Paulo in Brazil, and the Federal District and adjacent areas in Mexico – account for half the industrial product of their respective countries. The level of industrialization in these zones is such that they resemble the industrial areas of more developed countries. Elsewhere in the continent, except in Colombia, capital cities generate between 50 and 80 per cent of their respective national industrial product. Thus the bulk of Latin America's industry is concentrated in some thirty urban-industrial concentrations, separated by considerable spaces that are little industrialized. Such industry as does exist in these spaces tends to be smaller in scale and less complex in character. Traditional industries producing essentials of food, clothing and shelter tend to predominate in such areas; basic and intermediate industries tend to concentrate in the major centres.

Industrialization in Ceará, Brazil
Such a pattern can be seen in the industrial structure of the Brazilian state of Ceará (figure 6.8). The state is part of the poor, semi-arid north-east of the country, with low, seasonal rainfall and occasional drought. It has few natural resources and its principal products are cotton, cattle, oil palms and salt. Its industrial activity contains three elements. Most small settlements sustain small craft and artisan industries processing local materials for local use. These include food-processing activities such as grain milling, baking and sugar processing, the making of crude bricks and tiles from sun-dried mud, and the production of household furniture. Such activities are small scale, with few workers and little machinery; they may be seasonal or only work in response to specific orders; and they often form only part of essentially rural activities. Two-thirds of the state's industrial establishments employ less than five workers. In addition to the places shown in figure 6.8 there are over 100 other settlements with less than 100 industrial workers. Industrial activity in such places is confined almost entirely to the traditional consumer industries concerned with food and shelter.

A second industrial segment is concerned with the processing of produce,

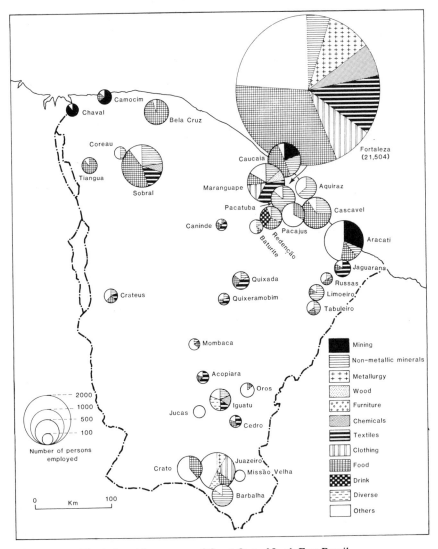

Figure 6.8 The industrial structure of Ceará State, North-East Brazil.

Source of data: IBGE, 1974.

mainly from agriculture, for export to more prosperous parts of Brazil or abroad. This includes the ginning of cotton, the tanning of hides and the processing of vegetable products such as cashew, oiticica, babaçu and carnauba. (The census classification of these generally rudimentary activities as part of the chemical industry explains the significance of this industry in some interior towns.) The mining activities of the coastal towns are derived mainly from the production of salt by evaporation of sea water.

Figure 6.8 shows that in most settlements in Ceará, industrial activity is largely confined to the two sectors of traditional consumer industries, and processing of primary products. Locally available cotton sustained the establishment of cotton-textile mills in Fortaleza, Aracati and Sobral, but only Fortaleza, the state capital, has developed a large and diverse industrial activity. Even so the non-metallic mineral, furniture, food and drink industries account for over 40 per cent of the city's industrial employment. However, it is also the focus of more 'modern' industries in the state, with most of the metallurgical, engineering, electrical and pharmaceutical factories. The capital's importance *vis-à-vis* the other towns of Ceará is clearly evident. In addition, regional development aid for the north-east which has gone to Ceará, has tended to concentrate in the most attractive location, Fortaleza, with the best infrastructure of skilled labour, transport, electricity and other urban services. This process has tended to increase the scale and diversity of the capital's industrial activity.

Patterns are similar in Africa. In several countries of tropical Africa in the early 1970s all manufacturing took place in the primate capital city – in Gambia, Liberia, Gabon and Rwanda. In a further nine countries over half of industrial activity was in the capital city. In Kenya, in 1979, 47 per cent of national employment in manufacturing was in Nairobi with only 5 per cent of the total population. Significant exceptions to this pattern, where the capital city contributes less than one-third of industry, occur where there are important

Plate 6.3 Industrial estate at Contagem, Minas Gerais, Brazil.
Developments such as this provide prepared sites and access to electricity, transport, water and other services in order to attract industry. This estate, established in 1941, is now one of the largest concentrations of industry in Brazil.

mineral processing activities elsewhere, as in the copper belts of Congo and Zambia.

These patterns of concentration have their origin in a number of factors. Settlements developed by the colonial powers became centres of administration and commerce. Before and after independence these were the centres of political power, of the élite, and major concentrations of population. Many of these colonial cities were also ports and thus foci of trading activity. The movement of goods for processing, the business ambience, the existence of the largest and most prosperous market, and proximity to political decision making, were all factors encouraging infant industries to develop in such centres. These cities were usually the first to benefit from the provision of services such as electricity, gas, water and urban transport. They were also the foci for the national networks of transport and communications, making them important centres for the assembly of raw materials and distribution of finished goods. In circumstances where infrastructural provision was and often still is incomplete, these centres provide important points of attraction for industry. As centres of government, location in such centres gives access to decision making that affects industrialization (through industrial finance, tariff protection, etc.). They are also the main concentrations of financial and commercial institutions, which are often little developed in the interior. As the principal foci of social and cultural activity the cities are most attractive to entrepreneurs, professionals and skilled workers who may be reluctant to live and work in the interior. Similarly they are major magnets for migrant labour, both skilled and unskilled, so that a substantial labour force is available.

Thus the industry which has developed in the Third World remains restricted in its diversity, relatively small in scale, spatially concentrated and of limited significance in world terms. There is one other dimension that must be noted, and which is, in some respects, probably its most crucial deficiency. It was noted above (p. 147) that a major function envisaged for industrialization was to create jobs; industry was seen as the vehicle whereby expanding population and the labour shed by agricultural modernization could be absorbed into productive employment. Whatever the success of Third World countries in expanding their industrial section, diversifying their economies and developing manufactured exports, their industrialization programmes have not been highly successful in this labour absorptive role.

The problem of employment

In Latin America, over the period 1945–60, the urban population increased by 4.3 per cent a year, the non-agricultural economically active population by 3.9 per cent, but manufacturing employment by only 2.8 per cent. Growth of industrial output has generally been more rapid than growth of industrial employment – in Brazil, Chile, Ethiopia and India, for example, the annual rate of growth of industrial output was more than twice that of the growth of industrial employment. As Table 6.8 indicates, the low and middle-income countries have achieved higher

Table 6.7 Employment patterns (per cent of total).

	Agriculture		Non-agricultural activities	
	1960	1979	1960	1979
Low-income countries	76	71	24	29
Middle-income countries	58	43	42	57
Industrialized capitalist countries	16	6	84	94

Source of data: World Bank, 1981: 170–1.

industrial growth rates than those of the industrialized capitalist countries over the period 1960–79 and have secured some change in the structure of their GDP; but they have failed to secure similar changes in their employment structure.

These imbalances reflect a number of factors. These include the sheer numbers involved in Third World population growth and the 'push–pull' influences that expel people from the countryside and draw them into the cities. Industrialization has thus failed to keep pace with population growth and with the concentration of people into the cities. But it also seems that the nature of the industrialization process in the Third World may have mitigated against job creation. One of the alleged advantages for Third World countries is that, unlike the industrializing countries of nineteenth-century Europe, they do not have to invent a technology, they can 'borrow' or, more realistically, buy it from the industrialized countries. The problem is that the industrial technology of the 1980s has advanced considerably over that of the nineteenth century. It is sophisticated, complex and costly. The input of labour per unit of output is often small; yet Third World countries have abundant labour to employ, but limited capital to spend. Available technology is therefore inappropriate to their needs. Thus the only industrial equipment available, because it is produced mainly in the developed world, is not designed to suit the particular circumstances of the developing countries. Third World countries have generally paid little attention to this problem. They have

Table 6.8 Average annual rates of growth 1960–70 and 1970–9 (per cent).

	GDP		Agriculture		Manufacturing		Services	
	1960–70	1970–9	1960–70	1970–9	1960–70	1970–9	1960–70	1970–9
Low-income countries	4.5	4.7	2.5	2.0	6.5	3.7	3.8	4.5
Middle-income countries	6.1	5.5	3.6	3.0	7.0	6.6	5.5	6.0
Industrialized capitalist countries	5.1	3.2	1.3	0.9	6.2	3.0	4.8	3.4

Source of data: World Bank, 1981: 136–7.

tended to adopt this technology, not only for lack of alternatives, but also because it is 'desirable' and 'modern'. Their industrialization policies have also tended to favour the adoption of this capital-intensive technology, by using tariff, tax and investment policies that artificially reduce the cost of equipment relative to the cost of labour, making it cheap for industrialists to import foreign machinery. It is true that some industries, such as metallurgy and chemicals, are by their nature capital intensive, but this is not the case for all industries. But even in the more traditional industries, capital-intensive strategies have often been adopted. Modernization of textile mills has made them more efficient and productive, but has reduced their employment capacity. Proposals to modernize the Brazilian cotton industry in the 1950s would have reduced the labour force in the spinning sector by 30 per cent and in weaving by 45 per cent. During the 1960s modernization of the industry in north-east Brazil, a region of considerable backwardness and poverty, resulted in the loss of 20,000 jobs, one-third of the labour force in the industry.

Thus industrial employment has not paralleled industrial expansion in the Third World. In 1971 the International Labour Office estimated that between 1970–80 there would be an increase of 177 million in the number of people employed in the region (excluding China and Southern Africa). Of that increase 26 per cent would be in agriculture, 29 per cent in industry and 45 per cent in the tertiary sector. Their estimate was that in 1980 agriculture would still provide 54 per cent of Third World employment, the tertiary sector 29 per cent and manufacturing and construction 17 per cent. This suggests that industrialization, at least in the provision of jobs, has not proved the panacea it was expected to be. The UN Economic Commission for Latin America has stated that industry has proved to be an inadequate source of employment in view of the magnitude of the problem faced and the urgency of the need for a solution.

In consequence of this failure, combined with the overall growth of population and migration to the cities, the Third World continues to face very high levels of unemployment and underemployment. Much of the expansion in the tertiary sector has been in marginal activities rather than in productive and secure jobs. Data on levels of unemployment and underemployment are both scarce and unreliable. In the 1960s levels of urban unemployment were in excess of 10 per cent in cities such as Bogotá, Caracas, Abidjan, Lagos, Calcutta and Jakarta. In São Paulo, in some ways one of the 'success' stories of Third World industrialization, with a very large and diverse industrial structure, it was estimated that in 1970 open unemployment was between 6 and 9 per cent, and underemployment around 34 per cent.

7 URBANIZATION

Since the Second World War, urbanization – the concentration of people in cities and towns – has taken place in the Third World at a pace and on a scale only paralleled by the experience of Western Europe and North America in the nineteenth century. The crisis of Third World urbanization, however, is expressed not in the speed or short history of city growth (table 7.1), but in the wide margin by which urban population increase (usually about 3 per cent per annum) has outstripped employment opportunities in manufacturing industry.

Patterns and processes of urbanization

Census data for urban areas show that over 20 per cent of the people in the Third World are living in towns of more than 20,000 – 17 per cent in South Asia, 18 per cent in Africa, 24 per cent in East Asia and 41 per cent in Latin America. But only Latin America closely approaches the level of urbanization in Europe (48 per cent) and in North America (65 per cent).

Third World cities are remarkable for their size. Settlements with more than a million inhabitants, which were rare in 1900, are now numerous in Latin America and the Middle East, and commonplace in India and China. In Latin America there are fifteen, and four of them – Buenos Aires, Rio de Janeiro, São Paulo and Mexico City – form the core of multimillion agglomerations which rank among the twenty-five largest urban regions in the world.

Despite the profusion of settlements with 250,000 inhabitants or more (figure 7.1), a major feature of Third World urbanization is the enormous concentration of each country's population in one city, usually the capital. Systems of cities in developed countries are generally graded, with the second settlement recording half the population of the largest, and so on. But in Third World countries this rank–size rule breaks down, especially near the top of the urban hierarchy, which is characterized by primacy.

The largest city in most Third World countries often contains between 10 and 25 per cent of the entire population, over half the urban-dwelling population and more than four times the number of inhabitants in the next largest city. Primacy occurs in an extreme form in the city-state of Singapore and city-colony of Hong Kong. Under more normal, yet exaggerated, circumstances Montevideo, the capital of Uruguay, contains approximately half the country's entire population. Exceptions to a high degree of primacy include Brazil, where São Paulo and Rio de Janeiro rival one another, though neither is the capital; China, where Shanghai and Peking vie for first place; and Turkey, where Ankara, the relatively recent capital, is growing more quickly than long-established Istanbul.

Where there is a pairing of cities of approximately equal size, commonly one is the capital and the other the major port or else they each head rival growth regions. Primacy, on the other hand, is linked to the amalgamation of commercial – usually port – and capital functions in one city, for example, Dakar or Kingston. This condition is particularly acute in small countries with undiversified economies, especially – as in Africa and the Caribbean – where colonialism persisted until the 1960s, or, in some instances, until the 1970s.

Table 7.1 Population of selected urban areas, 1950–2000 (in millions).

Urban area	1950	Average annual rate of growth (%)	1975	Average annual rate of growth (%)	2000 (estimated)
Underdeveloped countries					
Mexico City	2.9	5.4	10.9	4.4	31.5
Buenos Aires	4.5	2.9	9.3	1.5	13.7
São Paulo	2.5	5.7	9.9	3.9	26.0
Rio de Janeiro	2.9	4.4	8.3	3.4	19.3
Bogotá	0.7	6.5	3.4	4.2	9.5
Cairo	2.4	4.3	6.9	3.6	16.9
Seoul	1.0	8.3	7.3	3.8	18.7
Manila	1.5	4.4	4.4	4.3	12.8
Kinshasa	0.2	9.7	2.0	5.6	7.8
Lagos	0.3	8.1	2.1*	6.2	9.4
Shanghai	5.8	2.8	11.5	2.6	22.1
Peking	2.2	5.8	8.9	3.7	22.0
Jakarta	1.6	5.1	5.6	4.7	17.8
Calcutta	4.5	2.4	8.1	3.7	20.4
Bombay	2.9	3.7	7.1	4.2	19.8
Karachi	1.0	6.2	4.5	5.4	16.6
Developed countries					
New York	12.3	1.3	17.0	1.3	22.2
London	10.2	0.2	10.7	0.7	12.7
Paris	5.4	2.1	9.2	1.2	12.4
Tokyo	6.7	3.9	17.5	2.0	28.7

* The latest estimate for Greater Lagos is 3.3 million.

Source: IBRD (1975) *The Task Ahead for the Cities of the Developing World*, World Bank Staff Working Paper No. 209: 20; quoted in Sinclair, 1978: 15.

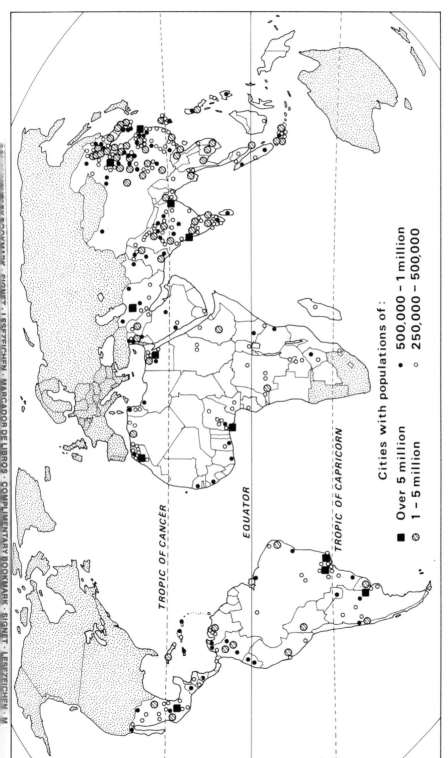

Figure 7.1 Third World cities with more than 250,000 inhabitants.

Source of data: Fullard, 1979.

Cities with populations of :

■ Over 5 million
⊘ 1 – 5 million
● 500,000 – 1 million
○ 250,000 – 500,000

TROPIC OF CANCER

EQUATOR

TROPIC OF CAPRICORN

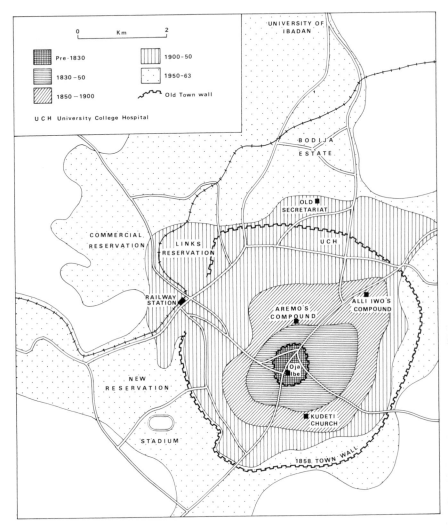

Figure 7.2   The growth of Ibadan, Nigeria, showing the indigenous Yoruba town and colonial additions to its layout.

Source: Mabogunje, 1968: 206.

Despite their recent growth, many Third World cities have long histories. This is obviously true of pre-colonial settlements, but, Africa south of the Sahara excepted, many colonial towns established by Europeans also have origins going back to the voyages of the Age of Discovery in the sixteenth and seventeenth centuries. Towns flourished in India, China, the Middle East, and in parts of North and West Africa before European contact; colonial settlements are the norm in Latin America, the Caribbean and most of Africa. Even where there were indigenous traditions of town-dwelling, it is common to find European colonial settlements added to the original town, as in the case of Ibadan in Nigeria (figure 7.2) and the company town of Abadan in Iran. Delhi and New Delhi in India exemplify this arrangement on the grand scale.

Third World cities for many decades, and often for centuries, have been agents of European imperialism, facilitating trade penetration and acting as gateways for the export of primary products and the import of manufactured goods. Many Third World cities remain essentially pre-industrial in their economic base, while their coastal locations in South-East Asia, Latin America, Africa, and, above all, in the Pacific and Caribbean, indicate their long association with colonial dependency (see figure 7.1).

Neo-Marxist economists extend the relationship between Third World towns and dependency further, and argue that not only are they agents of imperialism and external neo-colonialism but they also dominate their hinterlands through relationships of internal colonialism. According to this perspective, urban markets are locations at which unequal exchanges occur and are the means by which mercantile capitalists extract surplus value from the labour of agricultural

Plate 7.1 Urban scene, Peshawar, North-West Frontier Province, Pakistan.
Peshawar lies at the foot of the Khyber Pass, a major routeway between India and Europe, and a city has existed on the site at least since Alexander the Great passed through in 328 B.C. Many parts of modern Peshawar, in particular the military garrison of the canton-ment, were laid out during the British colonial period, but the old town exemplifies many of the features of the morphology, land use and activities of a pre-industrial city.

and handicraft workers. Clearly, the degree of domination depends upon a socio-economic gulf between town and country and upon distinctions in culture and language between the groups involved.

THE IMPACT OF MIGRATION

Whatever the origins of, or links between, Third World cities, their growth has been precipitated by high rates of natural increase – due principally to reduced mortality – added to which are large inflows of migrants (see chapter 3). Young migrants expand the urban population both by their presence and by their reproductive capacity; male migrants are usually in their twenties, but females are on average even younger, often predominantly in their teens. Many women migrate as part of the family and do not have separate motives for mobility, but such is the volume of independent female migration in Latin America and the Caribbean that most cities and towns record an excess of women. In Africa, Asia and the Middle East on the other hand, migration is a male phenomenon, and especially so in Africa and India where movements are circular rather than permanent: women and children stay on the land, maintain the cultivation of subsistence crops, and provide a secure village base to which men can return. Conditions vary in detail from country to country, from town to town, but migration is undoubtedly a major component of urban population growth throughout the Third World (table 7.2), notable exceptions being China and certain countries in the Middle East.

Table 7.2 Migrants as a percentage of recent urban population increases.

City	Period	Total population increase (thousands)	Migrants as a percentage of total population increase
Abidjan	1955–63	129	76
Bogotá	1956–66	930	33
Bombay	1951–61	1207	52
Caracas	1950–60	587	54
	1960–6	501	50
Djakarta	1961–8	1528	59
Istanbul	1950–60	672	68
	1960–5	428	65
Lagos	1952–62	393	75
Nairobi	1961–9	162	50
São Paulo	1950–60	2163	72
	1960–7	2543	68
Seoul	1955–65	1697	63
Taipei	1950–60	396	40
	1960–7	326	43

Source: IBRD (1972) *Urbanization*, World Bank Sector Working Paper No. 209: 80; quoted in Sinclair, 1978: 18.

Cityward migration operates in a number of ways. Those born in rural areas are drawn into the urban system and move either by way of smaller towns up the urban hierarchy towards the largest city – a common pattern in Latin America and the Middle East – or they may settle directly in the capital – a situation typical of West Africa and East and South-East Asia – depending on the distance and attraction of alternative destinations (table 7.3). Another possibility is for migrants to move through the settlement system in a less structured way in response to the availability of work and the location of friends and relatives from back home to assist them. Return migration from capitals and smaller towns to rural areas is the norm in many African countries; in Latin America, the Middle East and Asia it is generally a smaller-scale process. But even in these instances, rural links are maintained by migrants, who band together in regional associations for mutual support, remit cash to their families and occasionally raise funds for development projects in their areas of origin.

Size and spacing of towns and the way in which they are interconnected undoubtedly affect the type of migration recorded at various levels of the settlement hierarchy. Knowledge about the processes of urban migration is mainly derived from the largest cities, and evidence for urbanization in general is largely based on studies of capital cities. In some Third World countries with well-established urban systems migration is step-wise, the larger settlements drawing

Table 7.3   Distribution of migrant flows to and between urban areas.

Country Migration definition	Previous residence of urban migrants (%)	
	Other urban areas	Rural areas
Brazil Total population in urban areas (administratively defined) who had moved within one year of the 1970 census count	76	24
Ghana Adults in urban areas (5000 and over) who had moved within two years of the 1960 census count	38	62
Korea Total population in urban areas (50,000 and more) who had moved in 1965–70 period	26	74
India Total population in urban areas (5000 and more) who had moved within one year of the 1961 census count	37	63

Source: IBRD (1975) *Internal Migration in Less Developed Countries: a Survey of the Literature*, World Bank Staff Working Paper No. 215: 9; quoted in Sinclair, 1978: 42.

on smaller ones, and so on down the hierarchy. The major cities therefore receive many migrants who are familiar with urban life, though selectivity of this kind invariably declines as the movement continues over time.

There is no reason, of course, why families or individuals should divide their migration into stages, completed over the years or generations, if transport is cheap, there is an important city only a few hours away by bus or train, and relatives are at hand – as they so often are – to help a migrant in difficulties. Many Third World cities experience a mixture of direct and stage migration. Nevertheless, the distance–decay function usually holds good, and migratory flows generally cover short distances (figure 7.3).

Expansion of smaller towns of 2000, 5000 or 20,000 inhabitants, depending on definitions of what is urban, occurs principally through rural-to-urban migration. Reasons for the rural exodus are essentially economic, though in the Middle East and Asia political problems have generated vast flows of refugees (see chapter 3). Per capita agricultural output is either static or declining in many Third World countries. In parts of Africa where access to land is often communal and relatively free there is a lower level of migration and of urbanization, but in India and Latin America the bulk of arable land is in the hands of a small élite. Even in Mexico, where a land-reform programme has been in operation for over half a century, the penetration of the countryside by consumer goods has displaced local craft workers and helped to create a surplus population that has responded by out-migration to take its chance in the cities. Wage differentials everywhere explain the move to the towns, even in Jamaica where unemployment is far higher in Kingston than in the rural areas, though it is rarely perceived to be so by prospective migrants.

An additional stimulus to cityward migration is the educational system. Secondary schools and institutes of higher education – Cuba and China excepted – are located for the most part in large towns. Moreover, the value system in most Third World countries produces adolescents whose aspirations are to urban jobs. Their main objective is to live and work in a city or small town in preference to a rural district, where roads, electricity, piped-water supply and health facilities may be non-existent, the social status of families is common knowledge, and opportunities for non-agricultural work are negligible.

Employment and unemployment

Concentration of manufacturing activities in large Third World cities is as striking as primacy itself and has occurred because the major strategy for economic development has been one of industrialization by import substitution (see chapter 5). This policy has concentrated food, tobacco, drink, and textile industries in port-commercial centres or in pre-existing urban agglomerations where there is a ready market for consumer goods. In Latin America, where import substitution was introduced more than fifty years ago, the largest cities, São Paulo and Mexico City, now have branches of multinational firms manufacturing motor cars and electrical goods.

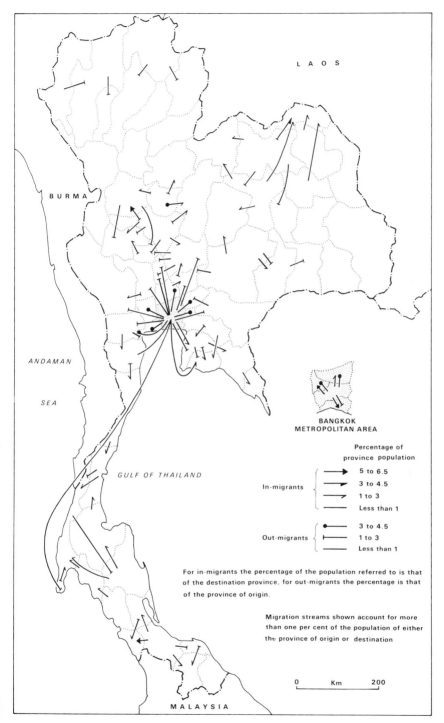

Figure 7.3   Short-distance migration to Bangkok, Thailand, 1970.
Most of the movement is short distance, but there is migration both into and out from many of the provinces and to and from Bangkok.

Source: Reprinted from Sternstein, *The Geographical Review*, 66 (1976), with the permission of the American Geographical Society.

Table 7.4 The growth of manufacturing employment and the labour force.

Region Countries	Employees in manufacturing (annual growth rate 1963-9)	GNP per capita (annual growth rate 1960-70)	Manufacturing labour force as % of total labour force, 1970
East Africa			
Botswana	—	—	1.0
Ethiopia	6.4	2.8	—
Kenya	—	3.6	—
Malawi	7.1[b]	2.1	—
Mauritius	1.4[d]	—	14.6
Somalia	−18.0[d]	−1.1	—
Sudan	—	1.0	5.0
Uganda	—	2.4	8.0
United Republic of Tanzania	14.0[e]	3.6	—
Zaire	—	2.7	3.1
Zambia	15.3[f]	7.1	2.6
West Africa			
Gabon	—	—	1.9
Ghana	6.3	−0.4	8.6
Ivory Coast	—	4.5	0.8
Liberia	—	0.9	2.1
Niger	—	−2.0	0.1
Nigeria	5.7[f]	0.1	—
Sierra Leone	—	4.7	4.4
Asia			
China	13.3[c]	7.1	—
Fiji Islands	—	—	7.0[a]
Hong Kong	9.2	—	41.4
India	—	1.2	9.5
Indonesia	—	1.0	5.6
Khmer	—	0.1	2.7
Korea	13.0	6.8	13.2
Malaysia (East Sabah)	12.3[d]	—	—
Malaysia (West)	8.1[c]	3.1	8.7
Nepal	—	0.5	1.9
Pakistan	2.6[f]	2.4[h]	9.5
Philippines	4.8	2.9	11.4
Singapore	17.4	—	13.9
Sri Lanka	—	1.5	9.1
Thailand	−12.0[g]	4.9	3.4
Latin America and the Caribbean			
Argentina	—	2.5	25.1
Barbados	—	—	14.6
Bolivia	−17.0[e]	2.5	10.3
Brazil	1.1	2.4	17.8[b]

Table 7.4—*cont.*

Region Countries	Employees in manufacturing (annual growth rate 1963–9)	GNP per capita (annual growth rate 1960–70)	Manufacturing labour force as % of total labour force, 1970
British Honduras	—	—	14.1
Chile	4.2[g]	1.6	23.2
Colombia	2.8	1.7	12.8
Costa Rica	2.8[f]	3.2	11.5
Dominican Republic	−3.3[f]	0.5	8.2
Ecuador	6.0	1.7	14.0
El Salvador	—	1.7	12.8
Guadaloupe	—	—	10.4
Guatemala	—	2.0	11.4
Guyana	—	—	15.1
Haiti	—	−0.9	4.9
Honduras	10.6[f]	1.8	7.8
Jamaica	—	—	13.7
Martinique	—	—	8.8
Mexico	—	3.7	16.7[b]
Netherlands Antilles	—	—	25.8
Nicaragua	—	2.8	12.0
Panama	7.4	4.2	7.6
Paraguay	—	1.3	15.1
Peru	—	1.4	13.2
Puerto Rico	—	—	17.2
Surinam	—	—	8.9
Trinidad and Tobago	20.0[c]	1.9	14.7
Uruguay	—	−0.4	21.6
Venezuela	—	2.3	18.6

a 1966 e 1966–8
b 1970 f 1963–8
c 1966–9 g 1963–7
d 1967–9 h Includes Bangladesh

Source: Sinclair, 1978: 71–2.

New port-side installations, such as the steel and fish-meal processing plants at Chimbote in Peru and oil refineries at Abadan in Iran, have created economically specialized urban settlements. Even more unique are inland concentrations of manufacturing industry based on indigenous raw materials exemplified by the towns of the Zambian copper belt or the more complex textile, mining, and iron and steel towns of central Minas Gerais in Brazil.

Excluding towns developed to exploit specific local resources and others like Hong Kong, which produce and export manufactured goods based on cheap labour, it is generally true that the accumulation of population in Third World cities has outstripped by a large margin the capacity of their manufacturing economies to absorb labour (table 7.4). In some countries like Zaire, Thailand and Haiti, sheer economic stagnation is responsible for the gap between the number of town dwellers and jobs: but in Brazil, India and Mexico, labour surplus in the towns has been exacerbated because their industrialization programmes are based on imported technology, which is capital intensive and employs few workers.

Comparison between indices of urban population concentration and industrialization compiled for Latin America about 30 years ago, produced the then puzzling conclusion that, at the macro scale, disharmony between these two social and economic processes was more acute in the most advanced countries. Now urban labour surplus is diagnosed as inherent in 'dependent' or 'peripheral-capitalist' development and associated with the prominent role played by the multinational corporations, many of whose factories are located in the cities of most advanced Third World countries.

Population growth in Third World cities has greatly inflated the service sector – in lieu of industrial employment – and in the largest settlements tertiary activities may account for more than half the jobs that are available. The ratio of employment in the service sector to that in manufacturing, in general, is higher than in Western Europe: the ratio approaches, and for many countries exceeds, that in the USA, where economic development has permitted a proliferation of services.

Most Third World countries are characterized by burgeoning urban bureaucracies that have expanded to administer newly independent or increasingly complex nations. Ministries, departments and agencies have been created or expanded, providing white-collar work for the educated, and unskilled jobs for porters, messengers and cleaners. National and local government are major, sometimes *the* major, employers of urban labour, and even small towns may have large numbers of officials to administer public works and collect taxes.

The largest Third World cities have sophisticated infrastructures – motorways, metros, bus services, telephone communications, water and sewerage facilities, electricity supplies – and require a substantial labour force to maintain and operate them. Finance houses, building societies and the head offices of national firms provide white-collar jobs in the principal cities, but even small towns linked by dirt roads may have branch banks. Universities, polytechnics, schools and hospitals are urban magnets for professionally qualified staff, while the retailing sector in most big cities requires tens of thousands of shop assistants.

Notwithstanding the existence of occupational structures comparable with those in the cities of developed countries, employment in Third World cities, in addition, is heavily reliant on petty services and manufacturing on a small scale – what has been called the 'bazaar' economy. Employment for the rapidly expanding labour force depends upon the absorptive capacity of small industries with high labour requirements but low productivity: shoemaking, traditional and modern handicrafts, metal work and machinery repair; trade, especially market and street selling of food and clothing; services, including domestic service, shoeshining, rickshaw operating, car watching; and casual labour of all kinds (notably in construction work and street cleaning). At the lowest level of living the urban poor

Plate 7.2 Underemployment, Mexico.
Artisans in need of day-labour stand outside the parochial church on the main square in Mexico City.

have no alternative but to raise and deal in small livestock or to scavenge the streets and garbage dumps for discarded food or for scrap material, such as metal and paper, which can be used for shelter or sold for small sums of money. But even a beggar in Cairo or Manila may do better than a landless labourer in the countryside.

The term 'the tertiary refuge sector' has been coined to describe these heterogeneous activities, which include small-scale workshops, repairing and recycling as well as services. A more appropriate term is the 'informal sector', which contrasts with the 'formal sector' (table 7.5), the latter implying large-scale activity, permanency of employment, set hours of work and pay, and sometimes the provision of pension and social-security rights. The informal sector lacks all these features and is, or appears to be, characterized by family labour, small-scale enterprise and self-employment. It is easy to enter informal occupations, most of which are at best semi-skilled and require little if any capital outlay.

Milton Santos (1979) has divided Third World employment into two circuits, superior and inferior (table 7.6), which are equivalent to the formal and informal sectors outlined above, though he contrasts the circuits more systematically than other authors, drawing attention to differences in technology, organization, capital, labour, wages, prices and credit. Bryan Roberts (1978) extends the dichotomy to the global scale and argues that formal-sector employment has

Table 7.5   Income opportunities in a Third World city.

Formal income opportunities
(a)   Public-sector wages
(b)   Private-sector wages
(c)   Transfer payments – pensions, unemployment benefits

Informal income opportunities: legitimate
(a)   Primary and secondary activities – farming, market gardening, building
      contractors and associated activities, self-employed artisans, shoemakers, tailors,
      manufacturers of beers and spirits
(b)   Tertiary enterprises with relatively large capital inputs – housing, transport,
      utilities, commodity speculation, rentier activities
(c)   Small-scale distribution – market operatives, petty traders, street hawkers, caterers
      in food and drink, bar attendants, carriers, commission agents and dealers
(d)   Other services – musicians, launderers, shoe-shiners, barbers, night-soil removers,
      photographers, vehicle-repair and other maintenance workers; brokerage and
      middlemanship; ritual services, magic and medicine
(e)   Private transfer payments – gifts and similar flows of money and goods between
      persons; borrowing; begging

Informal income opportunities: illegitimate
(a)   Services – confidence tricks; receiving stolen goods; usury and pawnbroking (at
      illegal interest rates); drug-pushing; prostitution; smuggling; bribery; political
      corruption; protection rackets
(b)   Transfers – petty theft (e.g., pickpockets); larceny (e.g., burglary and armed
      robbery); speculation and embezzlement; confidence tricksters (e.g., money
      doublers); gambling

Source: Hart, 1973: 69.

largely been pre-empted by the developed world, leaving Third World cities –
and the towns at the lower levels of the urban hierarchy in particular – essentially
dependent on small-scale, marginal employment. The basic difference between
the sectors or circuits can be reduced to finance capitalism versus penny capitalism (table 7.6). But how, if at all, do the sectors relate?

In the early 1970s it was usual to treat the two sectors as though they were
separate, and to focus on the absorptive capacity of the informal sector, whose
employees subsisted largely by earning from one another or, on a casual basis,
from the formal sector. In this way the urban lower class, and many of the middle
class too, were able to make ends meet by stringing together a number of low-paid
jobs. Santos has argued that growth of small-scale manufacturing and services,
which mostly cater to the urban poor, does not block expansion of the formal
sector; rather, the lower circuit responds to changes in urban consumption
patterns and to general conditions of employment and capital. Most commen-
tators now reject the dichotomy between formal and informal employment,
arguing that both are characterized by the profit motive, and that finance and
industrial capital dominate both sectors. Moreover, the two sectors interrelate in

Table 7.6 Characteristics of the two circuits of the urban economy in underdeveloped countries.

	Upper circuit	Lower circuit
Technology	capital intensive	labour intensive
Organization	bureaucratic	primitive
Capital	abundant	limited
Labour	limited	abundant
Regular wages	prevalent	exceptional
Inventories	large quantities and/or high quality	small quantities, poor quality
Prices	generally fixed	negotiable between buyer and seller (haggling)
Credit	from banks institutional	personal non-institutional
Profit margin	small per unit; but with large turnover, considerable in aggregate (excepting luxuries)	large per unit, but small turnover
Relations with customers	impersonal and/or on paper	direct, personalized
Fixed costs	substantial	negligible
Advertisement	necessary	none
Re-use of goods	none (waste)	frequent
Overhead capital	essential	not essential
Government aid	extensive	none or almost none
Direct dependence on foreign countries	great, externally orientated	small or none

Source: Santos, 1979: 22.

complex ways, the lower circuit selling cheap services and transformed goods to the upper circuit, and purchasing from it consumer goods such as electrical items.

Work in Colombia has shown that street sellers are rarely self-employed and self-financed, but act as a front for highly capitalized organizations. For example, paper pickers on refuse dumps in the city of Cali are not independent operators but outworkers for the local paper mill: by engaging their labour through middle-men and by keeping them off the official pay-roll, the company appropriates the surplus value created by the scavengers and avoids minimum-wage regulations and paying social-security contributions. Evidence from Lima, Calcutta, Dakar and Kashan confirms the existence of similar out-working systems in shoemaking, carpentry, tailoring and carpet-making, but it is too early to say firmly how formal and informal employment interlock in the context of street selling and petty services. However, domestic service, which is by far the largest employer of urban women in Latin America and the Caribbean, clearly depends almost entirely upon wages channelled directly from formal-sector employment.

If the dichotomy between formal and informal employment is being increasingly

Plate 7.3   Shanty town, Jamaica.
A squatter's home in Kingston, constructed from scavenged materials and lacking all basic services.

revealed as false, so too is the distinction between employment and unemployment. Measures of unemployment, if they are made, are likely to be inaccurate; where they are high, they are indicative of informal employment, much of it socially stigmatized or illegal. In the Caribbean, for example, where it is common for cities to record rates of unemployment of 20–30 per cent, idleness, in reality, is impossible, since in common with most Third World regions there is no unemployment benefit, and activities such as begging, stealing, prostitution and marijuana peddling are forms of social security. Under such circumstances it is impossible to differentiate clearly between employment, underemployment and unemployment, since some of the urban poor change their position within this range week by week as their fortunes shift. Third World cities, then, are characterized by enormous marginal populations. In Marxist terms, they form a lumpen proletariat that endures persistent poverty: the reserve army of labour, which in advanced capitalist countries is waiting to be drawn into use by new enterprise, is on permanent leave in Third World cities.

As most urban employment is in manual and service work, migrants reflect the same basic occupational pattern as the urban born. However, two additional factors help to explain this similarity: some migrants possess high levels of education relative to their areas of departure and are able to acquire secure employment; considerable numbers of migrants have been city dwellers for a long time and have achieved promotions in urban jobs. Even in the large cities of

Latin America, where educational credentials are important, newcomers rapidly resemble the local population in their employment, since migrants usually obtain work through the advice and influence of friends and relatives who are familiar with the system and can vouch for them. One migrant group in Mexico City, which originated in a rural community, has actually settled the same neighbourhood in the capital, and now works in collaboration as carpet fitters. In many African cities, quarters have developed a marked tribal character as this process of in-migration and informal-sector expansion has gathered momentum.

Housing conditions

Urbanization which occurs without adequate industrialization, sufficient formal employment or secure wages, has condemned burgeoning urban populations in the Third World to poor-quality housing. The problem has been compounded by a lack of government funds for housing subsidies, by inflated land prices boosted by housing needs and speculation, and by real-estate profiteering on the part of the upper and middle classes. The operation of the class structure of Third World cities is nowhere more geographically explicit than in the composition and working of the housing market.

Only the small upper and middle classes in Third World cities have the income, job security and credit worthiness to purchase or rent houses in properly surveyed, serviced and legally conveyanced developments. Even if mortgages are available, down-payments tend to be large, and the sum borrowed must be paid back over short periods. Middle-income housing schemes are often organized by trade unions or specific occupational groups, and thus automatically exclude those in informal jobs. Elites, of course, have the greatest capacity to choose building sites, house styles and ambiance. Upper and middle-class housing, especially that of recent construction, tends to be confined to formally employed workers and to match, or even excel, standards among equivalent groups in Europe.

Whereas the middle and upper classes are usually satisfactorily, even luxuriously, housed, the emergent working class and marginal population are confined to rented rooms in centrally located, high-density slums – *tugurios* in Latin America, *compounds* in the Middle East, *bazaars* in India – or to peripheral squatter settlements (table 7.7). In Mexico City, the older, stone and concrete tenements surround the commercial centre and occupy an area of almost 5 square miles. However, while central slum areas in Caribbean, West African, Middle Eastern and Indian cities are invariably dilapidated and grossly overcrowded, they usually have rudimentary, though often inadequate, shared services, such as piped water, toilets, sewerage systems and electricity.

The demand for low-cost shelter, in the context of rapid urban-population growth, has frequently been met by housing developments of illegal tenure. Known as *colonias proletarias* in Mexico, *favelas* in Brazil, squatter settlements in the English-speaking Caribbean and Africa, *bidonvilles* in former French colonies,

Table 7.7 Slums and uncontrolled settlements: percentage of total population in cities.

1970 GNP per capita ($ US)	City	Country	%	Year
980	Caracas	Venezuela	40	1960–6
920	Singapore		15	—
730	Panama City	Panama	17	—
720	Santiago	Chile	25	—
670	Mexico City	Mexico	46	—
670	Kingston	Jamaica	25	—
590	Beirut	Lebanon	15	—
450	Lima	Peru	40	—
420	Rio de Janeiro	Brazil	30	—
400	Lusaka	Zambia	58	1964
380	Kuala Lumpur	Malaysia	37	1947–57
360	Guatemala City	Guatemala	30	—
340	Bogotá	Colombia	60	—
320	Baghdad	Iraq	29	—
310	Istanbul	Turkey	40	1960–5
310	Abidjan	Ivory Coast	60	1955–63
310	Accra	Ghana	53	—
290	Guayaquil	Ecuador	49	—
280	Tegucigalpa	Honduras	25	—
250	Amman	Jordan	14	—
250	Seoul	Korea	30	1955–65
240	Monrovia	Liberia	50	—
230	Casablanca	Morocco	70	—
230	Dakar	Senegal	60	—
210	Manila	Philippines	35	—
180	Douala	Cameroon	80	—
150	Nairobi	Kenya	33	1963–73
140	Lomé	Togo	75	—
110	Calcutta	India	33	—
110	Colombo	Sri Lanka	43	—
100	Karachi	Pakistan	23	—
100	Dar es Salaam	Tanzania	50	—
90	Kinshasa	Zaire	60	—
80	Kabul	Afghanistan	21	—
80	Addis Ababa	Ethiopia	90	—
80	Blantyre	Malawi	56	—
80	Katmandu	Nepal	22	—
80	Djakarta	Indonesia	26	—
70	Mogadishu	Somalia	77	—
60	Ouagadougou	Upper Volta	70	—

— not available.
All estimates are extremely rough.

Source: O. F. Grimes, Jr, *Housing for Low-Income Urban Families*, London: Johns Hopkins Press for IBRD, 1976, Table A2: 118–27; quoted in Sinclair, 1978: 16.

and *bustees* in India, visually they are the most outstanding feature of Third World urbanization (figure 7.4). Squatters locate on any site that is outside the market for urban land. Abandoned plots, ravines, swamps and precipitous slopes are frequently colonized; settlements of houseboats or dwellings on stilts are established in harbours and creeks. The oldest of these squatter settlements are often adjacent to the city centre, as in Baghdad, but the most common location for squatters is the edge of the city, where land can be most easily expropriated. During the British colonial period in Nairobi, blacks were not allowed to settle within white residential areas and African peri-urban squatter settlements grew out of this proscription. In these ways the people who are economically and socially marginal become residentially and spatially marginal too. Initially, at least, squatter settlements are cut off from all types of public service, are prone to disease, and are usually located far from sources of formal employment.

Squatter settlements should be distinguished from shanty towns. Illegality of tenure is the hallmark of the squatter settlement, but shanties – huts or mean dwellings – are defined by their fabric. Some squatters occupy shanty towns, but shanties are more usually located on small, rented plots. In Mexico City rented shackyards make a limited contribution to urban housing, but in the Caribbean their residents outnumber squatters, in the strict sense of the term.

Squatting is more likely to be tolerated by the government than by private land-owners, though it is possible to find cities, such as Rio de Janeiro, where *favelas* are equally divided between public and private land. Squatter settlements are created in several ways. In Asia, the Middle East, the Caribbean and Africa, the process is usually gradual, essentially unorganized, and based on individual initiative. But in Mexico City, as in many other Latin-American cities, *colonias proletarias* are normally started either through illegal subdivisions, where estate agents market plots for which they lack title and fail to comply with planning requirements for service provision, or via illegal land captures organized to place thousands of households on the disputed property, literally overnight.

Squatter settlements were recorded for several Third World cities before the First World War, but only since 1945 have they become a significant aspect of urbanization. About half the entire population of 16 million in Mexico City is housed in illegal settlements that account for a similar proportion of the built-up area. By the 1970s more than 40 per cent of the inhabitants of Ankara, Lima and Casablanca were squatters. In contrast, squatters in West African towns rarely exceed a few per cent of the population, though dwellings erected without any control by public authorities nevertheless account for 30 per cent of the population of Dakar and Abidjan.

The spectacular growth of squatting in the last three decades is the result of the inability of the poor to pay rent or house-purchase prices, and a measure of the lack of public funds to rehouse slum dwellers or provide additional accommodation for new households. Despite government and international aid, long-term credit for housing is difficult to obtain and even white-collar workers find it hard to pay their rent and save enough money to purchase a plot outright – unless they

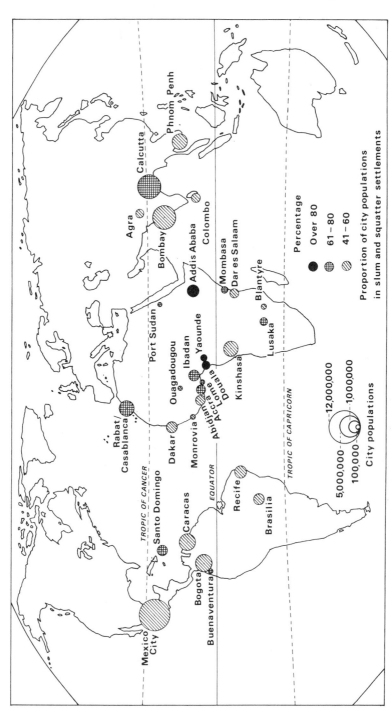

Figure 7.4 Proportion of slum and squatter populations in some Third World cities.

Source: Kidron and Segal, 1981: 50.

benefit from mortgage facilities provided by occupational organizations or unions. In some Third World countries a substantial proportion of the public money earmarked for housing is diverted into the banking system and used to finance private housing.

The necessity to provide some public housing is well understood by Third World government officials and planners, despite the lack of sufficient funds to finance anything more than token schemes. Projects are expensive and they are often strongly opposed by the middle and upper classes, especially if they involve the rehousing of squatters. Hong Kong has the largest and best-publicized, public-housing scheme – more than half the population live in government estates – but here the clearance of spontaneous settlements has been a response to the demand for sites for commercial and industrial purposes and minimal attention has been given to improvement of amenities among squatters. Oil-rich Venezuela provides an even more cautionary tale. The *superbloques* of Caracas, which were constructed by the dictator, Jimenez, in 1954–8, housed 159,000 people in eighty-five buildings and soon presented more problems of social control than the squatter settlements (*ranchos*) they partially replaced.

Politics and patronage are often deeply involved in the siting of housing schemes and the selection of occupants. Even the so-called beneficiaries encounter problems, as evidence from cities as diverse as Baghdad and Rio de Janeiro shows. Most schemes are located on the urban periphery: the journey to the city centre is long and costly; shops and other facilities in the immediate neighbourhood are often inadequate; and new residents are isolated from the various community supports, pastimes, and informal occupations that were once readily available in their old haunts. Despite modern design and layout, those accommodated in public housing remain as socially deprived as inhabitants of the inner sections of the city.

For most Third World governments public-housing schemes on a vast scale are too expensive to contemplate. Housing policy, with World Bank promptings, has therefore increasingly shifted to self-help schemes, using as a model the method of 'squatter autoconstruction'. What are the positive and negative aspects of squatter settlements and what implications do they have for self-help solutions to the housing problem?

Squatter settlements – problem or solution?

Squatter settlements were once stereotyped as collections of insanitary, flimsy dwellings, constructed by recent migrants who created a rural environment in the towns. Only by immediate eradication could Third World countries control this 'urban cancer'. Yet in the last decade squatting has been recognized as a positive feature of Third World urbanization. Squatter settlements are no longer viewed as rural slums recreated by new arrivals from the country, but residential areas that migrants of long standing, and many of the urban-born population, occupy as part of their adjustment to city life.

Overcrowded tenements or established squatter settlements usually act as initial footholds for recent migrants, and it is from them that the new waves of squatters come. While living in rented accommodation, migrants learn how to manipulate the housing system; but it is in the squatter settlements that they can gradually build their own houses by investing money that would otherwise be paid in rent. The move to peripheral squatter settlements from rented accommodation near the city centre frequently coincides with growing parental responsibilities; the availability of cheaper, spacious housing more than offsets the increased cost of the journey to work. As squatter settlements age, however, so their demographic composition and social role changes. The number of city born increases, and the squatter neighbourhoods themselves become reception areas for migrants who are joining friends or kin.

The largest squatter settlements are rarely single-class communities. On the contrary, they are well integrated with the employment structure of the city. In Lima, for example, almost 60 per cent of the labour force of the squatter settlements (*barriadas*) are artisans or labourers, 16 per cent domestic servants, 14 per cent street pedlars, shopkeepers or stallholders, and the remainder are white-collar workers or factory employees. This pattern is explained by the impoverished condition of the entire lower class, the magnitude of the housing shortage, and the low pay received even by white-collar workers. In the Caribbean, however, where squatting accommodates only a small percentage of the population, the occupants are uniformly lower class, impoverished, and drawn from the racially and ethnically most denigrated sections of the population.

Latin American squatter settlements have a well-documented history of dynamic change and improvement. The creation of a squatter settlement leads to the establishment of community organizations whose object is to defend the community and intercede for it with the government. Demands are made for recognition, title to land, water, sewerage, electricity and roads, and if these are successful requests may eventually include more sophisticated amenities – schools, clinics, community halls. Community and household improvement go hand-in-hand, and when title to land or some assurance of permanence is given, the original temporary dwellings are gradually replaced by more substantial home-made structures. This sequence of house and settlement development is often described as a trajectory, divided into incipient, consolidating and consolidated stages.

Successful squatting depends upon a positive government response. But government reactions to squatters' demands range from helpfulness to hostility. In Peru, some self-help settlements (*pueblos jovenes*) have been directed to specific locations where services are easy to install. Calcutta has encouraged *bustee* improvement (figure 7.5) and embarked upon massive site-and-service schemes to enable households to build on lots supplied with rudimentary amenities. Elsewhere in the Third World government attitudes have been less encouraging. Some presidential regimes in Mexico have acceded to squatter demands for security of tenure and sought to co-opt the local leadership; others have refused to

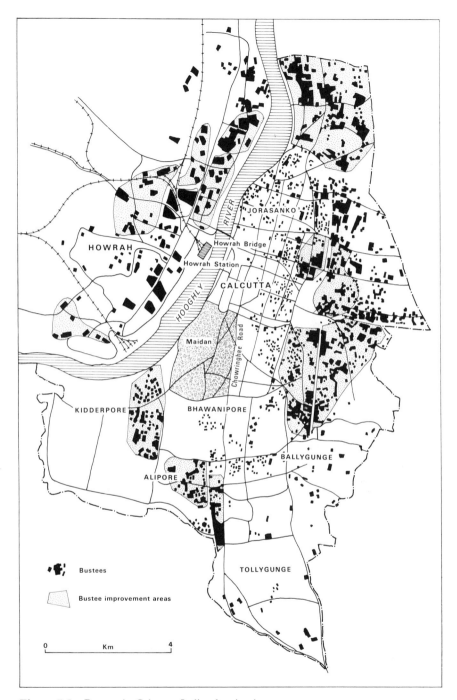

Figure 7.5 Bustees in Calcutta, India, showing improvement areas.
Source: Dwyer, 1975: 218.

recognize land grabs by squatters. In Jamaica, periodic eradication of insanitary squatter settlements punctuated Kingston's history of illegal settlement from the 1930s until the early 1970s, and bulldozing of shanty towns has been a common response in Africa.

However well disposed a government may be to encouraging the development trajectory of squatter settlements, micro-ecological and macro-economic circumstances may impede the process. The failure of shanty towns to improve over time is due to two different reasons, depending upon the tenurial category in which they fall. If they are based on rental, then that fact alone is usually sufficient to impede change and produce permanent shacks – as Jamaican experience illustrates. Squatter settlements that fail to develop are usually located on congested sites where hazards threaten or where redevelopment is impossible: in Jakarta, for example, 100,000 people squat on the city's pavements, as do countless millions in India's major cities. Of course, non-recognition and threats of eradication impose equal barriers to improvement, irrespective of ecology. But even where a government's attitude is benign and other circumstances are generally favourable to autoconstruction, the development trajectory may be cut short – as it almost certainly is in most Third World countries – by lack of economic development and the absence of household funds for investment. Recent evidence from Mexico City suggests that even when squatter settlements consolidate through autoconstruction, sometimes reaching a point where it is impossible to distinguish them from middle-class subdivisions, the original occupants have not been the ultimate beneficiaries. As squatter settlements consolidate, the cost of paying for a legal title, water and electricity installations, coupled to the provision of protection money for local bosses, squeezes out the poorest marginals who then have to move on to new land captures.

In addition to changes in residents, the Mexican development trajectory often involves tenurial change, in which squatting gives way to ownership and then to rental. Indeed, sub-letting is also present in the first stage of occupation, since speculators place families on plots and pay their outgoings as the settlement develops – only to remove them as the economic rent increases. Similar processes of crude capital accumulation threaten to undermine the development of site-and-service schemes. It is impossible to escape the conclusion that, in the economic circumstances of most Third World cities, only the humblest shack is viable for the poor, and even that dwelling is quite probably miniscule, lacking in furnishings and all basic services and tenurially insecure.

Social structure and the urban mosaic

Poverty and poor housing in Third World cities are closely related and – China and Cuba excepted – inherent in the social structure. In Latin America, the urban social stratification comprises a European or Europeanized élite, a small but growing middle class, and a mass of lower-class persons who are set apart from the bourgeoisie by an enormous social and economic gulf. In other Third World regions, notably the Middle East, the social structure is often more traditional and reflects non-class inequalities, such as those of race, religion, culture, tribe, language or ethnicity; and even if class distinctions are emerging they may remain subordinate to racial and cultural differences. But whatever the criteria of social differentiation, it is usual for them to be expressed in the urban mosaic. During the colonial period in West Africa, indigenous city dwellers were often segregated from the 'strangers' towns' which housed the migrants; since independence Africans who have succeeded to élite positions have taken over white housing areas and created an incipient class structure, which is reflected in the urban morphology.

In origin Third World cities and towns – both pre-colonial and colonial – are quintessentially pre-industrial. Gideon Sjoberg (1960) has described three main aspects of land use which, he argues, distinguish the pre-industrial city from Burgess's industrial model. These are: the pre-eminence of the central area over the periphery, particularly as portrayed in the distribution of social classes; certain small-scale spatial differences according to guild or family ties; and low levels of functional differentiation in other land-use patterns. A major aspect of the pre-industrial city is the absence of a central business district at the heart of the settlement; instead, religious and government buildings provide the focus. In contrast to the industrial city, so typical of the USA, homes of élite citizens cluster at the centre and disadvantaged members of the community fan out towards the periphery.

Sjoberg suggests these social patterns in pre-industrial cities may be explained by cultural values that define residence in the historic core as most prestigious. He also emphasizes that pre-industrial technology entailed foot and animal transport and placed a premium on face-to-face contact – or spatial proximity – for interpersonal communication. Many Third World cities, such as Ibadan and Peking, are pre-industrial in origin because they have pre-European foundations (see figure 7.2), while Caribbean and Latin American settlements at their inception incorporated the pre-industrial values and the systems of motive power which were available in Europe in the sixteenth, seventeenth and eighteenth centuries.

Indigenous settlements of the Muslim world whether planned or irregular, focus on the central mosque, citadel and bazaar (figure 7.6); cosmo-magical symbolism is expressed in the orientation of ceremonial cities in the pre-Colombian civilizations of Middle and South America and in pre-European Asia; European colonial settlements are usually laid out to conform to a simple grid pattern. Traditionally, the small, pre-industrial élite, whether in Guatemala City or Istanbul, lived in houses adjacent to the centre, while persons of low status were confined to the edge of the settlement. This declining social gradient from centre to periphery is still observable in many small Third World towns.

But large Third World cities, which have experienced rapid growth, have adopted modern technology since the mid-nineteenth century and now enjoy rapid communication by car and telephone, exemplify a partial reversal of the original, pre-industrial sequence (figure 7.7). Elites have left their old-fashioned homes as city-centre land values have rocketed, and now live in ostentatious modern properties that reveal more conspicuously their superior status and life-style. As in North America or Western Europe, the urban élite and middle class are suburban in location though often concentrated in a specific sector or wedge, and the pattern holds good for cities as far apart as Port-au-Prince, the capital of Haiti, and Calcutta. In general, the poor are concentrated in over-crowded compounds or tenements located near the city centre or in peripheral squatter settlements and government-housing schemes.

The establishment of multiple stores in the central business districts of Third World cities, the replacement of the old urban fabric by high-rise buildings, and

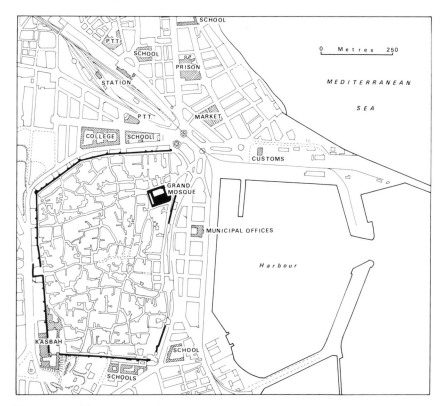

Figure 7.6   The urban morphology of Sousse, Tunisia.
The Arab core of the town, the medina, is surrounded by a wall, enclosing the mosque, the shopping area of the souks, a maze of narrow streets and alleys and secluded dwellings. Outside the walls the more regular and spacious layout of the modern commercial and residential areas was created by the French colonial administration after damage in the Second World War.

Source: Société Tunisienne de Topographie, Environs de Sousse, Flle 4, 1: 5000.

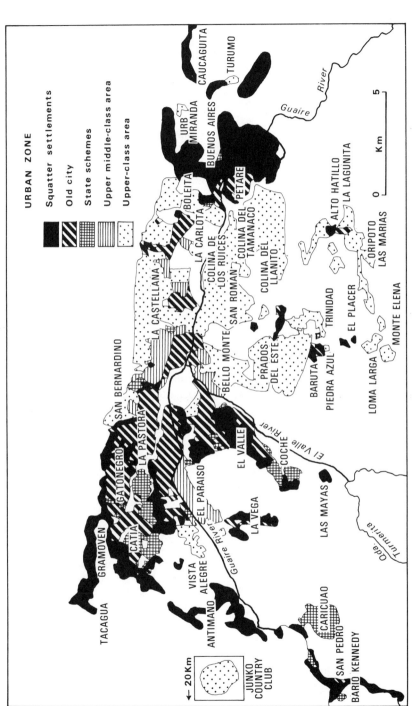

Figure 7.7 Housing and social class in Caracas, Venezuela.

Source: Franklin, 1979: 307.

the rapid growth of shopping precincts in the suburbs, are signs of the importation of the American style of life into Third World cities as diverse as Bangkok and Rio de Janeiro. But, in small towns, shops are often no more than lock-up sheds, and concrete construction and neon signs are appearing only slowly. There is, therefore, a pre-industrial to industrial continuum linking small traditional communities and large urban centres, which is reflected in fabric, economy and ecology.

However, the detailed residential morphology of each city depends upon the social structure of the country in which it is located, the proportions of different classes and races, and on topography. In Caracas the steep slopes which hem in the central business district are occupied by squatters, while the middle class form a buffer between the élite suburbs in the east and state-housing schemes in the old city (figure 7.7); in Port-au-Prince, Haiti, city-centre residence is associated with high population densities, low social status, black skin colour, and the practice of voodoo; in India caste distinctions give rise to residential segregation in which high-caste Brahmins and Kshattriyas take the prime locations.

Mexico City: a study of urban growth and marginality
Mexico City, laid out by the Spaniards over the ruins of Tenochtitlán, the capital of the Aztec empire, is now one of the largest and most rapidly growing settlements in the Third World. Since the beginning of this century its population has increased more than forty times and now approximates one-quarter of the nation's total. The census recorded 370,000 in Mexico City in 1900, 1 million in 1930, 5 million in 1960 and 8.5 million in 1970; estimates put its current population at about 16 million. Guadalajara, Mexico's second biggest city, lags way behind with barely 2 million inhabitants.

For many years Mexico City's annual growth rate has remained fairly constant at about 5 per cent, but each decade since the Second World War the contribution made by migration has fallen. During the 1970s provincial newcomers accounted for less than one-third of the addition to the population, the remainder being the result of natural increase – itself a consequence of the city's youthful age structure and the sharp decline in mortality, especially amongst children. Unless the demographic transition to low levels of fertility is rapidly achieved, Mexico City is likely to have over 30 million inhabitants at the end of the first decade of the twenty-first century.

Migration to Mexico City has declined in relative terms, but the absolute number of cityward movers continues to grow: net migration in the decade of the 1950s was 840,000 and rose to 1,800,000 in the 1960s. Three features characterize the migrants: they are young (mostly aged 15 to 45); the majority are women (1210 per 1000 males); and large numbers are drawn from states adjacent to the capital – Mexico, Puebla, Morelos, Hidalgo, Tlaxcala – or from impoverished regions in the southern states of Guerrero, Oaxaca and Chiapas. Most migrants, once established in homes and jobs through kin networks, remain in the capital yet retain close ties with their villages or towns of origin. Remittances are sent to support rural dependants, and organizations are created to stimulate and finance projects in the home regions.

Massive population concentration in Mexico City has generated spatial growth. As late as 1900 the capital still clustered around the Spanish-created plaza (*Zocalo*), which contained the country's principal administrative and ecclesiastical buildings, though there had already been some suburban expansion to the west

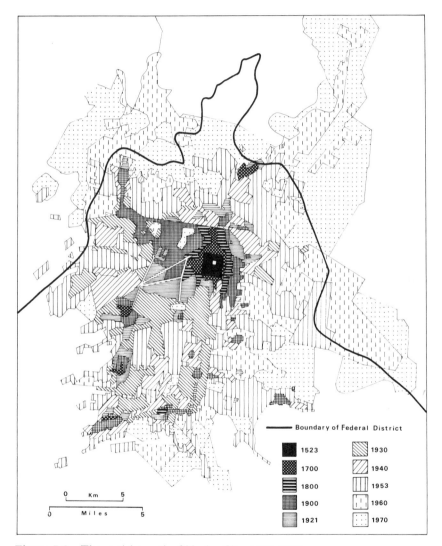

Boundary of Federal District

■ 1523	▨ 1930
▩ 1700	▨ 1940
☰ 1800	▥ 1953
▨ 1900	▦ 1960
▤ 1921	░ 1970

0   Km   5

0   Miles   5

Figure 7.8   The spatial growth of Mexico City, 1523–1970.

Source: Bataillon and Rivière d'Arc, 1973: 17.

and north in the direction of Guadalajara, and there were small satellite communities in the south, some of which had been occupied since colonial times
(figure 7.8). By the end of the Mexican Revolution in 1917, *colonias* had been
added to the east and south; developments in the 1920s took place essentially
to the south; and in the 1930s they concentrated in the west. Massive
encroachments in all directions were made into the surrounding countryside
after the Second World War. They were particularly large to the east of the
city, and caused settlement on the dry bed of Lake Texcoco to spill over the
Federal District boundary. By 1970 the district of Nazahualcoyotl recorded
more than 500,000 inhabitants; by the mid-1970s its population exceeded 1
million.

Official statistics suggest that less than one-third of Mexico City's population is
economically active. Industrial development in the capital was initially unusually
successful by Third World standards, and manufacturing accounts for 39 per cent
of jobs, followed by services (36.5 per cent), commerce (13.5 per cent) and transport (4 per cent). However, industrial growth in Mexico flagged during the 1970s,
and unemployment, underemployment, and marginality are immense and
increasing problems. Access to jobs in the coveted industrial sector has become
more and more selective and almost completely dependent on contacts – usually
through kin who will 'speak for' a job applicant – and sound credentials –
usually in the shape of a school-leaving certificate. In addition to those reckoned
to be in the formal and informal sectors of the labour force, there are over 100,000
minors who are employed in services, as bootblacks, petty salesmen, or as tip-
earning assistants in the supermarkets.

Income distribution in Mexico City is markedly skewed, so that the majority
receive less than the minimum wage. This pattern of purchasing power correlates
with the occupational and class structure of the city, has a direct bearing on the
quality of dwelling units and services, influences households' access to the housing market, and underpins the spatial structure of the city. A survey carried out by
the National Mortgage Bank in 1952 revealed that over one-third of Mexico
City's population lived in rented *tugurios* (slums), 10 per cent in *jacales* (shacks) in
rented yards, and 14 per cent in *colonias proletarias* (low-income neighbourhoods).
The remaining 42 per cent of the population was divided unequally between
decaying property near the city centre (28 per cent) and new housing (14 per cent)
of élite or middle-class status located near major routeways, especially those leading to the south.

During the last 30 years the low-income housing sector has been inflated to
accommodate the growth of the city's population: tenements have been built and
subdivided; enormous squatter settlements have been established through autoconstruction; and some government housing projects have been completed. By
the early 1970s 2 million people were living in *vecindades* (tenements) located in
dilapidated (often rent-controlled) colonial buildings, in overcrowded purpose-
built apartments, or in smaller suburban speculations.

Colonias proletarias fall into two categories, which together, in 1972, accounted

Plate 7.4 Tenement, Mexico.
A tenement or *vecinidad* in the centre of Mexico City.

for about 3.5 million inhabitants or 40 per cent of the capital's total. *Fracciona-mientos clandestinos* (illegal subdivisions) occur where the developer lacks legal title to the land or permission to sell it for housing, or more commonly where he lays out the lots but fails to provide the infrastructure that is required and thereby makes the project illegal. *Colonias paracaidistas* (parachutist settlements) are true squatter developments and are usually formed through invasion from *vecindades* or consolidating *colonias proletarias*.

The third major low-income housing system is that of the *ciudades perdidas* (lost cities) or shack yards. In 1972 they accounted for between 100,000 and 200,000 persons, and comprised concentrations of rough huts located on rented – usually privately owned – plots. A similar number lived in government-funded projects. However, the minimum income stipulated for entry to these schemes is beyond the earning capacity of one-third of the city's households, so the government has failed to eradicate *ciudades perdidas*, and has made no impression on popular housing demand as represented by the proliferation of *colonias paracaidistas*.

In view of the massive growth of Mexico City's population, it is to be expected that housing deprivation would be widespread. A quarter of all houses have only one room; 38 per cent lack a water supply piped into the house; 25 per cent have no sewerage; 43 per cent have no bath. These deficiencies persist despite the processes of legalization, service provision, fabric improvement, and auto-construction for which Mexico City has become justly famous. Moreover, they illustrate the persistent problems that characterize the *vecindades, ciudades perdidas* and those squatter settlements whose development trajectory has been cut short by government fiat or economic stagnation.

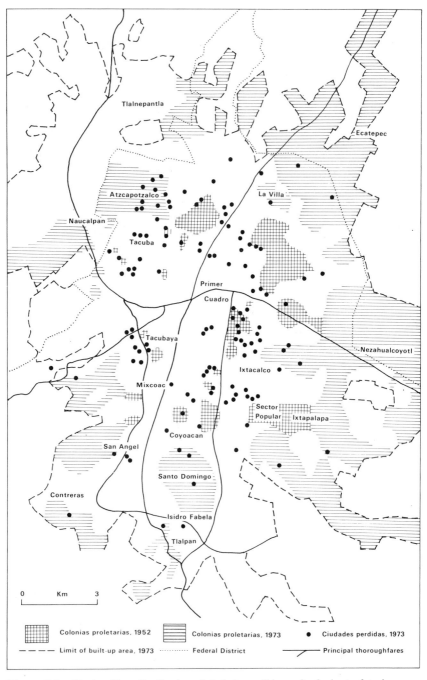

Figure 7.9 Mexico City: distribution of *ciudades perdidas* and *colonias proletarias*.
Source: Ward, 1976: 82.

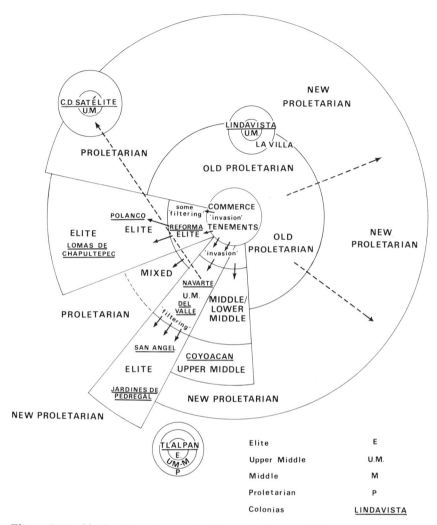

Figure 7.10 Mexico City: urban-ecological areas in the late 1970s.
Source: Ward, 1976: 50.

Mexico City's housing system crystallizes out into a number of clear-cut patterns (figure 7.9). *Colonias proletarias*, once concentrated in a horseshoe around the city centre, have been extended out to the city's periphery, in all directions. *Ciudades perdidas* are wrapped around the commercial centre of the capital where they occupy vacant lots and provide good access to service jobs. The remainder of the city is occupied by orthodox private housing and to a much lesser extent by schemes constructed by the state.

Processes of population growth, urban expansion, social deprivation and segregation have created a complex urban mosaic (figure 7.10). However, it is possible to discern some pattern to Mexico City's urban ecology and to decompose it into zones, sectors and nuclei that echo the various models of the industrial city developed, respectively, by Burgess, Hoyt and Harris and Ullman.

Inner and outer zones in the north and east are devoted to proletarian settlements. The middle class, in its various social fractions, concentrates – with status increasing towards the periphery – in the south-central wedge which follows Insurgentes Sur and incorporates the former independent colonial settlement of Coyoacan. Elite housing is confined to a western sector stretching via Polanco to the Lomas de Chapultepec and to an outer south-western sector incorporating San Angel and the Jardines de Pedregal. Finally, the outer *colonias*, Ciudad Satélite, Lindavista and Tlalpan, are set in vast expanses of *colonias proletarias*. Hence each of these three nuclei contains class stratifications organized in a pre-industrial fashion with a centralized élite or upper middle-class and a peripheral proletariat. As a generalization, the poor dominate the north and east; the south-west quadrant alone is unmistakably the preserve of the élite and middle class. However, the colonial palaces in the city centre and the peripheral poor illustrate the persistence of pre-industrial features.

Urban regions and planning

Cities are places as well as spaces. Third World cities articulate the economic system, and changes in economic conditions result in alterations to the urban hierarchy. Primacy, as we have seen, is indicative of urban imbalance: states in Africa and South America, for example, are dominated by coastal core regions surrounded by narrow belts of partially integrated territory.

Since the Second World War attempts have been made to establish poles of development in the interiors of countries in the Third World, and an excellent example is provided by Brasília, located in the state of Goiás in the interior of Brazil. Its function in the national planning strategy is to shift the political and psychological focus of the country away from the colonial centres on or near the coast and to create a real pioneer zone in Brazil's empty interior. Like the old, colonial towns, this new capital city has been imposed upon the landscape. Lucio Costa's layout resembles an aeroplane (figure 7.11); the scheme is based on modern planning principles that segregate pedestrians and vehicular traffic, and is greatly enhanced by Oscar Niemeyer's architecturally superb public buildings.

Civil servants were loath to leave Rio de Janeiro for the isolation of Brasília, yet the new city has gradually developed into a fully fledged capital. A substantial amount of road building has been completed around Brasília and has created a wave of rural colonization, much of it highly speculative. Within the new town a major planning task has been to harmonize housing, employment, shops, transport links and recreational facilities in combinations appropriate to the constantly changing needs of the rapidly growing city. But a conspicuous failure in the

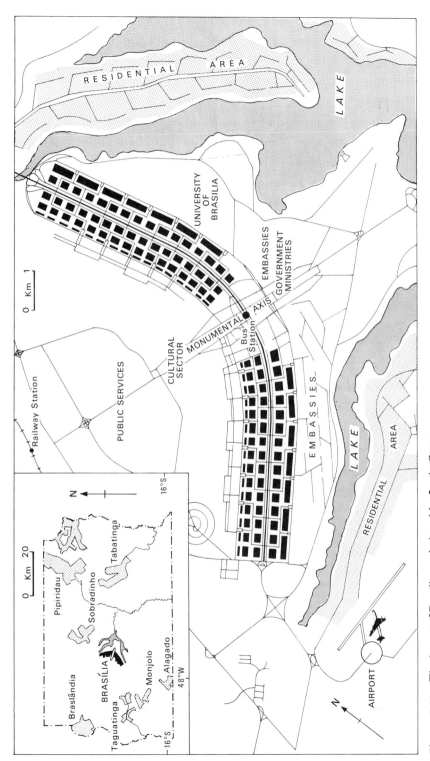

Figure 7.11 The layout of Brasília, as designed by Lucio Costa. The inset shows the unplanned, spontaneous settlements that have sprung up to house lower-income groups.

Plate 7.5 Brasília.
The National Congress building forms the monumental core of Brazil's planned capital city. The crowd is attending a concert to celebrate Independence Day.

project is the complete lack of working-class accommodation, and 60 per cent of the population of 1 million now lives in satellite communities situated outside 'the monumental city', where squatting and lack of water, light and sewage disposal are as problematical as in the old coastal capital of Rio de Janeiro.

Cuba and China, both socialist countries, provide an interesting contrast to the urban growth policy adopted by peripheral capitalist societies in Latin America, Africa and Asia, most of which have continuously reproduced marginality since the early 1960s. Migration to Cuban towns and cities is strictly controlled and forbidden without security of employment. Fidel Castro's revolutionary government has decentralized the economy and run down Havana, to the advantage of the provincial cities. *Pequeñas-ciudades* (small towns) have been established in the countryside to house landless labourers and deflect them from the capital. Government strategy is underpinned by central planning and by the emphasis placed on the sugar industry. But at least half the sugar crop is bought by the USSR and the socialist countries of Eastern Europe on terms highly favourable to Cuba, so it is unlikely that this model can be repeated elsewhere.

The Chinese, too, renounce urbanization and migration and base their economic development on regionally decentralized systems of peasant cultivation and rural industrialization. Big cities like Shanghai, though they persist, are rejected by the regime as hangovers from capitalism. Millions of people living in urban

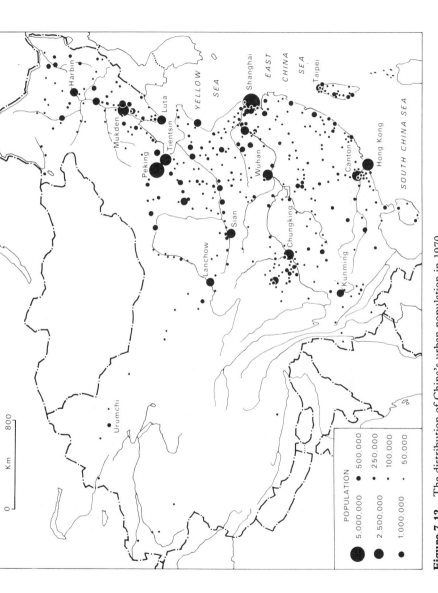

Figure 7.12 The distribution of China's urban population in 1970.

Source: Reprinted from Chen, *The Geographical Review*, 63 (1973), with the permission of the American Geographical Society.

slums and shanty towns (2 million in Shanghai alone) have been rehoused in vacated middle-class homes and in government-inspired schemes, or have been encouraged to renovate the fabric of their dwellings in response to government provision of services and subsidized materials. Admittedly urban growth has continued, and Shanghai now has a population of 10 million compared to 5 million in 1949. But it is no longer a city in the traditional sense because one-third of the active population is engaged in agriculture, and the increased area covered by the city includes a considerable number of communes that produce food for local consumption. Nevertheless, even China has a long way to go to solve its urban problems. Between 30 and 40 per cent of the country's industrial capacity is still concentrated in the eastern conurbations of Canton, Shanghai–Hangchow, Tiensin–Peking and Anchan–Fouchoun (figure 7.12).

Conclusion

Third World cities and towns confront problems that are more elementary than those experienced by settlements in the economically advanced countries. Yet some of the biggest Third World cities have literally the worst of both worlds. Mexico City, for example, is well on the way to becoming a squatter capital, yet with 2 million cars on its roads suffers from appalling smog and traffic jams. Many Third World cities combine pre-industrial and industrial morphologies and technologies, mansions and shanties, the richest and most impoverished people.

If urbanization has occurred without adequate industrial employment, it has also been achieved without breakdown. As the cities have expanded, employment has been created by informal means, and self-help housing has been married to self-employment to create do-it-yourself urbanization. Governments are gradually recognizing that it is impossible to deploy sufficient funds to build public housing for the urban poor, except in industrialized city colonies like Hong Kong. Most countries have attempted to eradicate squatting at one time or another only to find their efforts met by violent community resistance. Eradication may be worthwhile if the number of squatters is small and alternative accommodation can be supplied. But to make squatters or rent-yard dwellers homeless by destroying their communities only shifts the problem elsewhere.

Nevertheless, governments have considerable power to influence the urban situation. Encouragement of the positive aspects of squatting by the active planning of site and service schemes could become part of an urban strategy for the Third World, provided the loss of indigent settlers from improving communities can be prevented. Cuba exemplifies the wide-ranging impact that a government can have on the urban system. In addition to shifting the focus of economic growth down the urban hierarchy, the communist government eradicated unemployment in the 1960s by expanding the bureaucracy, socializing the labour force (and expatriating dissidents). Street sellers were branded petty capitalists and banned. Moreover, in Havana, strict rent controls have been imposed throughout the city and élite housing vacated by political refugees in the Vedado district has been taken over by the government and either allocated to poor families or converted into schools and dormitories. But at the end of the 1970s the Cuban sugar and tobacco harvests failed, and unemployment once more became a pressing problem. Cuba's achievements look frail, and they are probably unrepeatable in the larger, less-sophisticated and more capitalistic countries of the Third World.

Marginality is the hallmark of Third World urbanization, but its interpretation depends upon the model of development that is being used. Is it a temporary phenomenon, transitional to the absorption of surplus labour by the formal sector? Or is the informal sector a permanent feature of dependent development, the urban manifestation of the Third World's persistent poverty? Evidence suggests that marginality – informal employment and precarious squatting and renting – is growing not declining, that it is functionally related to dependent capitalism, and helps to sustain it by keeping wages low.

8 INTERNAL INTERACTION

Interaction and spatial structure

Rural and urban areas and agricultural and industrial sectors of the economy in countries of the Third World have been examined in their own right in the preceding chapters. However, they are not independent of each other, but interact as part of a spatially and economically cohesive whole. Incomes from crop production stimulate rural demand for locally made industrial and consumer products, which in turn have an effect on the urban economy by creating jobs. Expansion of cotton-textile production, for example, will mean not only more jobs in urban areas and increased rural/urban migration, but may also require an increase in cotton production by local farmers. Separately, town and country, industry and agriculture, comprise the essential building blocks of the geography of any country, but together they substantiate the view, outlined, in chapter 1, that the elements of spatial and economic structure are linked in the development process 'through a network of urban regions', arranged hierarchically to promote exchange or interaction as part of that process of development or underdevelopment. In this chapter we consider why and how a distinctive pattern of interaction has developed in Third World countries, and with what effect on the movement of goods, services, and people.

The essential features of any spatial structure are nodes, linkages and hierarchies. *Nodes* are points of exchange and control, and emerge at points of accessibility through *linkages* (roads, telecommunications, etc.) with their hinterlands. These nodes are not only related to each other through other linkages, but also tend to be arranged in *hierarchies*, levels of the hierarchies themselves being dependent on linkages with levels above and below. The most obvious type of interaction occurs through the linkages of the transportation system, by road, rail, air, river, lake and open sea, the relative importance of each of these being a matter of terrain, level of wealth and technology, and the size of the country. Movement by air, for example, could be expected to be more important (but still absolutely of minor importance) in a large and relatively prosperous country such as Brazil, or where surface transport is very difficult and costly as in Ethiopia, than in a poor, densely populated and relatively flat country such as India or Egypt. Island countries, such as Indonesia or Papua New Guinea, have inevitably developed networks of water transport. Other networks of movement are not related to transport in a formal sense, but to modes of communication such as electricity transmission grids or telecommunications networks. Even less formally they comprise person-to-person or village-to-village communication of information and ideas. Interaction between places at a similar level of the urban hierarchy involves a lot of short-distance, local exchange between local markets. Long-distance and interregional exchanges are mostly between different levels of the urban hierarchy, either moving upwards through it from rural areas to the capital, as in the case of export crops, or moving downwards, as in the case of imported pesticides (manufactured overseas or in the capital) for the use of farmers.

The mere existence of linkages and interaction in the Third World provides nothing that is unexpected or distinctive, for interaction is a universal spatial process. Certainly, in the Third World there are fewer roads or railways per head or per unit of area than in more-developed countries; there are fewer goods to be moved when a high proportion of them are consumed on the farms where they are produced; low-income levels generate a low overall demand for manufactured goods; newspapers are less widely read. The limited development of interaction is both a cause and an effect of low levels of economic activity and technology, and in all Third World countries the expansion and intensification of existing networks and linkages is an integral component of the overall development effort. An expanding system of transport and communications has been viewed both as a necessary condition for, and as a symptom of, economic advance and national integration.

However it is the nature of the interaction, its growth and its effect on the overall regional pattern of economic activity that merits particular attention. Patterns of interaction reflect the wider context of rural/urban and interregional relationships, and their distinctiveness in the Third World is part of the wider process of integration of the country as a whole, and of each part of it into the international and national systems of unequal exchange.

The growth of national transport networks

Most movement in subsistence societies was over short distances and on foot, but the availability of horses or camels in some areas gave some peoples a capability for movement denied to others. In tropical Africa, for example, there were no pack-animals and long-distance trading links were much more restricted than they were in the area to the north of the savanna belt, across the Sahara Desert to the Mediterranean, where horses and camels were used. Market places were everywhere the focus of local exchange, and in many areas they were linked to wider trading networks carrying long-distance trade, particularly in essential goods such as salt or iron, or in luxuries such as gold, spices or cloth. Many of the ancient states were essentially trading empires with an elaborate network of routes over land (for example, Songhai in interior West Africa, in what is now Mali, which was at its height in the fourteenth century) and sea (Sri Vijaya, for example, trading from the North-East Indian Ocean east to the China Sea in the sixth to the ninth centuries).

Ancient route networks were undermined by the new trading patterns associated with European expansion. Penetration was from the sea, and the colonial presence was first felt at seaports. Established ports and traditional routes inland by foot and animal transport were used initially, but once colonial control was established and new types of economic activity began to be introduced, the new technologies of rail (in the later nineteenth century) then road (in the twentieth century) transport developed. A network and hierarchy of settlement then developed round them.

The evolution of this superimposed network is described in the 'ideal–typical' sequence model of Taaffe, Morrill and Gould (1963) (figure 8.1a, b and c). This model considers the growth of transport routes in a colonial setting, from their origins in the ports of entry through their expansion into a national route network. In the earliest period transport is mainly in the coastal area with very limited communication inland (figure 8.1a). New routes are built inland, but only from one or two of the original ports and, as a result, these ports become larger at the expense of those with no new links to the interior as the growing trade is concentrated at a few trans-shipment points. The links inland are to areas of economic or strategic importance, whether pre-existent or of potential value for mineral, cash-crop or plantation development. These areas of early attraction then develop as major nodes for further expansion of transport routes, and as the basis for the newly emerging urban hierarchy (figure 8.1b). A more intensive pattern of feeder routes is then built, especially into areas of emerging export potential, eventually linking separate coast/interior routes into an integrated national network with increasing differentiation of settlement size and traffic volume to emphasize the main channels of import and export (figure 8.1c).

This has been an important model in the geographical study of the Third World, and it is based on the assumptions of those, like Rostow, who see development proceeding through stages of increasing incorporation into the world economy. This incorporation proceeds through the extension of transportation networks until the whole, previously undeveloped, area becomes part of the national and international system. The sequence is 'ideal' in the sense that it is consistent with the history and goals of colonial development. It assumes that the network is created primarily for the purpose of external trade, to facilitate the establishment, expansion and collection of exports of agricultural and mineral primary produce, and the import and distribution of manufactures, as well as for strategic and military control. It therefore assumes that the area is a *tabula rasa* – an area with little or no economic structure of its own on which the new economic and political order may be successfully built. The sequence is 'typical' in the sense that its essential structure can be traced historically in most countries of the Third World. Taaffe, Morrill and Gould used Ghana and Nigeria to develop and exemplify the sequence, but it can be identified in almost every

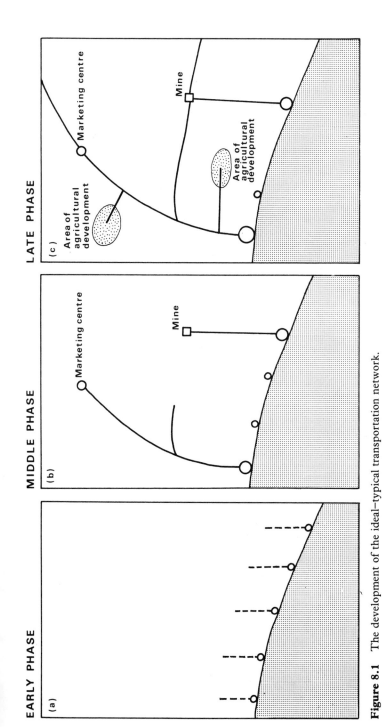

Figure 8.1 The development of the ideal–typical transportation network.

Source: After Taaffe, Morrill and Gould, 1963.

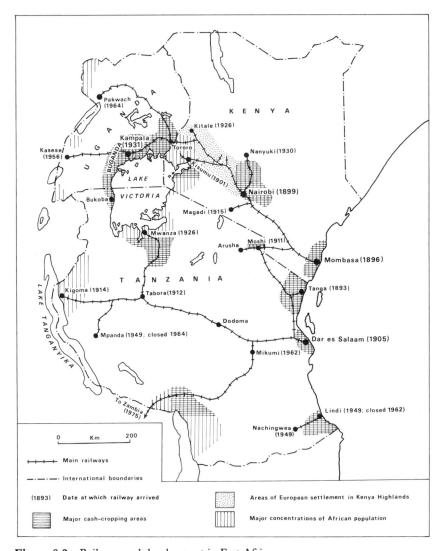

Figure 8.2 Railways and development in East Africa.

country of the Third World. In Africa, in particular, the radial pattern of railways emphasizes their close links with seaports and, by implication, with external trade (figure 8.2).

Railways in East Africa
In colonial East Africa, railways were built inland from four ports, Mombasa in Kenya (1896), and Tanga (1893), Dar es Salaam (1905) and Lindi (1949) in

Tanzania, each to link the coast with specific inland destinations: the already relatively well-developed and economically attractive southern Uganda and the Lake Victoria region to Mombasa; Kilimanjaro and the Usambara Mountains to Tanga; strategically important Lake Tanganyika to Dar es Salaam in the period of mounting political rivalry between Britain and Germany before the First World War; the ill-fated Groundnut Scheme around Nachingwea to Lindi after the Second World War. Some of the areas through which the railways passed quickly developed their own economic base, generated in part by the presence of the railway: notably the Highlands of Kenya which began to be settled for European farming along the Uganda Railway from the first decade of the twentieth century. Branch lines were built to serve areas of export production in Kenya or, as in Western Uganda, to serve the copper deposits of the Ruwenzori Mountains. The Central Tanzania line was extended in 1949 to the lead deposits of Mpanda. Lines were not, as a rule, built into areas of African settlement and subsistence farming unless there was a potential cash crop to generate traffic (such as the northern Uganda extension in the 1960s associated with the expansion of cotton production). Eventually the separate rail lines were linked by transverse routes, but these have never achieved the importance of the original axes. Even in the post-independence period the role of the railway for external trade has been confirmed by the building of the Tan-Zam railway from Dar es Salaam to landlocked Zambia. This enabled the export of copper, Zambia's main economic support, and the import of oil and other essentials for the mining economy, following the closure of Zambia's traditional routes through Rhodesia (now Zimbabwe) to Beira in Mozambique and to South Africa in 1965 during the period of political disruptions over the illegal independence of Rhodesia.

Within the last few decades rail has given way to road transport for long-distance interaction and export routes in many countries. The railways that were built remain important, but major highways are now being constructed to run parallel with them, and confirm the networks and hierarchies established in the earlier period – though they may considerably extend them into previously unserved areas, notably in the development of Amazonia in Brazil. As with railways, highways provide fast interregional links that are well suited to the movement of major products, but have relatively little direct local economic impact. Despite efforts to restructure the inherited colonial transportation network and associated urban hierarchy, as in the development of new non-coastal capitals such as Brasília in Brazil and Dodoma in Tanzania, national transportation networks continue to reflect the dependent exchange and productive relationships established at an earlier period. They may be far from ideal, operating as the means of creating and exacerbating internal and external inequalities.

Local transport

Alongside fundamental changes in the scale of interregional transportation linkages, there has been considerable continuity in local patterns of transport. Local exchange in the subsistence or non-commercial sector is dependent on movement by foot, by boat, by animal, or bicycle. The means of movement may have changed with increasing mechanization and the introduction of lorries or vans, but spatial patterns may continue to follow long-established links at the lowest level of the urban hierarchy. There is often, therefore, a functional relationship between local and national interactions, though they are not necessarily dependent on each other.

Plate 8.1   Forms of transportation, Burundi.
The old and the new in transportation technology crossing the Kagera River, Burundi.

The quality of local roads can vary from a bush track, suitable only for foot traffic, to all-weather roads for heavy vehicles. However, many areas of the Third World are well beyond reach of a motorable track, even seasonally. Not only is there a lack of funds for road building, but also in many areas of mountainous or swamp terrain, or of highly seasonal rainfall, the physical difficulties of building and maintaining roads are enormous. Alternatives may be available – notably rivers – but for many communities lack of access to adequate transport does impose severe limits on the possibility of producing goods for other than a very local market. Physical and economic isolation are thus closely related. Efforts are made, sometimes by government but often by the isolated communities themselves using communal labour, to build links to allow access to larger commercial markets, with acceptable and competitive prices, without the risk of goods' excessive deterioration (in the case of fresh fruit and vegetables) or complete loss. The opening up of sparsely settled but potentially productive areas has been hampered by the absence of local 'feeder' roads from the interregional highways, but major programmes have been launched to improve accessibility to and from such areas. The introduction of new cash crops has often been associated with the development of an adequate network of feeder roads to give farmers access to collecting or processing centres. Out-grower schemes for sugar-cane in Western Kenya, for example, have involved considerable investment in roads within 13 km of central sugar mills, so that farmers will, for the first time, have effective access to a processing plant and through it to the national market, and to advice and other benefits such as credit facilities.

But improvements in local mobility may also bring disadvantages. Just as goods and people can more easily move in or out to benefit rural communities, they can also do so to their disadvantage. Goods produced more cheaply elsewhere, even in another country, can be more competitive in the local market, and can undermine the traditional local production of such groups as potters, weavers, tinsmiths or iron-workers. Imported foodstuffs may equally undermine the traditional balance of agricultural activity. Roads may also facilitate considerable out-migration to the overall detriment of the local community. But, although the development of local roads has undoubtedly brought some unwelcome effects, the desire both within and beyond local communities to improve local transport suggests that the advantages considerably outweigh the disadvantages as the local community becomes more fully integrated into the national system.

Movement of goods

As levels of economic activity and income rise, an increasing proportion of agricultural produce leaves the farm in exchange for a rising volume of non-agricultural products. This exchange is at the heart of the development sequence implied by the Taaffe, Morrill and Gould model. At a national level exchange focuses on the chief port as the final collection point for exports and the initial entry point of imports. Rural products are brought to it through the urban hierarchy via a series of collection centres and, where appropriate, processing points; imports are distributed from it by that same hierarchy. The main, sometimes the only, economic activity in many smaller centres is collection and distribution, as would be the case in any market town in any country of the world. In most countries commodity flows are now a matter of internal rather than external movement of produce, and the larger and more economically complex the country, the more important internal trade must be. In a large country, like India or China, there are major flows of interregional trade that developed because of ecological differences between one part of the country and another, or as a result of the location of manufacturing industries in some areas but not in others.

The main flows of produce from rural to urban areas supply the urban food markets. With rapid population growth and rising incomes, the urban demand for food has risen rapidly. Some of that demand is met by food imports, and in some countries, such as Ghana and Nigeria, the level of import of basic commodities like rice and flour, has reached economically damaging levels. Internally, the sources of the urban food supply follow a familiar pattern anticipated by Von Thünen's model of intensity of land use, with more produce coming from the area immediately surrounding a focal settlement and declining in proportion with distance. Larger cities tend to have larger food hinterlands and capital cities are supplied from most parts of the country. In return some goods manufactured in the towns are taken out by the producers themselves or by middlemen to provide the small but expanding range of purchases from rural incomes, principal of which are kerosene for fuel, some food products, plastic utensils and clothing. The collection and distribution networks tend to be organized by small entrepreneurs each with a lorry or truck and operating as a general haulier (table 8.1).

Table 8.1   Traffic in foodstuffs to Brazzaville by product and method of transport, 1967.

Product	Rail		Road		River		Total	
	tonnes	%	tonnes	%	tonnes	%	tonnes	%
Yams	9,763	18.2	43,735	81.7	2	0.1	53,500	100
Fresh fish	2,437	62.9	—		1,438	37.1	3,875	100
Dried fish	1,659	73.7	3	0.2	588	26.1	2,250	100
Meat	16	100.0	—		—		16	100
Live animals	373	41.1	?		535	58.9	908	100
Rice	1,377	68.9	586	29.3	37	1.8	2,000	100
Groundnuts	82	5.5	56	3.7	1,362	90.8	1,500	100
Palm oil	101	7.3	148	10.8	1,126	81.9	1,375	100
Plantain bananas	1,406	93.7	94	6.3	—		1,500	100
Other fruits	109	7.3	1,391	92.7	—		1,500	100
Total	17,323	25.3	46,013	67.3	5,088	7.4	68,424	100

Source: Auger, 1972: 279.

Most local trade continues to be channelled through rural marketing systems, which can be very elaborate, and based on movement of traders between markets in regular cycles of varying length. The major Sunday market near a church depending on the sales and purchases of the congregation is a widespread feature in Latin America, and in West Africa there are particularly complex indigenous structures of local and long-distance marketing. Almost everywhere, however, there are daily markets with small hinterlands exchanging a small range of products. These are the most common, but least noticed means of exchange of goods.

Provision of economic and social services

The transportation system is also the means through which government and other agencies can provide many of the services that are thought to be necessary for the running of any modern state. These services are both economic, including power supply, agricultural advice, and telecommunications (telegram, telephone); and social, including health care, water supply, education, and media services (radio, television, newspapers). Ideally, each of these services is made available as widely as possible to the population, but in the conditions of scarcity of financial resources and qualified personnel that are all too familiar in the Third World, the services are normally not as widely available as governments and the population might wish. The distribution of service points such as schools, clinics and cattle dips, is highly uneven, and closely follows the spatial priorities implied by the urban hierarchy.

In many countries, and particularly in Africa and India, the most widely available directly economic service provided by government is the supply of information and advice to farmers. The nature and quality of the service will vary according to the historical, economic and cultural needs of any country, but most services are centrally controlled and hierarchically organized through a central agency that extends outwards and downwards through the urban system to provide a chain of communication between the centre and the farmer. In practice the benefits of such a service are felt disproportionately in areas near towns or in areas of already higher productivity, and by farmers who are already better off, and its impact is strongly related to the farmer's access to the transportation network.

Christallerian central place theory has been the basis of an Indian experiment to introduce services appropriate to the rank size of particular growth centres. So far, success of such mechanistic attempts to create an effective but artificial hierarchy has been limited even in socialist countries and may only be employed where population densities are high enough to sustain them. Similar plans to introduce growth centres to rural Zambia for example, where population densities rarely exceed five or six persons per square mile, have not succeeded, despite more than 30 years of colonial and post-colonial planning.

The supply of electricity is one of the most directly important of the higher economic services that can be provided, whether by government or by private generating companies. Power is distributed through its own communications network: the electricity grid. The principal flows in the grid are to the capital/primate cities, which have the heaviest demands, and subsequently to the smaller consuming centres, such that the pattern of the grid and of flows within it closely follows the national urban and industrial hierarchy. In Latin America, for example, much of the capacity remains close to the capital cities; it has been calculated that in the 1960s about 90 per cent of generating capacity was in only forty-one centres, particularly round Buenos Aires, São Paulo, Rio de Janeiro and Mexico City. Supplies may also extend quite considerably into some rural areas, particularly to the richer agricultural districts surrounding the major urban centres.

Electric power in Minas Gerais, Brazil
In 1950, the state of Minas Gerais in Brazil was estimated to have one-third of the country's hydro-electric power potential, but this resource was little exploited. Existing capacity was mainly in the hands of small private companies, which had

concessions to supply individual settlements, with small power stations and few transmission lines. There were 359 such companies, with over 400 power stations and a total installed capacity of 206 MW. This small and unreliable power supply was a discouragement to the industrialization programme which the state government was trying to foster, and the government therefore set up its own power company, Centrais Elétricas de Minas Gerais (CEMIG) in 1952 to generate and distribute electricity. It was recognized that it was impossible to create immediately a single-grid system to serve the whole state, so a number of regional systems supplied by moderate-size power stations, which could be interlinked at a later date, were developed. The main concentration of early growth was on the state capital, Belo Horizonte, which was regarded as the core area for any development programme, with a substantial population, established industrial structure and important local mineral resources. By 1957 CEMIG's dams had a capacity of over 100 MW. The power net that developed shows the concentration on Belo Horizonte, and the small regional nets (figure 8.3).

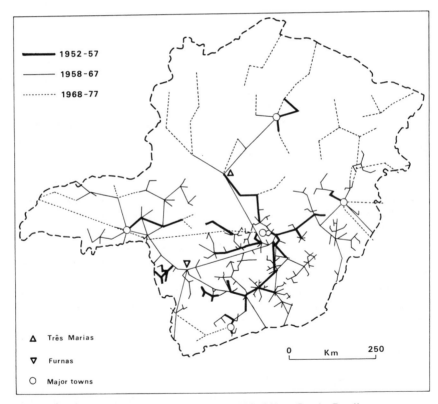

Figure 8.3   The evolution of the electricity grid in Minas Gerais, Brazil.
Source of data: CEMIG, 1952–77.

Over the next decade the system was expanded, and a number of larger dams, including those at Três Marias (390 MW) and Furnas (912 MW) were developed. The distribution system grew to link up the regional system and spread its tentacles into the more distant parts of the state. At the same time the local distribution system in the centre and south of the state became considerably denser. By 1967 installed capacity was over 520 MW. A federal power company, Eletrobras, had been established in 1961, and had begun to foster power production and distribution on a national scale. In 1967 the power grid linking the power supplies of south-east Brazil was completed, and with the development of a number of large power stations on the Rio Grande on its western border, Minas Gerais's power production and distribution became part of a regional network. The growth of the grid between 1967–77 shows both its extension into the poorer and less-developed north-west and north-east of the state, and the development of the inter-state grid. Provision of electricity from federally controlled power stations means that CEMIG, with an installed capacity of 1515 MW, now generates about one-fifth of the power consumed in Minas Gerais. The company, however, is responsible for the distribution of 90 per cent of the electricity consumed, and its transmission lines have grown from 1300 km in 1957 to over 12,000 km in 1977. In 1962 CEMIG created a subsidiary to supply electricity to rural consumers, and between 1962–77 the rural distribution net grew from 370 km to over 22,000 km.

Access to electricity is largely a function of ease of access to the wider network of communications. In order to provide electricity many Third World countries have begun to exploit major hydro-electric dam sites, with large generating capacity deriving from favourable physical conditions: for example, Cabora Bassa in Mozambique, Akosombo in Ghana, Aswan in Egypt.

Social services, in particular health care and education, existed in their traditional forms in all societies in the Third World. Now, they are provided in westernized institutions, in medical facilities and schools, each following the models provided by richer countries, and introduced in a fairly unsystematic way, often by unofficial agencies, notably Christian missions in Latin America and Africa. Here too there is a hierarchical structure of provision: medical facilities range from the large hospital with sophisticated medical technology to the small, rural one-room dispensary; for education the range is from university to the rural primary school. Inevitably, these facilities have been unevenly distributed with a very strong bias towards urban rather than rural provision, and to the richer districts rather than to the poorer ones. The pattern of service provision further confirms the overall pattern of internal disparities within each country of the Third World – high levels of health provision and school enrolments can be found in the urban and most economically productive districts. The areas with low levels of provision tend to be those further from the core area of the state and from areas of early colonial impact or advanced economic activity, or have populations that are politically, economically or socially apart from the rest of the state.

Social provision in Papua New Guinea

Papua New Guinea provides an example of a country of extreme economic and cultural diversity, and distinctly uneven levels of social provision (figure 8.4). The patterns of provincial levels of primary-school enrolment and the number of doctors per head of population, as an index of the availability of medical services, are similar to and confirm interprovincial imbalances in per-capita incomes. Higher levels of provision are evident in the outer island provinces, which are generally richer and have had longer and more intensive exposure to the outside world (largely through a 100 years of mission activity), and in Port Moresby, the capital. The provinces of the economically weak and physically (relatively) inaccessible highlands of the mainland have significantly lower levels of provision. These inequalities have remained in recent years despite strenuous efforts by the government, particularly since independence in 1974, to reduce interprovincial inequalities. There has been some success in narrowing the gap in

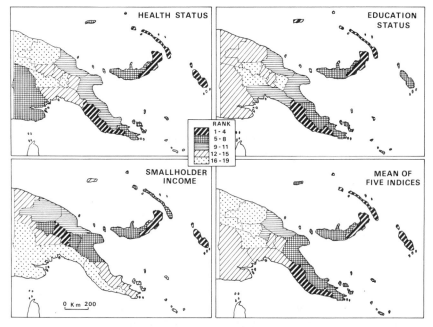

Figure 8.4 Papua New Guinea: provincial variation in development indices.
The maps are based on rankings of health status (measured by rural life expectancy, rural infant mortality and child malnutrition), education (adult literacy, proportion of 7-year-olds in first year of primary school and of 13-year-olds in first year of secondary school) and smallholder income (from export crops). These three rankings are combined with rankings for land transport and civil-service employment to give a composite mean index of development.

Source of data: Berry and Jackson, 1981.

social provision by allocating funds for schools and hospitals differentially to the poorer regions, but the government has found that it is less easy to induce any reduction in economic inequalities.

The similarities in the pattern and organization of provision of economic and social services suggest that they face similar problems in their attempts to achieve the goal of equality of access. The cost of providing for universal access is high, and resources are limited, so priorities in allocation need to be ordered. Since economic criteria generally dictate the ordering of priorities, services have been provided disproportionately in those areas where direct cost of provision is lowest; in urban and densely populated rural areas, where costs of transport are lowest; and where large facilities with considerable economies of scale can be provided. These are areas of highest total and per-capita demand, for they are the richest areas, but they are not necessarily the areas of greatest need.

Recent policies in many countries of the Third World, motivated by political criteria of equality of opportunity and access, have sought to spread services and economic infrastructures more evenly to permit better access to services in the remoter areas. Additional facilities have been allocated on the basis of criteria other than economic demand, often to achieve a more overtly equitable distribution. However, the economic basis of service provision has not been and cannot be ignored; so policies must seek to restructure the type of provision, to promote basic low-cost facilities rather than high-cost and technically sophisticated ones. Major examples of this trend are the shift to the development of rural health posts in Tanzania, and polyclinics in Cuba, rather than urban-based hospitals – part of overall national polices to promoting rural self-sufficiency. These further reduce rural/urban disparities and provide access to health care for more people, rather than increasing the quality of care for those already within reasonable access to a hospital.

Internal migration

The range of population movements in the Third World was discussed in chapter 3, emphasizing the importance of distinguishing between essentially short-term and repetitive movements (circulation) and permanent changes of residence (migrations) that result in changes in the overall distribution of population in the long term. While circulation occurs in all countries and is not necessarily directly related to the wider patterns of interaction and exchange that have been discussed above, migration has a much more obviously structured pattern, which resembles that of the movement of goods and services at both local and national levels.

The principal, but by no means only, motivation for migration is the expectation of economic benefit. Where there is rapid economic change with the introduction of new crops, industries and technologies for rural and urban production, it is likely that the geographical distribution of economic opportunities will change. Some areas decline and others expand. Changing population distribution is an expected and normal response to economic change and itself contributes to that change.

People will be attracted to newly developed or expanding areas; conversely, stagnating or declining areas will result in out-migration from them, either spontaneously or under environmental or economic pressure. The 'pull' of some areas and the 'push' from others creates an overall pattern of migration. The 'push' is generally from poor rural areas, and the 'pull' is to urban and rural areas with expanding opportunities. The scale and intensity of the movement will normally be influenced by the size of the differences in income and opportunity between the source and destination areas – the larger the differential, the greater the volume of movement.

The principal migrations are both rural/rural and rural/urban. In the rural sector they mostly comprise migrations from overcrowded areas to newly developed land, often as part of planned rural development. Such migrations have been widely encouraged to spread population and development into relatively empty areas, raising their productivity and the income of the settlers in them. Among the largest movements of this type are the so-called 'transmigrations' that have been a major feature of Indonesian development strategies since the mid 1950s, and continue into the 1980s, involving the migration and resettlement of several million people from the overcrowded central island of Java to the relatively empty outer islands, notably Sumatra. The Third Indonesian Five Year Plan, 1979–84, envisages the transmigration of 500,000 families, approximately $2\frac{1}{2}$ million people. Similar interregional migrations, but with much smaller numbers, have taken place, for example, in Peninsular Malaysia to promote the development of the eastern side of the peninsula with in-migrants from the relatively over-populated western side; and, on a much larger scale, in Brazil to develop parts of the Amazon Basin with migrants from areas of severe poverty and environmental difficulty in north-east Brazil. Other large-scale, long-distance rural/rural migrations have been associated with irrigation projects, bringing water and therefore greatly increased economic opportunity to previously dry areas. These include the Gezira Scheme in Sudan, developed in stages since the 1920s with water from the Blue Nile, and the Lower Indus Project in Pakistan.

More localized rural migrations have been part of planned settlement restructuring patterns, as in the villagization programme in Tanzania. This was designed to concentrate the population in nucleated villages, each with 250–1500 families, in a country where the traditional settlement pattern is that of dispersed homesteads and low overall population densities. The villagization policy was implemented in the mid 1970s as an essential part of a programme to improve rural productivity through increased communal effort and, as indicated previously in the context of rural health facilities, to facilitate the delivery of economic and social services, for each village is ideally on or near a road.

Rural/urban migration is more obviously significant in the changing production structure of any country, even though numerically it may be less than migration between rural areas. Massive differences in income between rural and urban areas generate temporary or permanent migrations to towns, even where there is open and considerable urban unemployment, for a precarious living in the urban informal sector may often be preferable to low incomes and few opportunities for improvement in rural areas. Movements out of rural areas tend to occur in a stepwise manner, first to the nearest town and subsequently to higher levels of the urban hierarchy. Most migrants to a capital or large city come from lower-order towns rather than directly from rural areas. The strength of the urban hierarchy as a channel in the migration pattern is very marked, and flows are much more markedly in one direction – upwards to larger centres – than is the case of the movement of goods and services. There is some reverse movement of individuals at all levels, and circulation between town and country remains important, especially in tropical Africa and throughout the Pacific Islands. But the overwhelming trend is cityward in particular to the larger and primate cities.

Migration in Uganda
Such patterns are indicated by the experience of Uganda, which achieved considerable international notoriety during the period of the military dictatorship and economic collapse of Idi Amin, 1971–9, but the period before that, as revealed by data collected in the national census of 1969, illustrated many of the principal characteristics of internal migration in countries of the Third World. Uganda is a compact state with about 10 million inhabitants but with sharp contrasts in population densities (figure 8.5) and economic conditions. There is a well-watered zone along the northern shore of Lake Victoria where there is considerable development of small-scale cash-crop agriculture of coffee and, to a lesser extent, cotton, with some estate production of sugar and tea. It contains the major centres of industrial and commercial development in the two largest towns, Kampala and Jinja. The outer districts of Uganda are characterized by low levels of commercial development and severe pressure on land resources, especially in the densely populated districts of the north-west and south-west. This pattern of development was largely created in the early colonial period, so that even by the early years of the twentieth century there was considerable migration of workers from the periphery of Uganda and also from neighbouring countries (notably Rwanda, Burundi and Sudan) into the burgeoning areas of rural and urban development of central Mengo. As the century progressed these movements gathered momentum, and the economic gap between the core and periphery was intensified by the greater expansion of cash cropping and wage labour in these areas of early colonial development.

The cumulative effect of migration was revealed by responses to a question in the national census of 1969 asking each person to state his or her district or country of birth. About 20 per cent of the population were not living in the district in which they were born, and half of them had been born outside Uganda. The districts of the south in general had net population gains through migration, while those of the north and the extreme periphery had net losses (figure 8.5b). The spatial pattern of the movement of over 10,000 people identifies two major types of interdistrict flow (figure 8.5c). There were four very

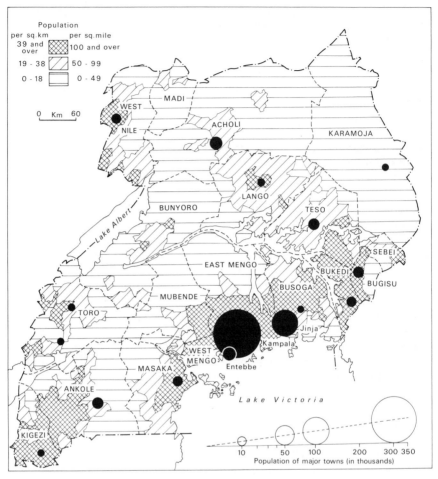

Figure 8.5(a) Population density and urban population, Uganda, 1969.

Source: After Masser and Gould, 1975: 30.

large, short-distance flows, each of over 50,000 people (Kigezi to Ankole and Toro, West Nile to Bunyoro, Bukedi to Busoga) from poor, peripheral districts with very high population densities into neighbouring districts with much lower densities. These were rural/rural migrations stimulated by land shortages at source, and, at destination, by agricultural developments, such as expansion of tobacco, tea and cotton crops and the introduction of exotic beef and dairy cattle; and land improvement and control of human and animal disease. Migrants included both organized, officially sponsored settlers and independent spontaneous movements of family groups. The other major flows were those from almost all parts of the country to Mengo. This was part rural/urban migration into Kampala,

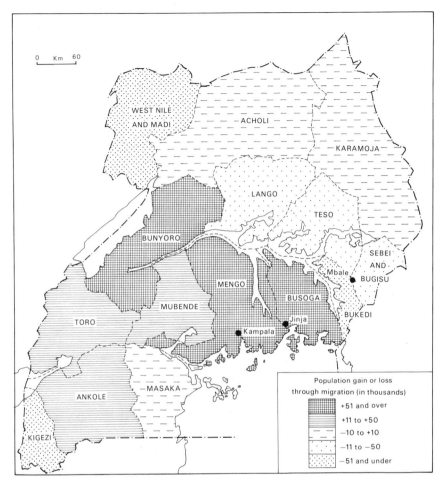

Figure 8.5(b) Net lifetime migration, Uganda, 1969.

Source: After Masser and Gould, 1975: 47.

the capital. Its growth has been very rapid in the present century, and it is likely that in 1969 less than 10 per cent of the adults among the 240,000 African residents were born in the city. The city dominates the highly primate urban hierarchy to such an extent that there is less step-wise migration in Uganda than in most Asian or Latin American countries. Although many of the migrants to Kampala are uneducated and unskilled, they include a relatively large number of the skilled and educated from the peripheral districts who seek the much wider range of opportunities that is available in the capital. Migration to Mengo recorded by the census also included migrations into rural areas by those who took jobs as wage labourers on the coffee farms and sugar estates, coming particularly from

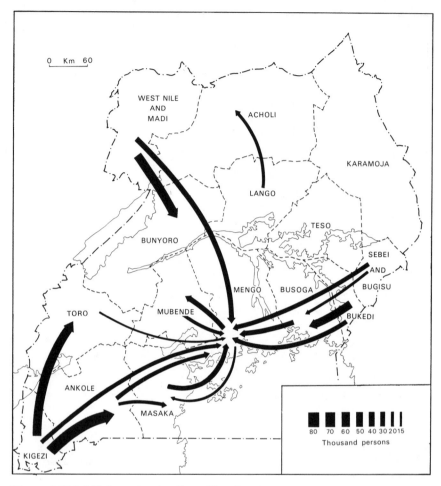

Figure 8.5(c) Lifetime migration flows, Uganda, 1969.
Source: After Masser and Gould, 1975: 52.

western Uganda and from the adjacent severely over-crowded and impoverished states of Rwanda and Burundi.

A strongly centripetal pattern of interdistrict migration reflects the overall spatial structure of Third World countries and the history of their development. Migration reinforces the inherited pattern of interdistrict inequalities in economic opportunity. Loss of people from poor districts may allow a short-term rise in per-capita productivity, especially of food, in over-crowded areas, but longer-term effects include falling capital inputs into agriculture, and smaller local markets with less incentive for rural innovation and urban development. The core area is strengthened by the immigration of additional labour, for not only is its productivity directly increased, but also the larger local market generated by these relatively affluent workers will enhance its economic potential.

Interaction and internal regional disequilibrium

We have considered above the movement of goods, services and people within Third World countries through national and local networks of transport and communications and the linkages developed through the urban hierarchy. Through these interactions regions of a country and sectors of an economy are integrated into a cohesive national economic and political entity. They also allow regional specialization to emerge, facilitated by the exchanges that may take place. The geographical distribution of economic activity is thus affected by the strength and directions of movements and exchanges. It is the result of conflicting pressures within each state that seek either to spread development throughout from the original foci or, conversely, to concentrate it in a few historically or ecologically favoured regions.

Spread effects are involved where there is a diffusion of developments and innovations from the national foci to all parts of the country. The development of an urban hierarchy and the transportation system associated with it is assumed in the Taaffe, Morrill and Gould ideal–typical sequence to facilitate the spread of goods and services initially provided in and organized from the core. However, the evidence presented in this chapter suggests that the hierarchy also generates flows in the opposite direction ('backwash effects') to attract from the periphery to the core, and widen any previous gap between them. Spread effects operate but are insufficiently strong to counter the opposite forces. The dominance of backwash effects would be expected, indeed were essential, for a colonial economy as the metropolitan countries sought to dominate internal production and external trade and integrate it with the world economy. The legacy of the colonial structures has ensured that, despite attempts to modify transportation networks and the urban hierarchy, there is still unequal interregional exchange. There is increasing divergence of interregional incomes and a growing internal disequilibrium in many countries of the Third World, and in response to this most countries have sought to develop a strong regional planning capability.

9 DEVELOPMENT PLANNING

It is clear that countries of the Third World are faced with a great variety of problems: substantial, rapidly growing and impoverished populations, inadequate medical and social provision, an agriculture often unable to meet basic food needs, limited and sometimes inappropriate industry, restricted and dependent trade, uncontrolled and rapidly growing cities. Colonialism left many Third World countries with underdeveloped or predeveloped economies incapable of meeting the needs and aspirations of their inhabitants. With few exceptions, the free play of market forces has generally proved incapable of overcoming the profound distortions in Third World economies and securing major and positive change in economic processes.

There are, therefore, many and diverse problems to be faced but, by definition, the Third World countries have only limited financial resources with which to tackle this multitude of problems. Some mechanism seems necessary to bring about change and provoke economic growth. It is not therefore surprising that they have resorted to some form of development planning in an attempt to identify an approach that will yield economic and social advance.

Development plans have been formulated in an effort to use scarce domestic resources carefully and productively. In addition, in seeking to develop, many Third World countries require external resources in addition to their own, and the drafting of precise, detailed plans outlining specific objectives makes it easier to secure foreign aid than a blanket request for funds for unspecified purposes. Development plans are also seen as symbols of political independence, through which Third World countries will make economic progress and secure economic independence from colonial and neo-colonial powers. They may also be the means of focusing the national consciousness of newly independent states, and securing the unity of new nation states which may contain populations divided on ethnic, religious or social grounds.

The objective of economic planning has been described as seeking to use national resources in the best interests of the nation as a whole. This involves some decisions as to what these best interests are and what the goals of development are to be. Once these have been determined, the process of economic planning tries to direct development along appropriate paths to achieve them. Planning therefore involves the choice of desired objectives, decisions about the best strategy by which these objectives may be secured, and the allocation of available resources to implement the strategies and fulfil the goals set.

Such a diverse and complex process inevitably means that the state has a crucial role in the planning process. The early association of the USSR with economic planning tends to equate planning and socialism, but this overlooks the role which the state plays in economic activity, even in market capitalist economies, in the provision of basic services. Even in the seemingly *laissez-faire* economies of industrializing nineteenth-century Europe, the state had a positive role in the development process. In consequence the role of the state may vary from those countries in which, as in socialist states, the government controls all, or most, of the means of production, to others where state control is restricted to a limited number of sectors. In the former, economic planning embraces the whole economy; in the latter it may be restricted to certain sectors with the government formulating guidelines or incentives for the objectives deemed desirable in the private sector.

Development plans, programmes and models

Within the planning process a number of levels may be distinguished. A 'plan' relates to the economy as whole, divided into major sectors – that is, sectoral planning – and possibly to areas within the country – regional planning. A 'programme' relates to the more detailed determination of specific objectives to be achieved within the various sectors or areas. 'Projects' are the individual components that together make up a programme.

The form of development plans and the techniques of planning show considerable apparent variety within the Third World, but most tend to derive from a limited number of more-or-less formalized economic models depending on differing interpretations of the factors that influence the rate and direction of development. Three major categories have been distinguished. The first, referred to as quantitative or aggregate models, emphasize the role of saving and investment as the determining element in development. Such models deal with the entire economy in terms of macro-economic variables such as saving, investment, production and consumption. They assume that lack of savings and investment are a major check to development, and seek to identify the amount of saving and investment necessary to secure a given rate of growth in GNP. Where domestic sources are inadequate such models give an indication of the amount of foreign assistance needed to secure the desired growth rate. Such an approach sets only the broadest objectives and may provide only background for a more comprehensive and operational plan which is concerned with economic activity *per se*.

Qualitative or sectoral models emphasize the generative role of specific activities or sectors. Here the economy is divided into component sectors such as agriculture and industry, so that the prospects and targets for these sectors can be identified, and an effort made to ensure that growth in one sector is consistent with growth in another and will contribute to the overall development of the economy.

In some cases concern may be with only a single sector, thought to be crucial to the economy or where data to facilitate comprehensive planning are unavailable. This gives rise to what is in essence a partial plan concerned with a single sector, or with a number of distinct sectors which lack any internal consistency. Such partial plans were characteristic of the pioneer schemes of a number of ex-British territories in Africa and the Caribbean in the early 1960s.

Changes in an economy are not independent from one another. Change in one sector may require or provoke change in another. Even the seemingly simple and primitive economies of poor countries are often complex so that, because of this interdependency, consistency is required between the various sectors. Planning at this level therefore seeks to take account of targets, resources and investment of production and consumption for the various sectors, and to interrelate the activities of all the productive sectors of the economy. All activities are viewed as producers of outputs and users of inputs. For example, an increase in agricultural output may require inputs from industry in the form of machinery and fertilizers. Thus the changes which might ensue from changing output in one activity, both direct and indirect, are sought, in terms of inputs, investment and employment in another using multi-sectoral or comprehensive input–output models. Given the selected targets of a development plan, these models can be used to trace all the implications for the economy and to produce a comprehensive plan with mutually consistent production levels and resource inputs. Complex models of this type require a considerable amount of data and sophisticated analysis, so that they tend to be more characteristic of more-advanced countries. However, Third World plans do seek both comprehensive goals and internal consistency.

In the formulation of any planning strategy a number of basic conditions have to be taken into consideration. The stage of development is clearly significant. In a very poor country, largely dependent on subsistence agriculture, with a little-developed money economy and few natural or financial resources, there is small possibility of formulating a complex multisectoral plan. Government priority would probably be to provoke some initial change to lay the foundation for later, more substantial development. On the other hand, a country with a prosperous, well-developed commercial, agricultural and mining economy may wish to begin a transformation to industrialization, and have the skills and resources to do so.

As indicated above, more sophisticated plans may require large inputs of demographic and economic information for analysis and prediction. In some Third World countries such data may be unavailable or unreliable, so that less-sophisticated planning structures may initially be more appropriate.

Resource endowments may impose particular constraints on development, or shape its form. Deficiencies in particular resources, such as fuel or water, may require particular strategies or major efforts to provide them. Shortage of labour skills requires an emphasis on education, while limited finances require careful assessment of what might be obtained from trade or aid sources.

In the choice of a planning path to be followed a major influence, of course, is the politico-economic context within which planning is to take place – capitalist, socialist or some indigenous alternative. Within such a context a country needs to decide which approaches are most suited to its particular needs and objectives. Having done so, the planning strategy decided upon should, within the political context of the country, define the goals to be achieved by the plan, set out a strategy by which these goals are to be achieved, and endeavour to ensure that the strategies for the various sectors are consistent with one another and with the overall objectives of the plan. Commonly a plan has some time-scale for its completion, say 5 or 7 years, though there may be a longer-term and more generalized perspective plan which sets out broader goals for the country and its development aspirations, and also shorter-term targets to be met, perhaps on an annual basis.

In formulating their plans, developing countries may wish to consider a whole range of alternative paths, such as the politico-economic framework for development. A fundamental choice exists between planning and development under socialism or under capitalism. These are not necessarily polarized choices, as all sorts of gradations between the two exist. The choice, however, will influence the nature of the economy and its organization, for under a socialist-command economy virtually all economic activity will be owned and controlled by the state, which can therefore determine and shape priorities. In such an economy decision making may be centralized and planning essentially coercive. In a capitalist economy direct control by the state may be restricted to a few sectors, and for the remainder the government may seek to influence the direction of development by indicating its priorities and trying to persuade the private sector to fulfil them.

In Kenya, for example, a country with an explicitly capitalist approach to development, the government offers incentives to certain types of industries and in certain parts of the country in the form of investment allowances and tax relief for each new job created. In addition, direct grants to small-scale enterprises permit their expansion where feasible, and these measures are currently being extended as part of Kenya's Fourth Development Plan, 1979–83.

A second area of apparent conflict involves the priority to be given to investment in public works or productive activity. These two sectors are sometimes referred to as social overhead capital (SOC) and directly productive activity (DPA). The former refers to basic services such as water and electricity supply, transport, law and order, and education without which productive activities cannot function. DPA refers to the directly productive primary, secondary and tertiary sectors. The debate here has something of a 'chicken and the egg' pattern. Is the provision of SOC essential before any DPA can develop, or will the creation of DPA stimulate provision of SOC?

In many African countries more than one-quarter of government expenditure is on education, most of which is teachers' salaries. Politically motivated policies to expand education, to make it more widely available, have increased the direct financial burden of the education service, but this change can be seen as investment in SOC for the future development of DPAs with a more educated labour force. There is, however, a growing feeling in many countries that the effects of this high level of SOC investment are small, and that better use of scarce resources would be in DPAs, notably small industries, rather than in schooling. A much more sinister issue, highlighted particularly by the Brandt Report, is expenditure on defence, with arms expenditure consuming a rising proportion of Third World expenditures – more in some countries than in others – and using funds that are necessarily diverted from other, more obviously development-oriented purposes.

Given that investment capital is scarce and living standards are low, what should be the balance between consumption and investment? Should any short-term improvements in the economy be made immediately available to the population to improve their condition, or should they be asked to maintain low levels of living, such that improvements can be saved, invested and used for a higher but later level of improvement? Would a modification of the pattern of income distribution, to provide greater equality or draw more people into the money economy, be beneficial to the overall rate of growth? A country may also wish to consider what is the most suitable pattern of ownership for achieving its development goals. What should be the balance between the state and the private sector in ownership of the means of production? What should be the balance of domestic ownership and foreign investment? Should a country invest in men or materials? To what extent should priority be given to improving the physical as opposed to the material lot of the population? Should scarce resources be invested in health care and education, to improve peoples' basic well-being, on the argument that a healthy, literate population will provide a more productive labour force; or will investment in productive activity provide funds for social improvement at a later date?

Countries may wish to restructure their trading patterns. Should a country seek to become more self-sufficient in the full range of economic activities and less dependent on exporting a few primary products and importing manufactures. Or, should it endeavour to expand and diversify its trade pattern, producing commodities it is best able to and thus benefit from comparative advantage?

A major debate in the development process, particularly in the early days of development planning, has been whether to give priority to developing agriculture or industry. If countries are dependent on traditional, low-productivity agriculture, should they give priority to developing a modern, efficient, industrial sector to give dynamism and diversity to their economies, or should they seek to transform agriculture which will, after change, be able to sustain the industrialization process?

More recently there has emerged a debate over the relative merits of capital-intensive and labour-intensive technology. It has been commonly argued that the development process should be easier for developing countries because, unlike Britain and the other now-developed countries which underwent economic revolution in the eighteenth and nineteenth centuries, they do not have to 'invent' a new technology, they can simply 'borrow' it from the developed countries (see p. 167). It has become apparent, however, that this technology, whether in agriculture or industry, developed to suit the peculiar conditions of those countries over a considerable period of time and it may not be suited to the distinct physical, cultural and economic environments of the Third World, especially where countries are anxious to achieve change in a couple of decades rather than centuries. Furthermore, the technology of the developed world has continued to change to take account of its changing factor structure, in which capital is relatively abundant and labour relatively scarce and expensive. In less-developed countries the factor mix is often reversed, with capital scarce and labour cheap and abundant, so that available technology is inappropriate. This has given rise to notions of an 'intermediate technology' more suited to the needs and resources of the Third World. This has not yet secured widespread acceptance, for a variety of reasons. The developed world remains the main source of technology and has expended little research on the particular needs of Third World countries for a cheaper and less complex technology, while Third World politicians have seen this technology as inferior and second rate in relation to the modern machines and equipment of the USA, Japan and Germany.

In fact, most of these 'choices' are not extreme and absolute; there are a whole range of compromises and intermediate positions. None the less, they do indicate the very complex nature of development and development planning: a whole range of elements of choice, balance and strategy have to be considered. Moreover, no single satisfactory model and plan for development has yet been formulated. In the relatively short time that development of the Third World has been a major priority (perhaps 30 years or so), few if any countries have achieved the breakthrough from developing to developed status, and no method of bringing about such a transformation in the short term is apparent. Moreover, the features of planning outlined above are essentially generalized. It will be evident from the earlier chapters that the Third World is not a homogeneous entity but a heterogeneous collection of nations with some common features but many contrasts. In consequence, no single model or plan is likely to be suitable to their varying circumstances. Each country and set of circumstances requires a procedure appropriate to its particular case. It has certainly come to be recognized that no single factor can account for success or failure in a process as complex as development. In addition, empirical research has not yet clearly identified all the significant factors in the development process or the means by which they operated in the now-developed nations.

Success or failure?

It is probably true that the mystique and euphoria that surrounded Third World development plans in the 1950s and 1960s has somewhat diminished as they have failed to deliver the progress expected or to secure economic transformation.

There has been a considerable gap between the aspirations and achievements of development planning. A number of reasons for this may be advanced. One is simply undue expectation as to what planning might achieve. Plans were overly ambitious, and did not fully recognize the often conflicting demands for scarce resources and inputs made by their own complexity. There was frequently a gap between declared, and grandiose, objectives and the practicalities of securing their achievement. Complex planning demands a good knowledge of the status quo, in terms of data and resources. This is often lacking or deficient in Third World countries such that plans and projections are based on inadequate or unreliable information.

Furthermore, the Third World does not exist in isolation from the wider world economy (see chapter 10), nor is it static, so that changes in external and internal circumstances have profoundly modified the situation in which planned change is to take place. As we have seen, many Third World countries are dependent on export earnings from a few primary products. They have little control over the price of these on world markets, such that fluctuations in world prices, and consequent variations in income, affect the availability of funds for development investment. In 1970 coffee provided at least 40 per cent of export earnings for nine countries in Africa and Latin America. Yet over the period 1967–76 the price of Colombian-grade coffee on the New York market ranged from 41.9 US cents per pound to 158 cents, a variation of over 300 per cent.

A general problem over the last decade has been the 'energy crisis'. In common with the more developed countries, the Third World had premised its development strategy on the assumption of the continuing availability of cheap oil imports. The rapid and continuing escalation of the price of oil and other fuels since 1974 has profoundly changed this and checked the anticipated progress of many countries. Between 1973–9 Brazil's oil imports increased by 20 per cent; her oil bill increased by over 1100 per cent. Influences as basic as climatic variations can be profound. India's First Five Year Plan (1951–6) saw considerable economic advance, in which a crucial factor was increased agricultural output, due partly to a series of exceptionally good harvests. The optimistic Second Plan (1956–61) conversely suffered severe setbacks, in which a significant element was a series of poor harvests.

Two particular areas of 'failure' of special relevance to geographers may be noted, namely the failure to create jobs, and the failure to redress spatial imbalance in the level of development. Most development theory and planning has been formulated by economists whose priorities have tended to be with economies in an abstract sense, to the neglect of the implications for people and places. Indeed, notwithstanding the suggestion above that planning, in strictly economic terms, has 'failed', Third World countries have made some advance. They have increased output, diversified their economies, reduced their dependence and achieved high rates of growth. As table 6.6 indicates, rates of growth in GDP and the three productive sectors have generally been higher in the Third World than in the developed capitalist countries.

In particular, the relative success of middle-income countries is notable. Over the period 1970–6 the highest annual rate of growth in GDP amongst developed countries was 5.6 per cent, achieved by Japan; over the same period twenty-six middle-income countries achieved growth rates in excess of this, with Brazil, Ecuador and Korea achieving rates in excess of 10 per cent. However, reference to rates of growth ignores a crucial feature of the Third World, its population: much of the benefit of these high rates of economic growth is lost to the high rates of population growth. Over the period 1970–5 population in the developed capitalist countries grew by 0.8 per cent a year; in low-income countries the rate was 2.4 per cent, and in middle-income countries 2.7 per cent. Thus, whereas Japan's population grew at 1.4 per cent, that of Brazil grew at 2.9 per cent, Ecuador at 3.5 per cent and Korea at 1.8 per cent. (The latter represents a decrease from a rate of 2.6 per cent in the 1960s and suggests the potential impact of population control policies when coupled with development progress.) In consequence of these high rates of population growth, whereas GNP per capita increased at 3.4 per cent a year over the period 1970–6 in developed countries, its rate was 2.8 per cent in middle-income countries and below 1 per cent in low-income countries. A number of the poorest countries – Bangladesh, Bhutan, Somalia, Chad and Niger – experienced negative growth rates – that is the level of GNP per capita fell. In 1976 these five countries had figures of below US $160 per capita, as against an average of US $6200 for developed countries.

In consequence, the high rates of economic growth achieved in the Third World have at best only kept pace with the growth of population; and progress in economic terms has not matched the need to provide jobs for the population unemployed and underemployed. One estimate, assuming a rate of population growth of 2.1 to 2.7 per cent a year between 1970–85, suggests that at least 130–170 million new jobs would be necessary to absorb the increase in the labour force, let alone reducing existing unemployment and underemployment. The same source suggests that in 1970 there were perhaps 130–200 million people in these conditions in the non-communist Third World. Thus despite economic planning and progress, the need for jobs is, and will continue to be, a major problem.

Regional planning

It will be apparent from previous chapters that there is considerable imbalance in levels of development: between countryside and town, and between regions within countries. Much early planning was aspatial and took little account of the location of projected development. Without control or concern new projects tended to locate in the economically most attractive and profitable places and areas. It gave rise to, or intensified, the core–periphery pattern within countries, so that the benefits of development tended to concentrate rather than spread. Even when the problem or imbalance was identified, there was a debate between the economic benefits of allowing growth to concentrate, which would maximize economic progress or, on grounds of social justice, of dispersing it, which might involve higher costs and lower returns for the nation as a whole. The need for some concern for the spatial aspects of development has come to be increasingly accepted, such that most countries now have some element of regional planning, either as an integral part of national planning policies or as an independent activity. The objective of such regional planning is to secure an equitable distribution of benefits from economic development for all geographic regions.

In attempting to achieve economic progress therefore, Third World countries are faced with many choices, and they have differing circumstances and differing levels of development. There is, in consequence, no single development plan that is equally applicable to all countries or regions.

Development plans: some examples

Brazil

For a century after independence in 1822, Brazil remained essentially a primary-product exporting country, in which items such as coffee, rubber and cocoa were important elements in the economic structure and trading pattern. The First World War and the interwar depression revealed the vulnerability of dependence on such a pattern, and in the 1930s the government set out to modify the economy diversifying the external sector by widening the range of commodities exported, and diversifying the internal economy by encouraging industrialization. The state sought greater influence in the use of mineral, petroleum and water resources. During the Second World War four specific development projects were fostered: a steel mill, alkali works, a lorry factory and iron-ore export. The strategy was to reshape the traditional agricultural, dependent economy, reducing such dependence by industrialization.

Tentative development programmes during the Second World War aimed at breaking perceived 'bottlenecks' to development, primarily in the transport infrastructure. The first formal plan, 1949–53, had as its objective the creation of an economic environment in which development might take place – improving health conditions, energy and transport provision and food supply. At this time it was believed that the state should not involve itself directly in the productive sector.

A second plan, 1956–60, took a much more positive role. It sought to stimulate growth in five areas: energy, transport, manufacturing, education and agriculture. It was particularly successful in the first three areas, securing considerable increase in energy production, extension of the highway system, and industrial expansion. This plan was undoubtedly a great stimulus to Brazil's economic advance, laying firm foundations for the 'economic miracle' of the late 1960s. The state was directly involved in highway building, railway improvement, electricity provision and petroleum production. It also participated directly in industrialization, particularly in the steel industry, and actively encouraged both basic industries and 'growth' industries such as automobiles, engineering and electrical goods.

Progress in the schemes for agricultural expansion was limited, reflecting both the low priority given to agriculture (for this was essentially an industrialization strategy) and also the difficulty of securing agricultural improvement without radical change in Brazil's patterns of land ownership and land use. Although the plan brought substantial increases in output of some goods, and high rates of economic growth, it was less successful in generating new jobs for a rapidly growing population.

The next plan, 1963–5, was not fully implemented, but it is of importance as the first national plan to recognize the need for a spatial dimension to planning. Previous plans had contained no regional perspective or locational controls, so many of the new developments had gone to south-east Brazil, and economic progress had been much more rapid there than in other regions of the country. The 1963–5 plan, while acknowledging the emerging spatial imbalances, raised the profound conflict facing most developing countries: should maximum economic growth be secured, by allowing it to concentrate at the most favourable locations; or should some attempt be made to diffuse it, at possibly higher cost, or lesser efficiency, to stimulate economic advance in other parts of the country?

Since 1964 there has been a continuous sequence of development plans in Brazil. They have been set in the framework of a 'market economic model' in which state, private, domestic and foreign capital have a role. The latter has been of great importance in some sectors such as the vehicle, electrical, chemical and pharmaceutical industries. The state has also been important both in shaping the overall strategy, and in its major participation in transport, electricity, petroleum provision, and in the steel industry. Of Brazil's twenty largest companies, thirteen are controlled by government and six by multinational corporations.

Plans have tended to concentrate on infrastructure and industry; programmes for agriculture have avoided the issue of reforming the pattern of land ownership, and have focused on improving agricultural support services and developing new areas for farming. Recent planning has also shown greater awareness of regional imbalances with the announcement in 1970 of a Programme of National Integration, designed to promote the development of the poorer areas of Amazonia and the North-East. Such a programme is still, however, a compromise, for much development continues to take place in the 'basic nucleus' of economic activity, focused on São Paulo, Rio de Janeiro and Belo Horizonte.

Brazilian planning presents a striking dichotomy in its structure, for although concern for regional imbalance was not made explicit in national plans until 1963, the country has a history of concern for less developed regions which is possibly the longest established of any Third World country. Attempts to relieve the problems of the impoverished North-East date back to 1877–9, when a major drought decimated the region, destroying crops, cattle and people. As the problem was perceived purely as one of drought, the response was to try and provide more reliable water supply by building dams. These were initially intended to support irrigated agriculture, but as that required altering existing land-tenure patterns, which reflected the established influence of powerful landowners and politicians, the dams and reservoirs became primarily sources of water for cattle and man in the dry season and dry years.

The problems of the North-East have been increasingly recognized as not merely the consequence of an environmental hazard, but the product of a whole complex of physical, social, historical and economic influences. In an effort to counter these, Brazil has applied a variety of regional development strategies copied from elsewhere. These include a multipurpose river basin project, focused on the region's principal perennial river, to provide irrigation, electricity and navigation; a regional development bank to provide credit for the introduction of drought-resistant crops and new industries; and a more comprehensive regional development agency, with major priorities in improving infrastructure and industrialization. Most recently the Transamazonica highway colonization projects were to decant excess population from the North-East. All of these programmes have had some impact on the region. They have generally made a contribution to economic advance, but the region remains poor when compared to average national levels of well-being, or those of the developed South-East (see figure 1.11). Within the region, totalling some 1.5 million km², economic progress has tended to concentrate in a few areas, particularly the coastlands and the large towns; there is pronounced intraregional inequality. As at the national level, progress measured in economic terms has not been matched by provision of jobs for an expanding impoverished population. Nor has the region been secured against the episodic recurrence of environmental catastrophe.

The North-East has not been the sole focus for regional development strategies in Brazil. At various times since 1945 much of the country has been encompassed within planning regions, for Amazonia, the Centre-West, the São Francisco and Paraiba valleys, and the southern borderlands. Such schemes were not part of a consistent strategy to provide a spatial dimension to national economic planning. Instead they were *ad hoc* responses to particular conditions, pressures and priorities, often totally divorced from national strategies. They were also subject to various and changing approaches to development. Since the announcement of the Programme of National Integration there has been a rather more coherent relationship between national and regional planning, and more consistent development strategies.

India
Planning in India differs from that in Brazil, in that it consists of a continuing sequence of plans, with declared long-term objectives, and incorporates much more concern for the rural sector. The country was committed to a programme of development planning before achieving independence in 1947, but its first Five Year Plan operated for the period 1951–6, followed by others for 1956–61, 1961–6, a series of annual plans, then 1969–74, 1974–9, 1978–83.

The government recognized major problems of demographic pressure, food shortage, basic poverty and a conservative, traditional society. It sought to bring about major economic change, following a compromise strategy which combined socialistic state-supervised economic programmes with private-sector development, rather than imposing total centralized planning or accepting a simple *laissez-faire* strategy. It aimed to transform a poor, traditional, agricultural country into a prosperous industrial and modern one, changing both the economic and social structure. Change in the countryside was essential to provide for the betterment of millions of rural dwellers. Each plan has therefore contained provisions for agricultural labourers, landless peasants, the unemployed, and for rural housing. The plans have also given major priority to providing the basis for change, by improving the infrastructure of highways, roads, electricity and education. In its broader efforts to diversify the economy, the government has also fostered basic industrialization, encouraging the steel, heavy engineering, electrical, aircraft, shipbuilding and fertilizer industries.

The objectives of the first and subsequent plans were to rejuvenate and expand the economy, and to develop both a strong private sector and also state-controlled steel, fertilizer and shipbuilding industries. The government was to supervise development, allocate resources, and encourage foreign investment. The basic aim was to create a mixed public–private economy, which was self-sufficient in agricultural and industrial output. The First Plan gave particular attention to agriculture but the second moved towards industrialization as the major priority, and successive plans have oscillated in their commitment to the two sectors.

Table 9.1 Sectoral allocation of investment funds in India's Five Year Plans (per cent).

	First 1951–6	Second 1956–61	Third 1961–6	Fourth 1969–74	Fifth 1974–9
Agriculture and irrigation	25	19	20	16	19
Major industry and electricity	23	29	35	39	40
Small industries	5	4	4	3	3
Transport	22	17	17	17	17
Other sectors	25	31	24	25	21

Progress has been hampered by a variety of influences. Food output has fluctuated in consequence of good and adverse monsoons; industrialization has required major imports of machine tools, creating foreign-exchange problems, and war with China in 1962 was a major setback. Bringing change in agriculture has been difficult, despite the increasing use of high-yielding seeds, machinery and chemical fertilizer. Growth in industrial output has not been matched by job creation, and the Fourth Plan tried to foster labour-intensive industry, developing small-scale urban industries producing items such as cycles, sewing machines and electrical goods.

Planning has undoubtedly brought progress for India. Most strategies were fulfilled to 80 per cent of their target. Between 1951–78 production of food grain and petroleum doubled; steel production rose from 1.7 million tons in 1951 to 9.3 million, and electricity production from 11 billion kW to 65 billion. Per-capita income rose from US $70 to $190. Therefore, there has been relative progress within the framework of economic planning yet, in absolute terms, Indians remain poor.

At the time of independence India had four major nodes of development, the commercial foci of the colonial economy. These were Calcutta, Bombay, Delhi and Madras, with some lesser inland centres. Beyond these centres was an extensive rural-based periphery, poorly articulated and with few services. Development planning has tried to improve the infrastructure in this periphery and there has been recognition of the existence of inequalities between the cores and the periphery, and between regions. The Indian Planning Commission acknowledged that such variations, together with contrasts in resource endowments, required consideration of the spatial dimension of planning. The Third Five Year Plan stated that regional planning was as important as national planning.

Despite this recognition, regional planning has not been comprehensive. Backward areas have been identified, where new enterprises might be located. There has been some decentralization of new industries to areas with low levels of industrial employment, with the location of steel mills in Orissa and Madhya Pradesh. Such diffusion may provide some stimulus to deprived areas, but strategies in the important rural sector have not had a comprehensive spatial programme. Provision of rural electricity and schools has not been on a spatially equitable basis and the development of rural–urban linkages has been neglected. Regional progress has therefore been largely a response to piecemeal projects rather than a comprehensive strategy. The 1969–74 and 1974–9 plans defined almost three-quarters of the country as backward due to environmental constraints of terrain or climate, cultural backwardness in tribal areas, or economic retardation, and the Fifth Plan sought to allocate more funds to these areas.

Papua New Guinea

Planning may also involve the decentralization of decision making to the regions themselves. The strength of the decentralized authority varies greatly from country to country in both its scale and areas of involvement. In large countries, like Brazil, India or Indonesia, the importance of decentralized planning is largely due to the size and complexity of the national economy, rather than to a commitment to decentralization in principle. In other countries, such as Pakistan, Malaysia and Nigeria, there are federal political structures, but the provinces or states of these countries have limited powers and can generally act only as the agents of central-government policy. In a few states, notably in Tanzania and Papua New Guinea, there has been a conscious attempt to devolve decision making to local authorities, so that the planning process reacts to local needs and concerns by acting 'from the bottom up' rather than 'from the top down', thus weakening the dominant flows of interaction between core and periphery through the urban hierarchy that were discussed in chapter 8. In Tanzania this has been part of the wider national policy of socialism and self-reliance, involving a decentralization of administration and decision making, not only from the primate city/port of Dar es Salaam to a new capital at Dodoma, inland in the sparsely populated centre of the country, but also to each of the twenty provinces, which now have responsibility for economic and physical planning. Each formulates its own plans and priorities with a minimum of central involvement.

In Papua New Guinea decentralization has been one of the main national objectives since independence in 1975. Each of the nineteen provinces of this country of 3 million people now has its own provincial assembly and administration, with powers to establish its own priorities for expenditure in major sectors such as health, education, transport, primary production and public works. Each also has the power to raise its own tax revenues, but in a country with such large regional variations in levels of development as Papua New Guinea (see figure 8.4), the size of the tax base varies enormously between the poorer provinces, mostly in the highlands of the mainland, and the richer provinces, mostly in the outer islands. About 50 per cent of the national income of the country is accounted for by government expenditure and central government collects funds from export royalties from minerals and cash crops, which it distributes for provincial finance. They are allocated partly to those provinces that generate the revenue, partly to the poorer provinces to redistribute the wealth. Thus, richer provinces, such as the copper-rich North Solomons and the island provinces with copra plantations and fishing industries, receive further and disproportionate additions to their financial resources. As a result, despite the fact that reduction of interprovincial inequalities is one of the national objectives, the system of financial allocations to provincial governments has effectively increased these inequalities. There is an obvious clash of interests in this case between the goal of provincial self-sufficiency and strong local planning responsibility on the one hand, and the goal of reducing spatial inequalities through the planning process on the other.

Cuba
Cuban planning under the socialist revolutionary government, which came to power in 1959, reflects the major changes that have occurred in policies relating to development strategy. In the pre-revolutionary situation, some 27 per cent of the total agricultural land was owned by large US or Cuban sugar companies. The dominance of the former sugar monoculture and the prevalent pattern of ownership led to a deliberate anti-sugar bias in the initial plans after 1959. This was accompanied by an attempt to diversify agricultural production on the collective farms established from the appropriated large, privately-owned units.

The planning framework for the implementation of the new strategies was, in the first phase (1961–3), characterized by the introduction of highly centralized control with an emphasis on physical planning. This was largely brought about with the aid of Soviet and other East-European technicians. The failure to raise productivity levels to aspired targets within the new framework led to the review and alteration of the plans after 1963, and a return to an emphasis on sugar. For planning purposes, all farms owned by the state were grouped on a geographical basis into some seventy units in an effort to rationalize the control of the labour force and equipment. Each grouping consisted of the contiguous land of about seven or eight state farms. Vertically integrated arrangements were also made with respect to the production of eggs, poultry and tobacco. Long-term 'macro' planning with centralized control was, by the end of the decade, substituted by short-term, more flexible 'micro' plans based on some decentralization of authority. The 1970s have seen the reestablishment of longer-term central planning with the utilization of computer techniques for handling information on a countrywide basis. In addition, the Institute of Physical Planning has initiated detailed ecological studies of terrain, soil and drainage conditions to determine regions for specialized agriculture and to achieve a greater measure of self-sufficiency in food at the provincial level.

In both the phases of macro and micro-planning, sectoral and regional considerations have featured. The main thrust of the plans has been to increase the productivity of the various economic sectors, while the development of the countryside at the expense of the towns and cities has also been a major priority. In the 1959 Reform Law, for example, twenty-seven agrarian development zones were created to promote the advancement of all aspects of rural life.

Economic planning in Cuba at all stages has been accompanied by important changes in social policies and programmes. The provision of free social services, especially in the fields of education and health, was an initial priority of the revolution that has been maintained throughout. Other programmes to bring about a more egalitarian society have included the rationing of essential foodstuffs and other consumer goods.

The period of planning between 1961 and 1963 included the reduction in individual material incentives and an emphasis on collective incentives for the good of the wider society. This was followed by a brief experiment in permitting personal concessions but it was discontinued in 1966 when the emphasis was again placed on moral stimuli and egalitarianism to bring about the unselfish 'New Man'. The obvious failure of this scheme led to the return to some measure of differential material reward for work in the 1970s, through a varied wage structure and a bonus system. The democratization of the bureaucracy through the formal separation of the party from the administration at that time also provided additional incentive to persons dedicated to the goals of the revolution to rise to positions of authority on behalf of the party at the local level.

10 EXTERNAL RELATIONSHIPS

The nature of the political and trading relationships that each country of the Third World has with other countries, and particularly with the rich countries of the First and Second Worlds, is the principal common feature of the Third World. These relationships have developed over several centuries of European overseas expansion and economic control, as discussed in chapter 2, and many of the *internal* geographical manifestations of global patterns of exchange and their restructuring have been examined in subsequent chapters. In this chapter, however, we return to the global scale and examine current features of *external* relationships of the countries of the Third World, and the possibilities for restructuring the continuing exchanges between rich and poor to promote a more equitable distribution of benefits. The discussion focuses primarily on four major interrelated aspects of external relationships, political and economic associations, trading patterns, aid and capital flows and international migration, and describes each of these as examples of the wider processes at work in the world economy. These features are of interest to geographers because they individually and jointly examine the patterns and processes of spatial integration and differentiation at a world scale, identifying how and why the Third World is both different from and interacts with the First and Second Worlds, and also how these patterns and processes operate within the Third World itself to create and maintain linkages between its countries.

A global view

Most political and economic discussion of the Third World in recent years has been at an international level. In the 1950s attention had been given to individual countries and their problems, especially as many countries were gaining political independence at that time, but by the end of the 1960s, notably with the publication of the Pearson Report *Partners in Development* (1969), a more generalized view of the problems affecting the Third World was taken. By the 1970s the global dimensions and causes of the gap between rich and poor countries were accepted not only by neo-Marxist analysts but also by those in the liberal tradition of Western classical economics and by those in the agencies of the UN which, under the stimulus of the increased political strength of the Third World, promoted such ideas as the New International Economic Order (NIEO) as part of a wider effort to provide the countries of the Third World with a larger share of the world's income. This approach reached its peak with the establishment of an Independent Commission on International Development Issues in 1978, chaired by a former Federal Chancellor of West Germany, Willy Brandt, whose report appeared in early 1980: *North South: a Programme for Survival.*

There were eighteen Commissioners, all senior public figures in their own countries, and the majority came from the Third World. They were asked to consider the problems of world poverty and development at a global scale (though the report does have one chapter on internal aspects: 'The task of the South'). Their report has received worldwide publicity and interest, and has brought the discussion of the Third World further into the centre of public affairs than it has been in the past. The findings of the Commission may be summarized under four headings:

Interdependence and mutuality
The North and the South are dependent on each other. The interests of the rich North are served by increasing prosperity in the poor South; the interests of the poor countries are served by increasing prosperity in the rich countries, for the flows of trade and aid will continue to rise if there is rising demand and purchasing power in the North and in the South.

Global Keynesianism
The method of economic management, associated with Keynes, developed to great effect in the countries of Western Europe between 1945 and the mid-1970s that sought to increase production and wealth by stimulating demand especially among the poorer sections of any community (see chapter 1), should be applied at a global scale. Rising incomes in the South would raise purchasing power in each country and stimulate demand, especially for manufactured products of the country and of other countries, including those in the North. Massive transfers from the North through aid and changing forms of trade are needed to stimulate that demand, and the scale of transfers should be substantially raised to the benefit of all countries.

Global disarmament
The large and growing expenditure on military hardware, both in the North and the South, is a gross waste of resources and should be halted so that these resources can be directed to more beneficial and productive uses.

World summit
A new strategy for restructuring global relationships should develop in the first instance out of a meeting of about twenty-five heads of governments, representing different viewpoints.

While the first three of these general findings require long-term discussion and planning, the suggestion of a world summit was designed to have a short-term impact, and it did so successfully in the North–South summit in Cancun, Mexico, in October, 1981, when twenty-two world leaders – nine from the North, thirteen from the South – met together for the first time to discuss global issues (figure 10.1). The results of this meeting seemed to fail to live up to the expectations of it raised by the Brandt Report, for there was no general agreement on either the causes or the means to remedy the increasing world income disparity. At its most general, three sets of views on the way forward for the Third World were apparent:

(a) *More investment, especially by private companies of the First World, in the economies of the Third World.* This approach, associated particularly with President Reagan of the USA, claims that existing global arrangements for trade and aid are adequate but have not been used sufficiently by the countries of the Third World in that they have thwarted private investment by foreign companies as a result of internal inefficiency and government interference; and suggests that more private investment would be beneficial to all.

(b) *Disengagement from the world economy.* The operation of the world economy is so manifestly inequitable, with active underdevelopment maintaining and enlarging the gap between rich and poor, that unless the structures of exchange are completely and fundamentally altered the countries of the Third World will always emerge badly from any exchange. This view was not directly expressed at the world summit since it is associated with the Communist block and the Second World, and (though invited) the USSR chose not to be represented at what it saw as a capitalist forum in which Marxist economic theory could not be accommodated.

(c) *A restructuring of global economic relationships along the lines suggested in the Brandt Report.* This was clearly a consensus view of most of the participants of the Cancun Summit, recognizing the problems of the existing structures, but recognizing also the validity of the ideas of interdependency and mutuality and the advantages of the massive transfers of resources to poor countries that would be a necessary feature of global Keynesianism. Although no agreements were reached at Cancun it is likely that pressure to implement Brandt's recommendations will continue, and that in the 1980s there will be attempts at the world scale, led by the agencies of the UN and by the International Monetary Fund (IMF) and the World Bank, to strengthen redistributive mechanisms within the existing institutional arrangements for global economic and political interaction.

Political and economic associations

Only Kampuchea, and that only briefly, has tried to completely sever all economic and political links with other countries. The coming of political independence

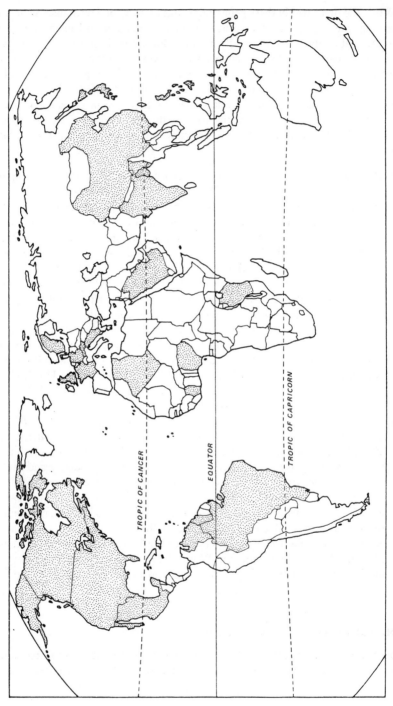

Figure 10.1 Countries represented at the Cancun conference.

throughout the Third World has often meant changing political and economic allegiances but seldom isolationist moves of the type taken to such extremes in Pol Pot's Kampuchea. Most ex-colonial countries have sought to maintain historical links with the metropolitan power, either on a bilateral basis or through wider associations of former colonies, such as the British Commonwealth or the French Community, which include First World and Third World members.

However, Third World countries have been anxious to diversify their political and economic relationships away from historically based linkages to those based more on regional and ideological criteria. Regional political groupings, such as the Organization of African Unity (OAU) and the Association of South-East Asian Nations (ASEAN), and economic groupings, such as the Central American Common Market and the now defunct East African Community (see p. 149), have emerged to enhance geographical cohesion within the Third World. They have had some impact in cementing political contacts between neighbours, but their ability to achieve economic integration has been very limited, as countries were reluctant to forgo their often hard-won sovereignty in political and economic affairs.

Much more important, and with rather better prospects of success, have been broader associations within the Third World as a whole to provide structures to rival the institutions of the First and Second Worlds. As was noted above, the struggle to win a NIEO brought countries of the Third World together as defence against continuing economic dominance by the rich countries of the Organization for Economic Co-operation and Development (OECD), the main inter-governmental economic alliance of the First World, and its Socialist bloc equivalent, the Council of Mutual Economic Assistance (COMECON) (figure 10.2). The Group of 77 (there are now more than 100 members) was formed in the mid-1970s to provide a stronger unified negotiating position for the Third World within UNCTAD. These major world economic groupings are mirrored in political groupings of the North Atlantic Treaty Organization (NATO) for the First World, the Warsaw Pact for the Socialist countries and the Non-aligned Summit for the Third World. Most countries in the Third World are members of the Non-aligned Summit, and some members of the Non-aligned Summit are associate members of the other groupings (for example, Cuba and Ethiopia are associate members of COMECON). These Third World associations are still fairly loose and informal, and do not approach the political, military or economic strength and cohesion of the First and Second Worlds, but their emergence within the last few years is indicative of the growing importance of the Third World taken as a whole. The Third World is now a positive force in world affairs, and not merely a heterogeneous residual.

International trade

The pattern of international trade established by the European control of the world economy was most evident in its classical form at about the turn of the

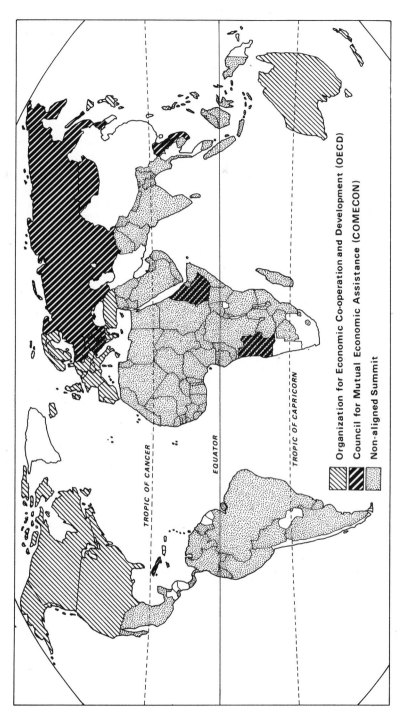

Figure 10.2 Membership of OECD, COMECON and Non-aligned Summit.

Organization for Economic Co-operation and Development (OECD)

Council for Mutual Economic Assistance (COMECON)

Non-aligned Summit

present century. It was based on the assumption of free trade and theoretically dependent on the economic doctrine of comparative advantage – that each country produced goods where it had a cost advantage over others. The pattern that emerged was of manufactured goods being most cheaply produced in the industrializing countries of Europe and North America, and being available for export in return for primary products that they either could not grow or mine, or could produce less efficiently. The pattern was thus dependent on what the industrialized countries could not nor did not want to produce. The imports came from colonies – whether colonies in a political sense or economically dependent countries – and included not only countries now identified in the Third World but also countries such as Australia and New Zealand with temperate environments capable of producing cereals and animal products for the European market. These countries have now been able to develop sufficiently to have an internal momentum that has taken them out of a dependent relationship, for their products did have the advantage of relatively high prices established by European competition. Tropical countries, however, provided imports in much smaller quantities to the industrialized areas of the North where, without the need to support at least some home production of coffee, cotton or tea, for example, world prices for these commodities could be kept low. But they were not so low that they were unable to support import of manufactured goods, particularly cotton textiles and machinery.

The main features of this colonial pattern persist at the present time, though in a rather more complex form and with less dependence on the theoretical assumptions and practical realities of the law of comparative advantage. However, three principal factors have undermined the classical structure somewhat. In the first place the predominance of free trade has declined, with, for example, commonwealth preference agreements in the 1930s, the General Agreement on Tariffs and Trade (GATT) in the 1950s, and common markets, notably the European Economic Community (EEC), from the 1960s. The Common Agricultural Policy of the EEC, for example, is designed to promote agricultural self-sufficiency within the Community to the exclusion of temperate and some tropical produce from elsewhere. One particular effect on Third World producers, especially in the Caribbean, has been due to the promotion of sugar-beet production within the EEC, and the consequent reduction of imports of tropical cane-sugar. Secondly, import substitution and primary-processing industries in Third World countries, particularly textiles and electronics from East Asia, have introduced a range of manufactured goods into the exports to Europe and North America, apparently as a result of changing comparative advantages for their production. Finally, world trade in food has been fundamentally restructured, partly as a response to food deficits in parts of the Third World. The USA and Canada in particular are major sources of cereals which are exported worldwide, notably to many Third World countries (for example, Nigeria, Ghana, Papua New Guinea) where, due to emphasis on industrial development and higher incomes which has brought changes in levels of demand for food and also new patterns of consumption, there is a rising demand for wheat flour and other imported foodstuffs. Taken as a whole, the Third World imports about as much food as it exports, but Africa in particular is now a food-deficit area.

World terms of trade were generally in favour of primary producers between 1930 and 1960, but have moved, in general, against them since 1960. In other words, Third World exports since 1960 have bought less and less imports from the developed countries. This turn-round is partly due to large expansions of production of agricultural and mineral products in a wider range of countries than has previously been the case. More effort is being made, especially by the newly independent countries of Africa, Asia and the Caribbean, to expand production of coffee, cocoa, tea, iron ore, bauxite and copper; and prices have fallen as supply exceeded a rising demand. But many countries had little alternative to expanding production even though unit revenues were falling.

The obvious exception that proves the rule is world trade in oil and the role of OPEC in altering the terms of trade, raising the price from just above the production cost of US $2.50 per barrel in 1973 to a level based on maximum short-term returns, fixed as $34 in 1981. The resulting massive redistribution of world income has created great capital surpluses in oil-rich countries, but the greatest disadvantage has been felt by oil-importing Third World countries who themselves pay the world price and find oil imports a crippling drain on foreign exchange. Sudan and Tanzania, for example, expend 60 per cent of their foreign-exchange earnings on oil imports.

Following the events of the 1970s and the Brandt recommendations, most countries of the world now accept the idea that development can be promoted by expanding trade within the Third World and between the richer and poorer

Plate 10.1 External trade links, Mexico.
Trading links between the developing and the developed world: zinc ingots being loaded at Tampico, Mexico.

countries, but in addition there must be some adjustment of the terms on which current trading relationships are based. UNCTAD has been the main forum for multilateral discussion of the problems and possibilities, but relatively little has been achieved. The rich countries in general see expansion of trade as in itself of sufficient importance to enhance development prospects, but Third World countries, individually and collectively in the Group of 77, are following Brandt, pressing for adjustments to the terms of trade in specific commodity agreements on price and quantity. However, with the weak state of the OECD economies and the political stance of the USA, short-term prospects for fundamental change in trading relationships are limited.

There is, however, much greater scope for increased trade between Third World countries themselves. This trade may be on a bilateral basis or through common-market agreements, but while these can in theory repay large dividends by expanding potential market sizes and allowing economies of scale, they tend to founder in practice on political issues surrounding the distribution of costs and benefits of co-operation.

Resource transfers and aid

The countries of the Third World, anxious to embark on ambitious development programmes, may seek capital support from the world money markets. In this they will be in direct competition with demands in the rich countries, where investment risks are perceived to be smaller, so that Third World countries are at a disadvantage. Not surprisingly, therefore, many countries do not find commercially raised capital an attractive prospect. Nor do banks wish to lend to high-risk projects in countries with very high levels of indebtedness and political instability. Nevertheless, commercial capital has been absorbed on a considerable scale by the larger, newly industrializing countries (NICs), such as Brazil, Mexico, Turkey, Taiwan and Malaysia. These countries can more readily absorb capital transfers, especially for industrialization, and stand to benefit most from the proposals of the Brandt Commission to greatly increase the capital flow to the Third World, and also within the Third World from the capital surplus OPEC countries.

The major alternative source of development capital that is available to governments is the World Bank. Like any other bank it raises capital in the world markets, but since it is 'owned' by the countries to which it lends it forgoes profits and can charge lower interest rates on its standard loans than commercial banks. The forty poorest countries of the world may borrow on special interest-free terms. World Bank borrowing is attractive to Third World governments and it is the principal foreign source of finance for most of them. But capacity to borrow is limited by the accumulated burden of loan repayments, and some countries, notably Pakistan, Zaire and Uganda, now find their previous borrowings have not had the financial effect they had hoped with the investment that had been made, and debt repayments have become a heavy burden on the national economy.

Capacity to borrow is also limited by the funds available, especially for the interest-free credits, but the Brandt recommendations are for a considerable increase in the funds available to the World Bank or similar institutions.

The ties of international capital set rigorous limits to the freedom of action of Third World countries. Loans may seem to be easily granted for major projects, countries have frequently embarked on development projects involving infrastructure, state-led industrial development, and even social welfare and education projects, only to find that at times of world economic depression, or a change in the fortunes of their exports, the burden of servicing their foreign debt precipitates a drastic reduction of their capacity to import, falling exchange rates and internal inflation. Internal economic crises can only be resolved by international agreement and a rescheduling of foreign debt through the International Monetary Fund (IMF), but this process, in turn, has usually been accompanied by draconian measures directed towards stabilization of the economy and the restriction of expansionist development projects. The relationship between the government of Jamaica and the IMF in the late 1970s became a *cause célèbre* as an illustration of how the policies of a government can be publicly altered under IMF pressure.

Increasingly, however, resource transfers, whether capital, technology or manpower, are made within multinational companies, the most obvious manifestation of the nature of global economic interdependence. While their operations may be based in a wide range of countries the firm is controlled at its headquarters, usually in New York, London, Paris or Tokyo; but there are a few Third World based multinationals, especially in India. These companies have certainly provided many types of developments, with important transfers of development capital and industrial technology to establish rural and urban industries in Third World countries. They may produce for a local market (as with European brewing companies such as Carlsberg or Guinness) using imported materials, and they may produce for export to Third World countries. They may also establish industries to use local materials (notably minerals) or cheap labour for production for the European or North American market. Japanese firms have been important in the rapid economic development of several East-Asian countries, notably South Korea, Taiwan, Malaysia and the Philippines, producing textiles and electronic goods for export.

A much more direct way of redistributing the world's wealth is in aid from richer to poorer countries. This is a purely redistributive method, unlike trade which seeks to promote overall increases in wealth in rich and poor countries. Aid may be bilateral, from one country to another directly, or multilateral, channelled through an agency such as the UN. It may comprise outright gifts, perhaps through organizations such as Oxfam, Christian Aid or Caritas, but much more important is aid in the form of capital, equipment or expertise at lower than commercial cost. Aid has been extremely important for the development of specific projects, but its scope is limited, both by the amount of aid that is available (even if the rich countries were to meet the UN aid targets of 0.7 per cent of GNP, which they generally do not) and the political strings that may be attached. These may include commitment to a given political position. The increase of economic and military assistance to Pakistan by the USA in 1981 was premised on Pakistan's support for the American position on the Russian invasion of Afghanistan, Pakistan's neighbour – a pattern that echoes US support for anti-communist governments in several Latin American countries.

With the weakening Western economies and general scepticism about its political value (especially in the USA, the largest donor), the amount of aid available has been declining in real terms, even though some of the capital surpluses accumulated by OPEC countries are available. Indeed, OPEC countries give as aid a higher proportion of their GNP than do European and North American countries.

Table 10.1 Official development assistance from OECD and OPEC members, 1979.

Total (million US dollars)		As percentage of GNP	
USA	7091	United Arab Emirates	6.17
France	4041	Qatar	5.89
West Germany	3512	Kuwait	4.08
Japan	3300	Saudi Arabia	3.01
Saudi Arabia	2298	Iraq	2.60
UK	2067	Sweden	0.94
Netherlands	1404	Netherlands	0.93
United Arab Emirates	1113	Norway	0.93
Kuwait	1053	Algeria	0.87
Canada	1042	Denmark	0.75
		France	0.59
		UK	0.52
		Canada	0.47
		West Germany	0.46
		Japan	0.26
		USA	0.19

Source: World Bank, 1981: 164–5.

However, if the logic of the Brandt Report were to be accepted, aid levels would rise if only to further the mutuality of interests of North and South. Nevertheless, it must be recognized that in some countries of the Third World there is a reluctance to accept aid, at least on a massive scale, as it not only undermines efforts to achieve self-sufficiency in the short term, but in the long term there are political and economic risks that might render it counterproductive. There is a widespread feeling in both the rich and poor countries that trade is preferable to aid, but that aid is necessary to support, in particular, social developments such as education and health improvements with the import of teachers and skilled medical personnel from the rich countries as part of the aid package.

International migration

The period between 1800 and 1939 saw a great deal of international migration from Europe to all parts of the world, including parts of countries we now include in the Third World. Also in that period and associated with the economic demands of the colonial presence was a certain redistribution of colonial peoples, notably workers from the Indian subcontinent to British plantations in Malaysia, Fiji, Mauritius, Natal (South Africa), Guyana, Trinidad and elsewhere.

These were all permanent migrations for settlement, but international movements of this type have now been largely replaced by movements over shorter distances and for temporary residence in neighbouring countries within the Third World. Notable amongst these are the seasonal and longer-term migrants within West Africa from the poor countries of the interior Savanna and Sahel regions, particularly from Upper Volta and Mali, to find work in towns and areas of cash cropping in the more prosperous coastal states. The oil-fed economic boom of Saudi Arabia and the Gulf States has attracted workers, skilled and unskilled, from all parts of the world, but particularly from the Islamic countries of the Middle East and the Indian subcontinent. Currently some 25 per cent of the adult males in Jordan are working abroad, mostly in Saudi Arabia and the Gulf States. As has been argued is the case with internal migration, this type of international migration strongly reflects varying levels of income and cash-earning opportunities between the source and destination of the flows, and the migrations confirm and extend that income gap to the extent that the source countries are deprived of labour for work on the land or in towns, but the host countries have a readily available supply of labour to maintain their development programmes.

More significant in global terms is the net movement out of the Third World to the richer countries of Western Europe and North America, both of skilled and unskilled workers (see chapter 3), but both primarily motivated by differential income-earning opportunities. Migration of unskilled and semi-skilled workers – such as West Indians, Indians, Bangladeshis and Pakistanis to Britain; North Africans and West Africans to France; Turks to West Germany; Mexicans to the USA – to occupy the poorest paid jobs in the developed countries has been associated with the urban racial problems in the host areas, but over time there has been considerable assimilation of Third World people. For some groups, however, institutional and legal arrangements ensure only a temporary sojourn for individual workers, who remit large proportions of their earnings back to the home country to support their families left behind and to provide finance for building a house, buying consumer goods, buying land or starting a business when the migrant returns. The most notorious flows of this type are in southern Africa. In a wide range of black African countries there is organized labour recruitment of single men to work in the gold mines of the Witwatersrand in the Republic of South Africa where they are segregated as a major element in the 'apartheid' structure of the society.

Much attention has been given to the 'brain drain', the migration of skilled and professional people, principally doctors and engineers, to the high-income countries where their skills are in short supply. They come disproportionately from India, Pakistan and Egypt and from several Latin American countries, and migrate mainly to the USA. The brain drain has gathered momentum in recent years as a result of changes in immigration regulations in many countries, including the USA, Canada and Australia, that established manpower shortage rather than race or country of origin as the main criterion for entry. The Third World professionals are, of course, in very short supply in their own country but since they can earn much more in the West they are attracted away from where they have been trained and where the demand for their skills is very high.

As a result of international migration of both brain and brawn there has been, as with trade, unequal exchange with benefits accruing disproportionately in the destination countries. Even where there is considerable remittance to the source country the money is often spent on consumption goods and luxuries, usually imported rather than being invested in productive activities. Stronger redistributive measures, such as taxing foreign earnings for a period of time by the source government, or having large payments at the time of emigration, or preventing migration of certain categories of labour, are contemplated by individual governments as part of a general strengthening of North–South exchange mechanisms implicit in global Keynesianism.

Conclusion

International associations, international trade, resource transfers and international migration are the main forms of global interaction between the countries of the Third World, individually and taken as a whole, and the countries of the First and Second Worlds. Each of these interactions exhibits major structural effects that tend to distribute the benefits of interaction in favour of the richer and stronger partner, and is marked by a weakness of redistributive mechanisms to ensure a more even distribution of benefit. Thus the gap between North and South grows as these interactions, mostly established in the colonial period, continue and in some cases intensify. The discussion has added weight to the view taken in chapters 1 and 2 that the countries of the Third World are enmeshed in a dependency relationship of unequal exchange with the rich countries and, despite much public discussion and changing political conditions after a major period of decolonization, the principal features of that relationship remain in the 1980s.

The importance of the Brandt Commission lies not so much in its conclusions and recommendations, for these have been current amongst those professionally concerned with development for some years, but more in bringing them forward to the forefront of public discussion. In Western Europe the findings have been presented with a very strong emphasis on mutual benefit: that it is in the medium and long-term economic and political interest of liberal democracies to promote Third World development; that global interaction is not a 'zero-sum game' (that is, benefit in one group occurs as a result of an equally large 'disbenefit' in the other);

and both rich and poor benefit, and will benefit further, from stronger redistributive mechanisms administered globally. Such a view has been strongly criticized from the political Right – that only when there is strong growth can redistribution be a practical reality – and from the political Left – that the Commission's findings are palliatives that will further the interests of corporate capitalism rather than the people of the Third World; and that only major structural changes in the type and mechanisms of trade and aid will reduce the development gap. It is certainly true that each of these views provides an alternative to Brandt, but it is equally likely in the 1980s that the Brandt approach will find more general support and be given more attention then either, particularly in the Third World itself.

The nature of the world economy and the processes operating to create spatial patterns of income and well-being at the global scale, have tended in the past to be less widely discussed by geographers than they might have been. Geographical studies in the 1960s and 1970s tended to focus on the individual behaviour and local and regional structures, and in the Third World geographers have been largely concerned with the state and its internal problems. The body of research at local, regional and national scales has contributed much to the understanding of the development process, but needs to be complemented by studies at the global scale. The Third World as a global phenomenon can only be fully appreciated through discussing the external relationships of each country and of the countries of the Third World as a whole.

11 CONCLUSION

This book has demonstrated that the use of the term the 'Third World' implies a degree of unity amongst the countries deemed to be part of it. Such countries have some similarities in their levels of income relative to the most affluent countries, and as measured by various other criteria, but the major feature they share is the constraints imposed by the nature of their past and contemporary involvement in the world economy. They are brought together mainly by the relationship they have with the global economy in their dependence on the economic conditions and social and political processes of the First and Second Worlds.

Yet the countries of the Third World also exhibit great diversity, in their physical environments, resource endowments, historical experience, cultural traditions, societal structures, economic organization and political practices. Diversity exists between these countries and within them. Moreover, there is not a great gulf between the First and Second Worlds and the Third. Annual GDPs per capita of US $80 in Bhutan and $13,920 in Switzerland may represent the extremes, but between them is a continuum from poor to rich; the precise placing of subdivisions along it is open to debate. The Third World does not consist of a precise number of uniform states; however defined it possesses great internal diversity. There is no single explanation of relative poverty or the essential geographical and economic characteristics of each Third World country; nor is there a single key to progress which, if turned, will set them all on the same path to development and to levels of well-being equivalent to those of the USA, Sweden, Saudi Arabia or West Germany.

Some Third World countries have already made progress. The special circumstances of the period since 1973 have created the distinctive group of the oil-exporting countries which have massive capital surpluses, but also a few other countries, if they have not leapt clearly into the First World, have at least progressed up the league table of per-capita income. Some countries at least have achieved high rates of economic growth. Between 1960 and 1979, for example, Syria, Hong Kong and Korea each achieved rates of increase in GDP in excess of 9 per cent a year. As table 11.1a shows, the poorer countries as a group achieved growth rates comparable with those of the more advanced countries, but when that growth is related to population the pattern is less favourable (table 11.1b). The per-capita figures suggest that the gap between the poorest countries and the industrialized First and Second Worlds continues to widen; there is also evidence of a growing gap between the poorest countries and middle-income countries such as Hong Kong, Korea, Brazil and Tunisia.

Table 11.1 Economic growth rates, 1960–79.

	(a) Average annual growth rate of GDP (per cent)		(b) Average annual growth rate of GNP per capita
	1960–70	1970–9	1960–79
Low-income countries	4.5	4.7	1.6
Middle-income countries	6.1	5.5	3.8
Industrial market economies	5.1	3.2	4.0
Capital surplus oil exporters	n.d.	6.5	5.0
Non-market industrial economies	4.8	5.2	4.3

Source: World Bank, 1981: 134–7.

One can nevertheless point to some signs of optimism and progress. In much of the Third World birth and death rates have fallen, infant mortality rates have declined and life expectancy has risen; access to health care and to education has improved; economic structures have diversified, reducing dependence on agriculture and a few primary-product exports; some countries at least have become effective competitors in the world market for manufactured goods. Yet many countries, regions and men, women and children, remain poor, in both relative and absolute terms.

Awareness of the problems of poverty has increased over the past three decades, on the part of both the less and the more-developed countries and their peoples, and there is greater concern by both rich and poor for securing progress. The Third World has been persistent in its efforts in this direction; the developed world has been less consistent, as its contributions to aid and concessions to trade have been periodically sacrificed to domestic 'needs', fashions and pressures. Coverage by the media has made people more aware of the horrors of poverty, whether persistent or catastrophic, and has prompted humanitarian response. The oil crisis brought home to many both the interdependence of the world economy, and the potential influences which might be exercised in the interests of the Third World; and the arguments of the Brandt Report have illuminated the mutual benefits of trade and development.

As part of this increasing interest in the development process there has been growing awareness of the potential available for advance in the Third World: greater knowledge of the resource endowment of soils, minerals and people, and increased utilization of new innovations, new crops, new equipment, new concepts. One area of particular concern is the formulation and spread of techniques of development that are most appropriate to the needs and endowments of Third World countries. Underdevelopment of the poor South may have been partially due to its exploitation by the rich North, yet in its attempts to secure development the Third World has been heavily dependent on concepts, methods and technologies largely formulated in the developed countries to meet their needs, aspirations and endowments. Such borrowing may not necessarily be the most appropriate for Third World countries to secure development in the best interests of their populations as a whole. There is a great need to develop more appropriate, replicable and indigenous development techniques.

This book has deliberately offered a geographical perspective on the Third World, in the belief that such a perspective has a positive contribution to make in identifying and analysing conditions affecting three-quarters of the world's population. Generalization is inevitable in a brief book of this sort, yet we have sought to identify the main common structural elements of interest to geographers. Study of the geography of any one country of the Third World would, of course, require more detailed consideration of these and other themes, in the context of the specific physical, historical, social, economic and political circumstances of that country.

A geographical contribution can be made at a variety of scales: global, international, national, regional or local. Although we have defined the Third World primarily in terms of global relationships, and explored these at some depth in chapters 2 and 10, it is evident that geography has a larger contribution to make at the national and subnational level, exploring structures, patterns and processes of spatial differentiation and integration. While it is true that many of the structural features of the Third World arise from and can be alleviated by international exchange and distribution mechanisms, a New International Economic Order, however defined, could not in itself solve many of the problems of resource availability, poverty and inequality that exist within Third World countries. It would need to be accompanied by changes and initiatives within each country and, given the internal diversity of these countries, would require many of the changes and initiatives to be specific to an individual country, or even to areas within it.

It is because of this very diversity that geographers may have special contributions to make to the study and process of development in three major but interrelated areas. The first is in the area of man–environment relations. Geographers have studied environment – soils, hydrology, climate, landforms – and man – distribution, society and economy – as geographical phenomena in their own right, but have also made important contributions, where man and environment interact, to topics such as land use, water management and resource utilization. It is at the local scale that human decisions about the use of environmental resources are most crucial.

The second major field is that of locational analysis. The conceptual revolution in geography in the 1960s and early 1970s pushed locational analysis to the forefront of geographical studies, particularly in the countries of the First World and, to a lesser extent, in the Second World. It also had an impact on the Third World. The description and analysis of space and man's organization of it requires an answer to the question: Why are geographical distributions structured the way they are? Geographers in the Third World have sought to consider the patterns of social and economic order, as they have evolved in the past and as they are currently changing. Studies of the patterns and processes governing the location of plantations, factories, rural schools and towns, or the diffusion of disease or new technologies, are not merely matters for the geographical record but may contribute to improvements in patterns of location, or checks to the spread of disease.

Thirdly, the geographer's traditional and continuing concern for regional analysis, both within and between regions, has brought geographical concepts and theories firmly into the centre of discussion of the nature and extent of spatial inequalities in Third World countries, and of means to diminish such imbalances. The broad thrust of concern within Third World studies derived from the existence of massive and growing international inequalities has inevitably been paralleled by a growing interest in the patterns and mechanisms of inequality within countries. Thus much work has been done on the problems of regional development.

In sum, the Third World offers geography an opportunity to put its theories and techniques to practical use, in the understanding and solution of at least some of the problems of a large part of the earth, and of its population.

Chapter 2

Buchanan, K. M. (1967) *The Southeast Asian World*, London: Bell.
Fieldhouse, D. K. (1966) *The Colonial Empires*, London: Weidenfeld & Nicolson.

Chapter 3

Malthus, T. (1970) *An Essay on the Principle of Population*, Harmondsworth: Penguin.
People (1975) 2, 4.
People (1979) 6, 2.
People (1981) 8, 2.
Segal, A. L. (1975) *Population Policies in the Caribbean*, Lexington, Mass.: Lexington Books, D. C. Heath & Co.
United Nations (1977) *Demographic Yearbook*, New York: UN.
United Nations (1978) *Demographic Yearbook*, New York: UN.
United States Bureau of Census (1977) *World Population*, Washington: US Dept of Commerce.
World Bank (1978) *World Development Report, 1978*, New York: World Bank.

Chapter 4

Clarke, C. G. (1974) *Jamaica in Maps*, London: University of London Press.
Food and Agriculture Organization (1979) *FAO Production Yearbook*, 33, Rome: FAO.
Food and Agriculture Organization (1980) *FAO Production Yearbook*, 34, Rome: FAO.
Hollier, G. (1981) The dynamics of rural marketing in N.W. Province, Cameroon. Unpublished PhD thesis, University of Liverpool.
Innis, D. Q. (1961) 'The efficiency of Jamaican peasant land use', *Canadian Geographer*, 5(2), 19–23.
Land Tenure Centre (1979) *Land Concentration in the Third World*, Madison: University of Wisconsin.
Mckim, W. (1972) 'Periodic markets in Ghana', *Economic Geography*, 48, 333–4.
Skinner, G. W. (1964) 'Marketing and social structure in rural China', *Journal of Asian Studies*, 34, 3–43.
United Nations (1978) *UN Statistical Yearbook*, New York: UN.
World Bank (1980) *Kenya: population and development*, Washington: World Bank.

Chapter 5

Clarke, C. G. (1974) *Jamaica in Maps*, London: University of London Press.
Hennessy, A. (1978) *The Frontier in Latin American History*, London: Edward Arnold.
Land Tenure Centre (1979) *Land Concentration in the Third World*, Madison: University of Wisconsin.

Lipton, M. (1977) *Why Poor People Stay Poor*, London: Temple Smith.

Schumacher, E. F. (1974) *Small is Beautiful*, London: Abacus.

Turner, F. J. (1961) *Frontier and Section: selected readings of Frederick Jackson Turner*, Englewood Cliffs, NJ: Prentice Hall.

Chapter 6

Drucker, P. (1971) *The Age of Discontinuity*, London: Pan.

Dunkerley, J., Ramsay, W., Gordon, L. and Cecelski, E. (1981) *Energy Strategies for Developing Nations*, Baltimore and London: Johns Hopkins University Press.

IBGE (Instituto Brasileiro de Geografia e Estatistica) (1974) *Censo Industrial Ceará, VIII Recenseamento Geral*, Rio de Janeiro: IBGE.

Lonrho (1980) *Lonrho 1979*, London: Lonrho.

Odell, P. R. and Preston, D. A. (1978) (2nd ed.) *Economies and Societies in Latin America*, Chichester: Wiley.

UN (1978) *Statistical Yearbook*, New York: UN.

UN (1981) *Statistical Yearbook 1979/80*, New York: UN.

World Bank (1980) *World Development Report 1980*, New York: World Bank.

Chapter 7

Bataillon, C. and Rivière d'Arc, H. (1973) *La Cuidad de Mexico*, Mexico: Sep-Setentas/Diana.

Cheng-Siang Chen (1973) 'Population growth and urbanisation in China 1953–70', *Geographical Review*, 63, 55–72.

Dwyer, D. J. (1975) *People and Housing in Third World Cities*, London: Longman.

de Franklin, E. H. M. (1979) The housing problem in Caracas, Venezuela. Unpublished PhD thesis, University of Liverpool.

Fullard, H. (ed.) (1979) *The Geographical Digest*, London: Philips.

Hart, K. (1973) 'Informal income opportunities and urban employment in Ghana', *Journal of Modern African Studies*, 11, 61–81.

Kidron, M. and Segal, R. (1981) *State of the World Atlas*, London: Pluto Press in association with Heinemann and Pan.

Mabogunje, A. L. (1968) *Urbanisation in Nigeria*, London: University of London Press.

Roberts, B. (1978) *Cities of Peasants*, London: Edward Arnold.

Santos, M. (1979) *The Shared Space*, London: Methuen.

Sinclair, S. (1978) *Urbanisation and Labour Markets in Developing Countries*, London: Croom Helm.

Sjoberg, G. (1960) *The Pre-industrial City*, New York: Free Press.

Sternstein, L. (1976) 'Migration and development in Thailand', *Geographical Review*, 66, 401–19.

Ward, P. M. (1976) In search of a home: social and economic characteristics of squatter settlements and the role of self-help housing in Mexico City. Unpublished PhD thesis, University of Liverpool.

Chapter 8

Auger, A. (1972) 'Le ravitaillement vivrier traditionnel de la population africaine de Brazzaville', in P. Vennetier (ed.) *La Croissance Urbaine en Afrique Noire et a Madagascar*, Paris: CNRS, 273–98.

Berry, R. and Jackson, R. (1981) 'Interprovincial inequalities and decentralisation in Papua New Guinea', *Third World Planning Review*, 3, 57–77.

CEMIG (Centrais Elétricas de Minas Gerais) (1952–77) *Relatório Annual*, Belo Horizonte: CEMIG.

Masser, I. and Gould, W. T. S. (1975) *Inter-Regional Migration in Tropical Africa*, London: Institute of British Geographers Special Publication 8.

Taaffe, E. J., Morrill, R. and Gould, P. R. (1963) 'Transport expansion in underdeveloped countries: a comparative analysis', *Geographical Review*, 53, 503–29.

Chapter 10

Pearson, L. B. (1969) *Partners in Development: Report of the Commission on International Development*, London: Pall Mall.

World Bank (1981) *World Development Report 1981*, New York: Oxford University Press.

Chapter 11

World Bank (1981) *World Development Report 1981*, New York: Oxford University Press.

SUGGESTIONS FOR FURTHER READING

General texts

Bernstein, H. (ed.) (1973) *Underdevelopment and Development: the Third World Today*, Harmondsworth: Penguin.

Brookfield, H. (1975) *Interdependent Development*, London: Methuen.

Caldwell, M. (1977) *The Wealth of Some Nations*, London: Zed Press.

Cole, J. P. (1981) *The Development Gap: a spatial analysis of world poverty and inequality*, Chichester: Wiley.

Harrison, P. (1979) *Inside the Third World*, Harmondsworth: Penguin.

Harrison, P. (1980) *The Third World Tomorrow*, Harmondsworth: Penguin.

Hayter, T. (1980) *The Creation of World Poverty*, London: Pluto Press.

Kidron, M. and Segal, R. (1981) *The State of the World Atlas*, London: Pan.

Mabogunje, A. (1980) *The Development Process*, London: Hutchinson.

Mountjoy, A. B. (ed.) (1978) *The Third World: problems and perspectives*, London: Macmillan.

de Souza, A. R. and Porter, P. W. (1974) 'The underdevelopment and modernisation of the Third World', *Association of American Geographers Commission on College Geography Resource*, 28.

Steel, R. W. and Prothero, R. M. (1964) *Geographers and the Tropics. Liverpool Essays in Geography*, London: Longman.

Todaro, M. (1977) *Economics for a Developing World*, London: Longman.

Regional texts

Beaumont, P., Blake, G. H. and Wagstaff, J. M. (eds) (1974) *The Middle East: a geographical survey*, Chichester: Wiley.

Best, A. C. G. and de Blij, H. J. (eds) (1977) *African Survey*, New York: Wiley.

Brookfield, H. (ed.) (1973) *The Pacific in Transition*, New York: St Martins Press.

Buchanan, K. M. (1966) *The Chinese People and the Chinese Earth*, London: Bell.

Buchanan, K. M. (1967) *The South-east Asian World*, London: Bell.

Gilbert, A. (1974) *Latin American Development*, Harmondsworth: Penguin.
Johnson, B. C. L. (1979) *India: resources and development*, London: Heinemann.
Morris, A. (1981) *Latin America*, London: Hutchinson.
Odell, P. R. and Preston, D. (1978) *Economies and Societies in Latin America*, Chichester: Wiley.
Prothero, R. M. (ed.) (1972) *People and Land in Africa South of the Sahara*, New York: Oxford University Press.

Journals containing Third World material

Economic Development and Cultural Change
Geographical Magazine
Journal of Developing Areas
Journal of Development Studies
New Internationalist
Third World Quarterly
World Development
Cahiers d'Outre Mer
East African Geographical Review
Indian Geographical Journal
Malayan Journal of Tropical Geography
Nigerian Geographical Journal
Revista Geografica
Singapore Journal of Tropical Geography

Sources of data on the Third World

UN Demographic Yearbooks
UN Food and Agriculture Organization
UN Statistical Yearbooks
World Bank World Development Reports

Preface

Brookfield, H. (1975) op.cit.
Gourou, P. (1953) *The Tropical World*, London: Longman.
Lawton, R. (1964) 'Liverpool and the tropics', in R. W. Steel and R. M. Prothero (eds) op.cit., 349–75.
McGee, T. G. (1978) 'Western geography and the Third World', *American Behavioural Scientist*, 22, 93–114.
Steel, R. W. (1964) 'Geographers and the Tropics', in R. W. Steel and R. M. Prothero (eds) *op.cit.*, 1–29.
Steel, R. W. (1974) 'The Third World: geography in practice', *Geography*, 59, 189–207.

Chapter 1

Brookfield, H. (1975) *op.cit.*
Dwyer, D. J. (1977) 'Economic development: development for whom?', *Geography*, 62, 325–34.
Mabogunje, A. (1980) *op.cit.*
Odell, P. R. (1974) 'Geography and economic development with special reference to Latin America', *Geography*, 54, 208–22.

There is only limited discussion of theories relating to development at various scales in this book. It has been assumed that general theories in human geography (Burgess, Christaller, Rostow, Von Thünen, etc.) will be familiar to the reader. Some specific references to particular theoretical work is included in the references and reading list. More general discussion may be found in:
Brookfield, H. (1975) *Interdependent Development*, London: Methuen.
Haggett, P. (1975) *Geography: a modern synthesis*, London: Harper & Row.
Keeble, D. (1967) Models of economic development, in R. J. Chorley and P. Haggett (eds) *Models in Geography*, London: Methuen, 243–302.

Chapter 2

Amin, S. (1973) *Neo-colonialism in West Africa*, Harmondsworth: Penguin.
Bairoch, P. (1975) *The Economic Development of the World Since 1900*, London: Methuen.
Beckford, G. (1972) *Persistent Poverty: underdevelopment in plantation economies of the Third World*, Oxford: Oxford University Press.
Brookfield, H. (1972) *Colonialism, Development and Independence*, Cambridge: Cambridge University Press.
Fanon, F. (1967) *Black Skin, White Masks*, New York: Grove Press.
Fieldhouse, D. K. (1966) *The Colonial Empires*, London: Weidenfeld & Nicolson.
Ginsberg, N. (1973) 'From colonialism to national development: geographical perspectives on patterns and policies', *Annals of the Association of American Geographers*, 63, 1–21.
Lewis, W. A. (1970) *Tropical Development 1880–1913*, London: Allen & Unwin.
Rodney, W. (1972) *How Europe Underdeveloped Africa*, London: Bogle-l'ouverture.
Sachs, I. (1976) *The Discovery of the Third World*, Cambridge, Mass.: MIT Press.
Tate, D. J. M. (1979) *The Making of Modern South-east Asia*, Oxford: Oxford University Press.
Worsley, P. (1964) *The Third World*, London: Weidenfeld & Nicolson.

Chapter 3

Clarke, J. I. (1971) *Population Geography and the Developing Countries*, London: Pergamon.

Gould, W. T. S. and Prothero, R. M. (1974) 'Space and time in African population mobility', in L. A. Kosinski and R. M. Prothero (eds) *People on the Move*, London: Methuen, 39–49.

Heer, D. M. (1975) *Society and Population*, Englewood Cliffs, NJ: Prentice-Hall.

Jackson, S. H. (1981) 'Population policy in the People's Republic of China', *Geography*, 66, 235–7.

Moraes, D. (1974) *A Matter of People*, London: Deutsch.

Prothero, R. M. (1974) 'Nigeria loses count', *Geographical Magazine*, 47, 24–8.

Prothero, R. M., Zelinsky, W. and Kosinski, L. A. (eds) (1970) *Geography and a Crowding World: a symposium on population pressure upon physical and social resources in the developing land*, New York: Oxford University Press.

Sánchez-Albornoz, N. (1974) *The Population of Latin America*, Berkeley: University of California Press.

Trewartha, G. T. (1969) *A Geography of Population: world patterns*, London: Wiley.

Trewartha, G. T. (1972) *The Less-Developed Realm: a geography of its population*, London: Wiley.

Chapter 4

Bromley, R. (1971) 'Markets in the developing countries: a review', *Geography*, 56, 124–32.

Dumont, R. and Rosier, B. (1969) *The Hungry Future*, London: Methuen.

Grigg, D. B. (1970) *The Harsh Lands*, London: Macmillan.

Grigg, D. B. (1974) 'The growth and distribution of the world's arable land 1870–1970', *Geography*, 59, 111–20.

Grigg, D. B. (1975) 'The world's agricultural labour force 1800–1970', *Geography*, 60, 194–202.

Grigg, D. B. (1981) 'The historiography of hunger, changing views on the world food problem', *Transactions of the Institute of British Geographers*, New Series, 6, 279–92.

Grossman, L. (1981) 'The cultural ecology of economic development', *Annals of the Association of American Geographers*, 71, 220–36.

Jackson, R. T. (1971) 'Periodic markets in southern Ethiopia', *Transactions of the Institute of British Geographers*, 53, 31–42.

Manshard, W. (1974) *Tropical Agriculture*, London: Longman.

Morgan, W. B. (1977) *Third World Agriculture*, London: Bell.

Preston, D. (1974) 'Geographers among the peasants', *Progress in Human Geography*, 6, 143–78.

Riddell, J. B. (1974) 'Periodic markets in Sierra Leone', *Annals of the Association of American Geographers*, 64, 541–8.

Ruthenberg, H. (1980) *Farming Systems in the Tropics*, Oxford: Oxford University Press.

Stewart, N. and Belute, J. and L. (1976) 'Transhumance in the Central Andes', *Annals of the Association of American Geographers*, 66, 377–97.

Wanmali, S. (1980) 'The regulated and periodic markets and rural development in India', *Transactions of the Institute of British Geographers*, New Series, 5, 466–87.

Webster, C. C. and Wilson, P. N. (1980) *Agriculture in the Tropics*, London: Longman.

Chapter 5

Baker, P. R. (1971) 'Stages in the development of a dairy industry in Bunyoro, Western Uganda', *Transactions of the Institute of British Geographers*, 53, 43–54.

Blaikie, P. M. (1971) 'Spatial organisation of agriculture in some north Indian villages', *Transactions of the Institute of British Geographers*, 52, 1–40; 53, 15–30.

Briggs, J. A. (1978) 'Farmers' response to planned agricultural development in the Sudan', *Transactions of the Institute of British Geographers*, New Series, 3, 464–75.

Chakravati, A. K. (1973) 'Green Revolution in India', *Annals of the Association of American Geographers*, 63, 319–30.

Courtenay, P. P. (1965) *Plantation Agriculture*, London: Bell.

Fanon, F. (1965) *The Wretched of the Earth*, London: MacGibbon & Kee.

Farmer, B. H. (1981) 'The "Green Revolution" in southern Asia', *Geography*, 66, 202–7.

Floyd, B. and Tandap, L. (1980) 'Intensification of agriculture in the Republique Unie du Cameroun', *Geography*, 65, 324–7.

Hirst, M. (1978) 'Recent villagisation in Tanzania', *Geography*, 63, 122–5.

Jefferies, A. (1971) 'Agrarian reform in Chile', *Geography*, 56, 221–30.

King, R. (1977) *Land Reform*, London: Bell.

Krinks, P. A. (1978) 'Rural change in Java: an end to involution', *Geography*, 63, 31–6.

Ng, R. (1974) 'Rural change in South east Asia', *Geography*, 59, 251–6.

O'Connor, A. M. (1975) 'Sugar in tropical Africa', *Geography*, 60, 24–30.

Preston, D. A. (1969) 'The revolutionary landscape of highland Bolivia', *Geographical Journal*, 135, 1–16.

Rogerson, C. M. (1981) 'The communal village of Mozambique: an experiment in rural socialist transformation', *Geography*, 66, 232–5.

Williams, O. (1981) 'Irrigated farming in the south-east low veldt of Zimbabwe: retrospect and prospect', *Geography*, 66, 228–32.

Wood, A. (1981) 'Rural development and national integration: the experience of post-revolutionary Ethiopia', *Geography*, 66, 131–3.

enquiry into the Middle East labour market', *International Migration Review*, 13, 122–35.

Buchanan, K. M. (1972) *The Geography of Empire*, Nottingham: Spokesman.

Frank, A. G. (1980) *Crisis in the World Economy*, London: Heinemann.

Glaser, W. (1978) *The Brain Drain: emigration and return*, London: Pergamon.

Hayter, T. (1981) *The Creation of World Poverty*, London: Pluto Press.

International Migration Review (1978) 'Mexican immigrants to the United States', *special issue*, 12(4).

International Migration Review (1979) 'International migration in Latin America', *special issue*, 13(3).

Mabogunje, A. (1980) 'The dynamics of centre–periphery relations: the need for a new geography of resource development', *Transactions of the Institute of British Geographers*, New Series, 5, 277–96.

Prothero, R. M. (1974) 'Foreign migrant labour for South Africa', *International Migration Review*, 8, 383–94.

Salt, J. and Clout, H. (1976) 'International labour migration: the sources of supply', in J. Salt and H. Clout (eds) *Migration in Post-war Europe*, Oxford: Oxford University Press, 126–67.

Thomas-Hope, E. M. (1983) 'Off the island: population mobility among the Caribbean middle class', in A. F. Marks and H. M. C. Vessuri (eds) *White Collar Migrants in the Americas and Caribbean*, Leiden: Royal Institute of Linguistics and Anthropology, 39–57.

INDEX